Black Chameleons

Written, Created and Arranged by;

Jonathan P. Mance

Written in Concord, North Carolina

The Black House Publishing Inc.

All Rights Reserved

2018 Copyright©

Book Cover Illustration by: MNSartsstudionew

Edited by: Stella Joy   Contact at: Editorstellajoy@gmail.com

Executive Producer: Cendra S. Clarke-Mance

Copyright © Jonathan P. Mance/Cendra S. Mance

The Black House Publishing Inc.

ISBN 13: 978-0-9972731-4-4

ISBN 10: 0-9972731-4-3

Library of Congress Cat Num. in-pub.-Data

PRINTED IN THE UNITED STATES OF AMERICA

ALSO AVAILABLE IN EBOOK

Audio Book Forthcoming.

Jonathan P. Mance writes courtesy of The Black House Publishing Inc.

The Black House Publishing Inc. Presents:

Black Chameleons

Government has lost all trust within itself due to political corruption. Foreign influence has permeated multiple levels in Washington DC. That leaves FBI Agent Sabrina Morgan working with no oversight or support in Baltimore. She does have ample resources though. She begins to weave a web of deceit. One that connects two brothers who are on opposite sides of the law. Until now they've avoided one another for decades. Now greed and opportunity has them on a collision course. As their worlds get more intertwined, they learn that everybody has secrets. There is no one you can take at face value. Sabrina just wants to blend in with her new lover. Having her wildest fantasies while her wildest dream is in reach. Is she fooling everyone by hiding her true colors? Or does everyone else have a coloring book too?

The Black House Publishing Inc.

Baltimore, Maryland USA

Contact

P.O. Box 941

Harrisburg, NC. 28075

443-904-0649

BlackHousePublish@gmail.com email

On the web

Jonathanpmance.com

Shop.jonathanpmance.com

www.Amazon.com

www.Amazon.co.uk

All rights reserved. Unauthorized duplication is a violation of Federal Law. 2018 Copyright The Black House Publishing Inc. No portion of this book may be copied, retransmitted, published, transferred, or otherwise shared without express written consent of the Author, The Black House Publishing Inc. and/or their representatives.

This book is a work of fiction. Any similarities to any actual persons either living or dead is strictly coincidental and is based entirely on imagination and creative thoughts. While actual places, events and other circumstances may exist, they do not change the fact that the author drew upon his knowledge of such places or events and interlaced fictitious characters to make the story more intense and realistic.

Black Chameleons
Table of Contents

Chapter 1. A Bump in the Road	Page 1
Chapter 2. The Comfort Zone	Page 26
Chapter 3. Duty Calls	Page 45
Chapter 4. The Black House	Page 77
Chapter 5. Brotherly Love	Page 101
Chapter 6. The Submission Forms	Page 114
Chapter 7. What Kind of Ship?	Page 160
Chapter 8. Sign and a Date	Page 194
Chapter 9. The Clean Up	Page 215
Chapter 10. We Had No Idea	Page 230
Chapter 11. Dog and Pony	Page 252

From Red Stick, to Charm City, to the Queen City and around the Globe

The Black House is Blackening Your Eyes and dropping knowledge in your Ear hole.

Experience is the greatest school, but a fool will learn no other way-Favorite quote of the late, great and wise **Janie Mance**

These are the times that try men's souls-**Thomas Paine.**

Black Chameleons

Chapter 1

A Bump in the Road

The morning crispness of early spring held the promise of a beautiful Tuesday. Captain André Nichols of the Maryland Transit Police, was on his way to work. As he headed into downtown Baltimore Maryland. He was all smiles. He heard the radio stating temperatures will reach high 60s. That just made his smile brighter. He listened to his radio going back and forth between 92.3 and 95.9. They both seemed to be overly long with radio commercials. He was driving along with rush hour traffic southbound on I-83.

He was just approaching the Northern Pkwy exit. The radio traffic update alerted him. To an accident just before North Ave. that was blocking traffic. Quickly, he decided to exit onto W. Coldspring Lane. To take the scenic route. Traffic was already beginning to back up. So he turned on his blue lights of his unmarked patrol car. He rode down the shoulder. Making his way to the exit. As he did, a vehicle behind him joined on the shoulder. The vehicle started following him. "I should give your ass a ticket." He mumbles. "I know you'll say, 'you were doing it too.'" He smiled at the humor of it all. He said to himself, "Membership has its privileges."

As he continued down the shoulder. Another car tried to cut out immediately after him. The vehicle already behind him sped up. So the oncoming one wouldn't cut it off. The vehicle trying to come out honked in an angry 4-second burst. Captain Nichols is startled and applied his brakes suddenly. Just then, the car behind him. Rammed into his vehicle at about 30 mph. His coffee fell from his hand. His chest hit the steering wheel. His bullet proof vest absorbed most of the impact.

Now he's pissed. This motherfucker behind him just hit his shit. If this bitch has any kind of violations whatsoever. I'm going to have one of my officers lock her the fuck up. He thinks. He got out of his car and kept his jacket open. So that the person could clearly see his gun on his hip. Being the professional that he was. He tried desperately to hide his anger. If he does end up locking her up. He doesn't want any indication given that it was personal. Captain Nichols called on his Police radio. Saying that he had been involved in a Signal-30.

He was Southbound on the Jones Falls Expressway. Just before the W. Coldspring exit. He could see another vehicle just behind the one that hit him. It had Washington DC tags. It had also pulled onto the shoulder. The female driver that struck him quickly exited her vehicle. Captain Nichols put his hand on his gun. "Get back in your vehicle ma'am!" He yelled. "I just need to explain." The woman replied. She stepped from behind her vehicle door. Captain Nichols could see she was a very shapely woman. In fact, she was gorgeous. Damn, I might be able to let this go. He thought to himself.

"Ma'am, I need you to get back into your vehicle now! Are you okay? Do you need medical attention?" He asked. "No, I'm fine." She replied. He looked at the other vehicle trapped on the shoulder. Due to the Jersey wall on the right side of them. Heavy traffic on the left side. Captain Nichols stepped out into the slow-moving traffic. He pointed at a vehicle to stop in the right lane. He then directed the vehicle behind the female. To drive on its way. The vehicle, a black Chevy Impala. Had two men inside.

One was wearing a suit. One was dressed like he just came off the corner, selling drugs. An odd combination. Captain Nichols thought to himself. Then again, it's Baltimore. The vehicle slowly entered traffic. The passenger appeared to be placing something under his seat. "I should stop those fools." Captain Nichols thought.

There's probably is some weird criminal shit, going on in that car. That I don't feel like getting into today. The car stopped next to the female. With passenger window down, the driver in the suit asked her. "Are you okay, ma'am? Do you need a ride anywhere?" The female driver nervously looked at them and said, "No I'm good, but thank you." Captain Nichols walked back to her. She was seated in the vehicle. "I'm going to need to get your license and registration." He said. "Plus proof of insurance ma'am."

"Alright." She replied. "I'm reaching for my license and registration. I'm not trying to be on the six o'clock news. As no story about how you feared for your life. I've seen how you cops, do us sisters and brothers out here." She smiled as she handed him her information. "I've never shot anyone in my life." Captain Nichols replied. "I don't intend to change that today. In fact, here comes two of my officers now. I'll get one of them to shoot you." He smiled back at her and they both laughed. "Ummm, a man of authority with a sense of humor." She said.

"I think I could like you Officer..?" She looked at his name tag.... "Officer Nichols." "It's Captain Nichols." He said. I'll forgive you for not knowing my rank. Provided your information checks out. Sabrina Marie Morgan, from Washington DC. A Southeast girl. I spent my summers in Southeast at my aunt's house. Around Minnesota Ave and 34th." He said. "I used to run through the car shows. In Anacostia Park back in the day. I can't believe I missed a woman as fine as you.

"Actually, I'm from the Atlanta area in Marietta." She replied. "Not too far from the big Chicken." "The what?" Captain Nichols asked. "It's a well-known landmark in the ATL." She replied. "Oh, you think I'm fine, do you Captain? Does that mean you won't be handcuffing me? That's too bad if you aren't. I think I might like that." Captain Nichols smiled and turned to his approaching officers. Officers Glover and Bellamy Walked up. After they parked behind the lady's vehicle.

"Run this information through KMT." Captain Nichols said. Let me know if she escaped from prison. Then gather all pertinent information. So the Major can do this Departmental vehicle accident report." Officer Glover asked, "Captain, do you want me to run your license? Or do you think you still have Warrants out for your arrest?" "Oh, you've got jokes Officer Glover?" He asked. We'll see how funny you are the next time it's pouring rain. Then you're standing in the intersection directing traffic. I'm going to request you personally." "No Captain, I was saying." Officer Glover said. "I know you don't have any warrants. So there is no need to run your information."

You're getting old and not hearing so well." She joked. "Oh, now I'm old? Captain Nichols asked. "Just wait until the coldest day of winter comes. I'm going to put you out on foot patrol. Over at Lake Clifton. Checking the water for any evidence. Find out who ate that candy off my desk." Officer Glover said, "I'm going to shut up now." Officer Bellamy added. "Hey Captain, I didn't say anything. Just remember that when you're giving out shit details." "You just did say something, Officer Bellamy." Captain Nichols replied. "Let me go to the office. See how many of your reports need to be rewritten."

"You guys are hilarious." Ms. Morgan said. "I never knew cops had this kind of sense of humor." "Yeah, they are a regular Laurel and Hardy these two." Captain Nichols said. "Uh Captain." Officer Glover said. "Laurel and Hardy were men. I'm a woman if you haven't noticed. Officer Adrianne Glover. Not Anthony Glover. A very feminine and often called a beautiful woman." "Okay, so you're Mrs. Hardy." Captain Nichols said. "I remember when Stevie Wonder called you beautiful. He tells every woman they're beautiful." "Oh Mrs. Hardy." Officer Glover said. "I got to be the fat one huh, Captain? I'm cutting down on your birthday gifts this year. Just for that."

"You didn't get me shit last year." Captain Nichols said. "You're talking about cutting down? In fact, you cut my damn cake the squad gave me. Before I ate a piece. Now look, you got me cursing. In front of Ms. Morgan Officer Glover. I apologize ma'am. These two sometimes work my last nerve." Ms. Morgan laughed hysterically. "No, it's quite alright. You guys are making an otherwise bad day. Feel much better right now." "Well, here is some more good news for you." Officer Bellamy said. "No warrants and her license is valid." "Okay." Captain Nichols said. Here is the registration on the State-owned vehicle, my license too."

"Oh, Captain André Nichols." Ms. Morgan said. "Of the Maryland Transit Police Department. Is that like you guys patrol the subways and buses?" "Yeah, we do that and the Light Rail too." Captain Nichols said. Plus we patrol the streets of Baltimore City and surrounding counties. We get into a few things. You'd be surprised." "Well, I have to run. I have to give roll call in about 35 minutes." Ms. Morgan looked down the highway. At the sitting Impala. "Wait Captain." She said. "Let me at least buy you a cup of coffee or breakfast. To try and make up for hitting you this morning." "I can't." He replied. Like I said. I have to be in roll call soon." "Well, that's okay." She said. I can wait until you're done with roll call. Then I'll buy you a quick bite to eat afterwards."

"Oh, now that may work." Captain Nichols said. "You can follow me to the office. Wait for me outside. I'll be about 30 minutes. With roll call and a few things I need to do." "That sounds fine with me." Ms. Morgan said. "We'll see you back at the house Captain." Officer Bellamy said. He and Officer Glover walked back to their patrol vehicles. Then drove off. Captain Nichols drove down W. Coldspring Lane to Park Heights Ave. Ms. Morgan followed. They turn towards downtown. He was all smiles. This very attractive woman was giving him every indication. She wanted to get to know him better.

He checked his rearview mirror. To make sure he wasn't driving too fast. Or would lose her at a red light. Behind him, Ms. Morgan was also checking her rearview mirror. They arrived at the Southern District Building. For the Maryland Transit Police. Captain Nichols got out of his vehicle. He walked to Ms. Morgan. "You can sit right here in front of this building." He said. Wait for me on this street. If any officer comes up to you and asks you to move. Give them my card." He handed her his business card. "Tell them to call me before they give you a ticket. Ms. Morgan smiled. "Aww, that's so sweet."

She looked in her rearview again. Captain Nichols was walking back up to his vehicle. "André!" She yelled. "I mean, Captain Nichols. Do you guys have a bathroom I can use? Sitting on the side of that road and being so nervous. I really have to tinkle." "It's okay, you can call me André." He said. "Yes, we have a bathroom. I tell you what. I'm going to swipe you in. To our parking garage with my key card. Make sure you go all the way up top please? You can park in the guest parking spaces. We have a reception area inside. You can sit and wait for me. After you use the restroom. There are some magazines and what not to read. Sorry, no Essence or Ebony is in there. I'm working on that."

"Oh, that's more than fine André." She said. I feel like I owe you so much already." "No, you don't owe me anything." He replied. I will take that breakfast if you still want to go." He said. "Of course, I want to go." She replied. As they eased towards the gate of the parking lot. She could hear a car drive off behind her. She had a sigh of relief. She parked where instructed and met Captain Nichols. They went inside and he showed her the restroom. After roll call is over. A squad of officers came into the lobby area. They were loud and cracked jokes on each other. The receptionist was in the middle of talking to Ms. Morgan. Her voice was overpowered. By the noise of the officers in the squad.

Suddenly their police radios were blasting. "KMT to 9 Baker 86?" "9 Baker 89 to KMT." Replied the officer. 10-63 for assault in progress. Subject possibly armed with a 10-39A. The officer took out his pad and pen. "I'm ready to copy KMT. Go ahead with the information." The dispatcher began. "Subjects last seen in the 1600 block of Pennsylvania Ave. Number two and number one males. Both dark green colored jackets. The number two male has a red hoodie under his jacket. The number one has a yellow hoodie under his. One wearing black jeans. The other blue jeans. Victim is a number two female. With an apparent head wound. Unknown if wound is severe or superficial.

She states both men assaulted and tried to rob her. The number two male was armed. With a handgun during assault. The Sergeant responded over the radio. 9 Baker 84, 85, 92 91 and 99 are all responding with 9 Baker 86 KMT. They all ran out of office at a frantic pace. The Sergeants of the squad rushed out behind the officers. Captain Nichols came briskly walking behind them. "Do you mind sitting here a few more minutes? He asked. "I just have to listen to the radio. To see if this turns into something I need to respond to." "No, of course not." She answered. Was this a home invasion or something?" She asked. "Not hardly." Captain Nichols replied. "A white female and a white male down on Pennsylvania Ave. Probably are there for drugs."

"Oh okay." She said. "You don't have to call me Ms. Morgan. Sabrina is fine." "Okay, Sabrina it is." He said. "Give me a second." He talked into his radio. "KMT, do I have any units on 20?" Officers responded. "9 Baker 86, 92, and 85 are 10-23 the call. Other units are canvassing area for the suspects. KMT we're going to need a Medic at this location. Number 2 female bleeding from a head wound. She says she was struck with the 10-39A. She is conscious and breathing." Captain Nichols speaks again into his radio. "KMT, have one of my Sergeants call me on my cell. With an update as soon as possible."

Captain Nichols walked her to the parking garage. They drove a short distance to a restaurant. "What is this place?" Sabrina asked. "This is a spot owned by a friend of mine." André responded. It's The Darker than Blue Café." André responded. "It's black-owned and the food is out of this world." André opened her car door for her. Then put some money into her parking meter. He took her hand as they walked into the restaurant. Sabrina took a quick look up and down the street. Then walked inside. "André my man." A voice called. "You're eating here a lot. I'm starting to think you like my food." "It's pretty good bro. André replied. Mr. Jenkins this is Sabrina. Sabrina this is Mr. Jenkins…he owns this place."

"Nice to meet you Mr. Jenkins." Sabrina said. "Likewise, the pleasure is mine." Mr. Jenkins said. André I see you have good taste in food and women. You might actually have some sense in your head." "Oh wait." Sabrina said. "Does he have some mental issues I should know about?" "Anybody who runs towards gun fire." Mr. Jenkins replied. "Is plain crazy to me. Now I know what he wants to eat. What can I get you, pretty lady?" "I'll have whatever he's having." Sabrina said. "With a cup of coffee." "So, Sabrina from Atlanta." André said. "How long have you lived here in the DMV?" "Well, I lived in P.G. County Maryland." She replied. "When I first came here two years ago.

Then I moved into DC. I have never lived in Virginia. So, I guess you could say. I'm from just the DM and not the V." Normally, people move out of DC into Maryland." André said. Or Virginia. You did the reverse, why was that?" "Especially not moving out of Maryland into Southeast DC." "Well, I had some interest that I…" She paused. At that moment, André's phone rang. "Captain Nichols speaking." Sabrina could hear a man's voice on the phone. "How bad is her injury? Does she know her assailants? Where exactly did the incident take place? What was she doing on Pennsylvania Ave? Do we have an I.D. on the suspects? Oh, they're in custody. That's beautiful."

"I don't need to know anymore by phone." Captain Nichols continued. "Get on your laptop in your vehicle. Email me a notification so I can forward it up the chain. Contact Citi-watch. See if they have video of this incident. Send someone to go pick up the tape. Later." He hangs up his phone. "Now, where were we?" He continued. "You said you had interest?" "Yes, I had some interest in the District." She said. That I needed to be close to." She replied. "Oh, that's woman code talk." André said. For I moved there for some dude." "Oh, my God, you're terrible." She replied. Why would you say something like that?" "I might be terrible but am I right?" He asked. "That's kind of the reason." She said. It's not that black and white." "Kind of the reason." André repeated. That's woman code talk. For the shit didn't work out like I thought it would."

"My God, you are killing me." She said. "What did I do to deserve this abuse? No, it didn't work out like I planned but that's okay. I learn from my mistakes. I will eventually win. So, what about you, André? What's your story?" The waitress brought them their coffee and juice. "Well, I'm Baltimore born and raised." He said. Westside brother. Spent some summers in D.C. at my aunt's house. Did my four years in the Marines and got out. Had a few jobs until I fell into this one 21 years ago. It was 10 years before I got promoted to Sergeant. After that, I moved up the ranks pretty quickly." "So, what are your plans?" She asked. Are you just doing 25 and getting out?"

"Well actually, the State takes my Military time. As part of my service. So technically, I have 25 years now. I probably will stick around another 10 years. I'll be just over 50 and ready to travel. So, what is it that you do for a living Sabrina?" He asked. "Me?" She replied. "Well, I'm between jobs right now. I worked for this Defense contractor down at the NSA. For the last six and a half years. They just lost the contract." "Well, you still have your Top-Secret Clearance right?" He asked. So why didn't you get on with the company that won the contract?" "I probably will do that." Sabrina said. "I have time to make that decision."

"My old job gave us a six-month severance package. Of our entire salary so I'm okay for now." "Damn!" André replied. "I need to get with one of those Federal contractors. These MoFos I work for. Will hand you an ink pen and tell you good luck. So, do you have any family in the area Sabrina? He asked. Any kids?" "No and no." She replied. I don't have any kids yet. My mom lives in Arizona. She moved out there with her boyfriend. A few years after my dad died." She said. The waitress brought their breakfast and their conversation continued. "Damn!" André said. "Women in your family will move for a man. Won't they?"

"I hope your ass doesn't meet an astronaut." André continued. "He'll be like, 'Sabrina, I'm moving to the Moon. Pack your shit." "You are not right!" She replied. "I don't know why you are giving me so much grief. I thought we were going to be cool. I see already this is starting to be an abusive relationship." She laughed. "Oh, now we're in a relationship already?" André asked. "You haven't even finished your grits yet. Don't call me tonight. Saying you're seven months pregnant and it's mine." He joked. "I wouldn't do that to you André." She replied. "What kind of a girl do you think I am? I'm only going to be five months pregnant tonight. So, what about you Sir? Do you have any kids? Is most of your family still here?"

"Yeah, I have two kids." He said. "A son and a daughter both out of State. My parents are both deceased. I have three brothers. My brother Lincoln use to be a lobbyist in Washington. He is now a College Professor at Howard University. My brother Justin has his own Information Technology business. They are both overseas. Helping to clean up a government mess. Then there's Drexler. They call him Count Drexler on the streets. Drexler has always been involved in some type of drama. My other brothers and I don't really talk to him too often." "What kind of drama is he involved in?" Sabrina asked. "Drugs, of course." André said. "Who knows what else? I haven't seen or talked to Drexler since our Aunt Emma died."

"Death is the only time. I can justify being in the same circle as him." "So, you don't know where your brother hangs out?" Sabrina asked. "Oh, I know exactly where he is right now." André replied. "I just don't go to that part of the Eastside." "So, you can drive by and check on him?" She asked. See that he is okay, can't you?" "I can if he's out on his corners." André replied. "When he's feeling some heat. He has a couple of spots he lays low at." "Oh really, where are his lay low spots?" She asked. "I don't know the addresses on purpose." He responded. "I know how to find him." If I would ever need to reach him." "You couldn't call to reach him?" She asked. "Nah, he doesn't keep a cell phone." He said. "Not even a burner phone. I think the way he works is. He gets a phone from one of his guys. When the phone has 20 minutes left in pre-paid minutes."

In a vacant warehouse in East Baltimore. Drexler is seated eating some chicken wings. "Damn, where did you get these wings from O?" Drexler asks. "Down on Eutaw and Saratoga? Would you like a wing sweetie?" He looked over at a woman who was stripped naked. Her hands were tied over her head to a pole. Her mouth was gagged. "You're probably not hungry." Drexler said. "Now that I think about it, Cynthia. A pending excruciating death. Can really fuck with your appetite. Tell me where you hid my shit. I'll let you walk out of here alive."

"However in 15 minutes." He continued. "That train is going to pass by outside. The last sounds you make. Aren't going to be heard by anybody, who gives a fuck about you. Speaking of giving a fuck. Hey O! I mean Deer Dog. Hand me that wire brush right there." Deer Dog handed him the brush. Drexler held the brush up to her face. "I use this to clean my shotguns. It's made of steel bristle brush. I shove it down the barrel. To clean out all the burned residue. Left when you fire the weapon."

"I bet you have some residue." Drexler said. "Inside that little pussy of yours. Don't you darling? Now you can go home and clean it out. With some Summers Eve douche shit. Or whatever the fuck you use. Or, I can clean it out for you with this brush. Now that train will be passing. On its way to Aberdeen in about 10 minutes. You might want to think real fucking hard. About where you bitches hid my shit. Or I'm going to clean the fuck out your ass. Literally." He took the gag from her mouth. The woman was crying desperately. "Please Drexler." She plead. "I swear to God. I didn't have anything to do with someone taking your stash. Please don't kill me. I'll do anything you say. I'll do anything." She began to cry uncontrollably. She saw her pleas had no effect on Count Drexler.

"Unfortunately for you." He replied. That is not the answer I wanted to hear." "You still have two minutes to tell me something good." "I DON'T KNOW ANYTHING DREXLER!" She yelled. "I SWEAR, I DON'T KNOW!" "Then, you're wasting my time you worthless bitch." He said. He grabbed her by the throat with his left hand. He began to choke her. He told Deer Dog and Fats to grab her legs. She fought desperately but it was futile. Drexler took the long wire brush. Shoving it deep inside her vagina. She screamed the most horrific, agonizing scream. Drexler placed his eyes an inch from hers. He continued to choke her as he watched her die. He then turned to Fats and Deer Dog. "Hey O! I mean Deer Dog. Take this bitch and dump her in Westport somewhere. Don't forget to clean the ride once you're finished."

Back on Greenmount Ave. André was standing next to Sabrina, outside of her car. "Aren't you fancy?" André asked. "You out here pushing a 6 series Benz. I can't wait until I grow up. To make moves like this." "Don't get it twisted." She replied. "I bought this used. After I let someone else lose their money in depreciation."

"Oh and you're fiscally responsible too." André said. "I'm liking you more and more, Sabrina." "Oh, does that mean I can see you again?" She asked. "Yes, you can definitely see me again." He said. "I'll be off from work this evening, about 6pm. There is a nice little spot on Charles Street. We can go have drinks. It's not too far from Penn Station. You do drink, don't you woman?" He asked. "Oh yes, I have a drink or two socially." She said. Every now and then." "Just two drinks?" He teased. "Don't tell me you're one of those goodie two shoes girls," "Well, that depends." She retorted. "On what you're hoping I'm good at." "I'm hoping you're good." He replied. "At whatever it is you like to do."

"Watch yourself Captain." Sabrina said. "You may be very surprised at what I like to do. In fact, you may not be able to handle it." "Is that some kind of challenge?" He asked. "Not a challenge, just a warning." She stated. "You're probably not on my level." "Oh shit! André exclaimed. "What kind of level are you on? How do I get up there?" "I'll show you if I ever think you're ready André." She said. "For now, I have to go call my insurance company. Then move a few things before we meet tonight." "Damn, you have moved me." He replied. "At least in some places. I guess I better get to my office and do some work. I'll see you later tonight." "Oh I don't get a goodbye hug or anything?" Sabrina asked playfully.

André walked up to her. As she stood between her car door and frame. "I didn't want to seem like I was trying to rush you." He joked. "Into the back seat so soon." "Oh, so now you're going to try to do me in the back seat?" She asked. "You won't even spring for the Motel 6? It's just around the corner?" They embraced and held it for a few seconds. Sabrina took her seat in her car and André closed her door. She started the engine and rolled down her window. "Thank you André for a lovely morning." She said. "Thank you." He responded. "For the pleasure of your company as well Sabrina. I'll see you tonight." She drove off and André walked back to his vehicle.

He headed back to his office. He had a stack of reports and paperwork were waiting for him. He began to review the latest Robbery/Assault reports. His presentation was due at the end of the week to the Chief of Police. Detailing his plans to curtail the crimes in his District. That's what he was supposed to be doing. All he could think about was Sabrina. She has the most gorgeous brown skin with beautiful white teeth. Her body is straight out of a 2-Live Crew video. Her conversation is also very pleasant he thought. She wears her hair natural in Afro. Which makes her even sexier to the tenth power.

He decided to text her. To let her know he was thinking about her. *Awwww, that's so sweet, she responds. I've been thinking about you too.* She replied. "*I just hope you're careful because I'm addictive.*" She texted. Along with a photo of her face. *Good Lord, you're beautiful*! He texted back to her. "*I think I may already have a habit.*" LOL. She responded. *I'll see you in a few hours*. Was her next text. André tried to get back to work but couldn't clear his head. "Lieutenant Johnson!" He yelled. "Yes Sir." An approaching voice responded. "Have Sergeant Mays or Sergeant Womack get these reports ready." Captain Nichols said. "For CompStat. I'm going to check on things around Mondawmin. See if our officers need anything."

"Okay Captain." Lieutenant Johnson said. "I'll make sure this gets taken care of right away." "Thank you Lew." Captain Nichols responded. "I owe you one. When I win the lottery. You know you've got a Coke or Pepsi on me." "Oh wow Sir. You are too kind." Lieutenant Johnson replied. "All I really need is a ski mask. And where you'll be keeping all that money." "Whatever nigga." Captain Nichols said. "I might be rich but I'll still be carrying something. Waiting on your ass to come creeping to my door." "I wouldn't creep to your door Captain." Lieutenant Johnson said. "If you hit the lottery. I'm going to put some C4 to your door. No beef no more."

Captain Nichols responded, "You don't want to see me in pain. I'll leave that ass like Toni Braxton, never breathing again." "You crazy as shit Captain." Lieutenant Johnson said. "Let me go find my Sergeants and get this work done." The two of them then walked out of the room. Arriving at the Mondawmin Mall. Captain Nichols looked at the massive amount of people. Going to and fro. Many waiting on a bus to arrive. While others were just waiting. He soon saw two of his officers. One of them was Officer Gaines. Gaines had managed to get three complaints against him. In the last 45 days. Captain Nichols wanted to have an informal talk with him. To try and get him to settle down.

He knew having an informal discussion, with an officer was risky to him. Still he wanted to help this young brother if he could. "Officer Gaines!" The Captain called out. "Let's take a walk. We'll be back, Officer Stewart. We're on the radio if you need us." He and Officer Gaines began walking towards Gwynn Falls Pkwy. They eventually ended on Bentalou Street. They stopped. Captain Nichols asked. "Why do you think you're getting so many complaints?" Officer Gaines replied, "I just ask people to not break the law in front of me. A few of them try to make it into this big ordeal." "Maybe it's not what you're asking them to do." Captain Nichols said. "It's how you're asking them."

"You see, I grew up in this neighborhood." Captain Nichols continued. "I knew every drug dealer and every hoe. Every killer and moarfuggers that were up to no good. I still know quite a few of them. Now, do you know what I call them? If I have to deal with one of them today Officer?" He asked. "No Sir." Replied Officer Gaines. "I call them Sir or Ma'am." Captain Nichols said. "Look, you have the power to take these people's freedom. If they are breaking the law. You don't have to go back and forth. Word for word. Every time somebody is giving you a lot of mouth. Your presence there says all you need to say. I'm not telling you to be no punk and get abused out here."

"I'm just saying if you ask somebody to move off the corner. Captain Nichols continued. They call you a bitch or whatever." "You can say something like, you don't believe that. If you did, you wouldn't be leaving. He knows the law enough. To know once you tell him to leave, he better bounce. What's he going to do after that? Not stand there talking shit. Unless he wants to go to jail. So, you just pulled his punk card. You don't have to say anything else. When you get to cursing at them because they cursed at you. You're in the wrong. You're the professional and should always remain professional."

"Just because you have the power. Doesn't make you any better. Than anybody you meet out here on the streets." "I'm not trying to act like I'm better." Officer Gaines said. "Than anybody out here Captain." "See, there you go." Captain Nichols said. "You just have to say something when somebody is talking to you. Just be quiet. As long as they are not talking about getting a weapon. Or doing something to you. It's probably just talk. They're mad at you because you made them leave the corner. They can't do anything about it. So they talk trash. It's the same thing you would do. If I told you in front of your boys to leave the corner."

"Now, let's walk up here to the block I grew up on." Captain Nichols continued. "I went to school right over there. My mom made me and my brothers, go to this church right here. St. Mary Baptist Church. One of the biggest in West Baltimore. Those guys standing in front of the store. I grew up with them. See that old lady sitting over there on the porch?" Captain Nichols asked. "Yeah, I see her." Officer Gaines replied. "That's Ms. Katherine "Kitty" Parsons. She has lived in that house since before I was born. Legend says she was the neighborhood hoe. Way back in the day before she got old. They say she was fucking the previous Pastor at our church before he died. Now that they have this younger Pastor in there. She's all sanctified and holy. She never did like me. When I was growing up around here.

"For some reasons, she loved my brother Drexler." "Who is that coming out the house Captain?" Officer Gaines asked. Oh, that's her son. Captain Nichols replied. "Crazy Ronnie James. He's always had some mental issues. That must be his State case worker visiting him. He barely talks. At least not anything more than you can barely understand. He grunts and growls a lot. When he looks at you. It's hard to tell if he is smiling because he likes you or wants to kill you." "Damn, that's a big dude Captain." Officer Gaines said. "I would hate to have to fight him." "I doubt Crazy Ronnie James is coordinated enough." Captain Nichols said. "To throw a punch. But if he ever grabs your ass. They say he's strong as a bull."

"Anyhow, if you're up this way. Or you see Ms. Parsons up by Mondawmin. Look out for her. I know she doesn't like me. I have never been crazy about her. I just have a soft spot for the elderly. She's always over at St. Mary across the street. So stop in. Let them know you're in the area. In case they need you. So they can feel safe." "Alright Captain, I can do that." Officer Gaines said. "They have a parking lot." Captain Nichols said. "In the back of the church that's fenced in." As he pointed. He saw a car that looked like Sabrina's car. It was leaving the lot behind the church. On the next street over.

Every car I see. Is going to look like hers he thought to himself. "Okay, I have to get back to the office." Captain Nichols said. "So we better walk back up to Mondawmin. Before these bad ass kids get out of school." "Yo! What's happening? Little brother?" A voice said. Captain Nichols turned around to see his brother Drexler. Stepping out of his SUV. "I didn't expect to see the law around here." Drexler said. "What happened? Are they opening a doughnut shop on this block or something?" "Officer Gaines." Captain Nichols said. "This is my infamous brother Drexler. "Aka Count Drexler." "Nice to meet you Sir." Officer Gaines said. "Sir? Drexler repeated. "You must be getting that bullshit speech from my little brother."

"Whatever nigga." Captain Nichols said. "What are you doing back over here in our old neighborhood?" "Oh Ms. Kitty, I mean Ms. Parsons called me." Drexler replied. "She had some trash I was going to go dump for her. I was going to talk to her for a minute." "I know you're not hauling trash in your brand-new Jeep Cherokee." Captain Nichols said. "I know better than that." "Well, sometimes, you have to do what you have to do." Drexler answered. "I wouldn't want Ms. Parsons to have a house full of trash. Then not be able to get rid of it." "It's a miracle, Officer Gaines." Captain Nichols said.

"My brother is more concerned, with helping the elderly than running the streets." "I guess I should repent right Captain?" Officer Gaines asked. "You make it seem like the end of the world is near." "We may both have to repent." Captain Nichols answered. "I can't stay around here. "I'm sure my brother will do something." "To make me have to lock his ass up." Captain Nichols said. "Nigga I told you." Drexler said. "If you try that shit again we will fight to death." "Let the best man win." "Your ass ain't bullet proof Count Drexler." Captain Nichols said. "You either, Captain brother." Drexler replied. "Stay out of this part of town. Before people think you're up to no good."

"Everybody knows which one of us is up to no good." Captain Nichols replied. "That's why I'm surprised at the holy lady. Why Ms. Parsons even fools with you? I guess opposites attract." Opposites? Drexler asks. "Man, you have always been wearing those rose-colored glasses." Drexler said. "Your entire life." "What's that supposed to mean?" Captain Nichols asked. "Nothing." Drexler said. "Good seeing you again little brother. Let's get together. The second Thursday of Not-ever. I'll buy you a drink." Captain Nichols and Officer Gaines started walking back to Mondawmin. "He seems pretty cool Captain." Officer Gaines said. "There's nothing cool about my brother Drexler." Captain Nichols said.

"He's a cold, calculating, manipulative, violent, and sadistic motherfucker. When we were kids. My brother used to torture animals for the fun of it. I won't even turn your stomach. With the kind of sick stuff he did. I'm sure in his adult life. He's done some twisted evil stuff. This is why we don't associate very much. We run into each other. We speak and keep moving. It would tear my family up. If I had to put my brother away for a long time. He's an evil motherfucker but he's still my brother." "Yeah, that's a rough one Captain." Officer Gaines said. "All of us have at least one bad seed in our family."

"My brother is not just a bad seed." Captain Nichols said. "That Negro is toxic poison. Unstable chemicals and a vicious animal all rolled into one." "How did he get like that Sir?" Officer Gaines asked? If you don't mind me asking?" "I wish I knew." Captain Nichols responded. "Our Pops rolled out when I was about seven. Drexler was about twelve. So, he was right at that teenage time. He started hanging out on the streets. Next thing we know. He was a big-time drug dealer. Word on the streets is he's killed a few people. Police have either found no bodies, proof or witnesses." They arrived back at Mondawmin and approached Officer Stewart. "Is everything all quiet up here Stewart?" Officer Gaines asked.

"Yes, nothing has happened while you were away." She said. "Were you snitching to the Captain? About me taking an extra 5 minutes for lunch?" "That's a lie." Officer Gaines replied. "I didn't tell him you took an extra 5 minutes for lunch. I told him you abandoned your post. Then went shopping in the Mall. She didn't pay for shit Captain. She came running out with a fat gold rope. Security was chasing her. Oh, my bad. You told me not to say anything. About what you did to those Security guards. Damn shame how they died." Officer Gaines joked. "Boy you're stupid." Officer Stewart said. "If I had to kill any Security Guards and you knew about it. I'd have to kill you too. I'd be afraid you might snitch like you're doing now."

"I was taught when I was growing up." She continued. "Snitches get stitches and found in ditches." "Damn, she's always trying to resort to violence Captain." Officer Gaines said. "Did you all do a psychological exam on her?" Before you hired her? I think she needs another one." "I don't have time to be fooling with you two nut cases." Captain Nichols said. "I have somewhere to be after work. I'm going to the office to get cleaned up and change." "Don't get into any trouble Captain!" Officer Stewart yelled. "You know how I do!" Captain Nichols yelled back. "That's what I'm afraid of." Officer Stewart laughed.

André walked into XS restaurant and found the table where Sabrina was waiting. "I'm sorry I'm running a few minutes late." He said. "I had to park a few blocks up Charles Street. On the other side of Penn Station." "Well, I parked in one of the parking garages." Sabrina replied. "Around the corner on Cathedral Street. I didn't feel like going out to check the meter. I ordered you a Henny and coke already." "Thank you." André said. "So, tell me, how was your day André?" She asked. "My day was good." He replied. "I had to have a talk with one of our young Officers. He has been getting a few complaints lately. I need him to settle down. If I have to talk to him in my office. It won't be good for him."

"Wait, Cops actually get in trouble?" Sabrina asked. "If people file a complaint on them?" "Yeah, they can get in trouble." André replied. "We get demoted or even get fired. If the complainant follows through on the complaint. Don't believe everything you see on T.V." He said. "Oh well, you learn something new every day." Sabrina remarked. "I could teach you a few things." He said. "The way you were talking this morning. You sounded like you know more than I do." "Well, let's just say I've never been shy." Sabrina responded. "About exploring my options." "What kind of options are we talking?" André asked. "It's too early in the game." She said. I don't want to shock you so soon." "Damn, you're rolling like that?" He asked.

"What the hell kind of stuff are you into?" He asked. "Look, I'm not into that pain and torture bullshit. Don't cut me, don't burn any candles on me. No electrical wires on me. Or none of that crazy white people shit." "You forgot no poop or piss." Sabrina said. "That's on my don't-do list as well." "I'm definitely not into having nobody's poop on me." André said. "What about piss?" Sabrina asked. "Hell no!" André exclaimed. "I have never drank no woman's piss before!" "I have no plans to ever!" "I may have licked a little residue. In the heat of the moment. That's about it." They both laughed.

"Oh, I see you have dealt with some skanks in your day." Sabrina said. "They wouldn't even wash up. Before they let you down there?" "Like I said, it was in the heat of the moment." André said. "So what else did you do today?" Sabrina asked. "Oh, I walked over to my old neighborhood. With that Officer I was talking to. We were across the street from my old church. I thought I saw your car leaving off the back-parking lot. Of course, there are million silver Mercedes in this city. Now I'll think they all are yours." "No, that definitely was not me." She said. "I was down on K. St in DC, this afternoon." "Oh snap, that's where the money is." André said. "What were you doing on K. St?"

"Oh, I had an interview." Sabrina replied. "With this Defense Contractor Company." "Well, why didn't you tell me?" André asked. "I would have wished you good luck." "Well I didn't want to say anything." Sabrina said. "Until I see which way it may go. You know how it is when you're looking for a job. You're hopeful but don't want to get your hopes up too high." "Yeah, I feel you." André said. "So, did you go over to your old church?" Sabrina asked. "While you were in the area?" "No, I didn't go over there." André said. "I saw the new Pastor was there. I've been wanting to go talk to him. I just haven't gotten around to it."

"Then what was crazy." André continued. "I rarely visit over there anymore. I don't think my brother does either. But he showed up out of the blue." "Your brother Drexler?" Sabrina asked. "Yes." André said. "He said he was helping out the old lady named Ms. Parsons." "Is she the neighborhood old lady?" Sabrina asked. "I guess you could call her that." André responded. "She was up there in my mom's age group. When she was younger, she was nothing like my mom. They say that old lady. Used to raise hell out on the streets. Now you can find her over at the church most of the time. If she's not at home."

"She's probably a sweet little old lady." Sabrina said. "She has now found the Lord and is sea of wisdom." For anybody that will go talk to her" "I don't know about all that." André said. "She never did talk to me too much. She loved my brother Drexler for some reasons." "Well, there you go." Sabrina replied. "She probably figured. He needed more guidance and wisdom than you. Where did your brother Drexler say he was going when he left?" "I didn't ask." André replied. "Well, did he say anything about being over there?" Sabrina asked. "Other than helping Ms. Parsons?" "Anything like what?" André asked. "Like where he had just come from?" Sabrina inquired. "Where he was going? Anything?"

"Why would he tell me all of that?" André asked. "I told you my brother and I don't bond like that. Why are you so interested in what he's doing?" "Who said I was interested in what he's doing?" Sabrina asked. "Well, you're sure asking a lot of questions about him." André said. "Do you know my brother from somewhere?" "Don't be silly André." She said. "Do I look like that kind of girl? Who runs around in that type of environment?" "Nah." André said. "You look like you're one of those good girls. You try to act bad sometimes." "You think I'm a good girl?" She asked. "Man, you do wear those rose-colored glasses." "What!" André uttered. "What, what?" Sabrina responded. "What did you just say?" André asked. "You said I wear rose-colored glasses.

"That's the second time I've heard that today." He said. "Who else said that to you?" She asked. "Nobody." André said. He looked at her somewhat suspicious. His Police instincts were humming. Telling him to take a more investigative observation of Sabrina. "Hey, why don't we get out of here?" Sabrina asked. "Let's go to your place." She interrupted his thought process. "Oh, you want to go back to my place do you?" André asked. "We may need to stop at the store. Pick up a few things. I haven't gone grocery shopping yet" He said. "Oh, that's okay." Sabrina replied. "I just need a glass of wine. A stick of bubble gum and your dick."

"You could be out of bubble gum for all I care." She continued. "Well damn!" André said. "Nobody can accuse you of being shy." "I may be a lot of things." Sabrina said. "Shy is not at the top of my list." "Let me get the waitress over here." André said. "So we can pay for these drinks and can get out of here. Fuck it. I'll just leave fifty dollars on the table. She can figure that shit out and have a nice tip." "Oh, a generous man." Sabrina remarked. "I hope you don't get all stingy when we get to your house." "No, you can have all the bubble gum you want." André said. "Oh, you've got jokes huh, Mister?" Sabrina said.

He helped her put on her jacket. They walked out the front door. He walked her to her car and she drove him to his. She then followed him home. Parking in his garage. Just next to his car. They walked into his kitchen. Through the garage door entrance. "Oh, you've got a nice-looking place here Captain." She said. "Don't be trying to get all formal on me in here lady." André replied. "Let me take your jacket. Go make yourself comfortable." André walked over to his stereo. He connected his mp3 player. He selected a song and Luther Vandross began to sing. "Oh, that's not fair." Sabrina said. "Luther will definitely make the mood irresistible. Are we listening to his greatest hits?" "No, this is a playlist I have." André answered. "On my player. It's called Slow Jam Tapes."

"Oh, I remember them." She said. "My older brothers used to make those slow jam tapes. Back in the day. I used to love it when they would play them. I just knew I'd fall in love to one of those songs." Sabrina said. "So, did you ever fall in love?" André asked. "I thought I was a couple of times." She replied. I realized other things were in the cards for me. So I just grab the feeling of love. Whenever I can get it. For however long I can." "That sounds kind of lonely." André said. "No, I'm not lonely at all." Sabrina said. "I have my needs met. Probably a lot more than the average wife or girlfriend."

André selected a bottle of wine from his wine rack. Then put it on ice. "What about you Mr. Interrogator?" Sabrina asked. "Have you ever been in love?" She asked. "I was in love just a couple of years ago." He answered. "I reconnected with this woman I used to date. From Newark New Jersey. I found her on social media after 22 years apart. We started talking and it was like no time had passed. We started making plans to get married and everything. I flew her up to visit me. For the long Labor Day weekend that year. We had the greatest time or so I thought. When she got back home, we talked. We were still planning for her to move in here with me."

"She has two kids. Their father lives up that way too. She was supposed to talk to him about moving the kids. How we'd work out him being able to see his kids. I wasn't trying to interfere with him being able to do that. Since he was active in their lives. I don't know how that went over. Shortly after they were supposed to talk. The bitch tells me she doesn't ever want to talk to me again. She threatened to call my job. If I ever called her again. Just broke everything off cold turkey. I was devastated. The shit was unreal and unbelievable. We both seemed so much in love." "She probably was getting drama from her babies' daddy." Sabrina said.

"He may have said, he was going to try to take the kids. If she moved. Most women can't handle something like that. So she did what was safe." "Fuck that!" André replied. "The bitch could have talked to me about it. We could have worked shit out. Hell, I would have been willing, to take an early retirement. Then move there. Then I see the bitch's picture on social media. She married the motherfucker. That didn't want her sorry ass until she was about to move. Now if I ever see that bitch. I'll slap the shit out of her and her nigga." "Awwww, she really hurt you, didn't she?" Sabrina said. "I don't think it was intentional." "Bring me a glass of wine. Let me see if I can make you feel better."

Chapter 2

The Comfort Zone

He brought over the two glasses of wine. Giving her one. "Yeah, I think I can forget about her." André said. "I have someone beautiful and fine. Standing in my living room. Damn, you're fine, Sabrina. Do you work out?" "I do when I have the time." She replied. "Most of this is God-given though. Also, I found out when I was 21. That I can't have any kids. Not having all that trauma beat up on my body. Has helped me keep my assets." She continued. "What a nice asset you have too." André said. Oh, my damn!" He exclaimed.

"Come here!" Sabrina commanded. He moved closer to her and she kissed him. He sat his glass of wine on a coaster. She soon placed hers on a coaster too. They began kissing passionately. Their hands searched each other in an intense effort. To disrobe and please each other. André found her neck and began to kiss and suck on it. Sabrina flowed into the moment and surrendered her neck to him. "I don't have to worry about marking your neck up, do I? André asked. "I don't want any jealous boyfriends or husbands coming to look for me." "No, neither won't mind." Sabrina replied playfully.

André allowed his hand to open her blouse. Revealing her bra. Sabrina in turn, unbuttoned his shirt. He quickly removed his t-shirt as well. She leaned forward so he could undo her bra. He soon had her breast exposed. "Wow, you have some nice Tits Sabrina." He said. "I could suck on them all night." "Ummmm, now that's a dedicated man." Sabrina replied. André lowered his head and began to suck on her right nipple. While caressing her left with his hand. Sabrina moaned in delightful approval. The next song on the playlist was an Anita Baker classic.

"Ah, you want the best that I've got?" Sabrina inquired. André just moaned in approval. He continued to suck on her right breast. "I just hope you can handle it Mr. Officer." She said. At that moment, she let her right hand wander down to his waist. After a brief, frantic search, she found his belt buckle. She began to undo it. His pants were quickly opened and unzipped. Her hand went straight for his rod. She began stroking and caressing it with her hand. André awkwardly contorted his body. So that she could have access. While he continued his oral assault on her body. Her hands felt so good and her chocolate skin smelled so delicious.

He sat her down so that he could remove her shoes. Her pants and panties quickly followed. "What are you about to do to me?" She asked playfully. "I'm about to eat your pussy woman if you must know." He responded. "You're all up in my business." "Well excuse me, carry on." She said sarcastically. He laid her back on the sofa. Then began to pull her pants down to her ankles. She sat up and made him stand. So that she could lower his pants as well. André then extended his hand and invited her to his bedroom. They both began walking. With no tops on but their pants around their ankles. They smiled like children.

However, at that moment. Far more serious things were on their minds. He pulled the covers down. On his neatly-made bed and sat her down. They removed their clothing completely. André stared at her perfectly pedicured feet. He began kissing each one. He then started sucking her toes to Sabrina's delight. "You're a good boy." She said. "You know what mama likes." André moved up her legs with his lips. Kissing the meaty part of the back of her legs. His hands led a trail higher and higher up her thighs. As they gently spread her legs apart. His face soon followed as he began alternating kisses. On her right and left inner thigh. He could see the glistening of her pearl. Her labia waited in eager anticipation of what was soon to come.

He sucked the meat on her inner thighs. Trying to leave a light mark as to his visit. Sabrina moaned in excited coercion. For him to not stop what he was doing. Taking the hint from her fevered breathing. He moved slow and teasingly towards her treasure. He savored the aroma of her scent. Then kissed her vaginal lips as if he were kissing her mouth. "Ummmmm." Sabrina moaned. His tongue soon pierced her lips and entered her. Before flickering up and down. Sabrina gasped as his tongue met her clitoris for the first time. Sensing that was what she wanted. André quickly went to work. His tongue began a wicked back and forth. Like a switch blade all over her pussy.

She pressed her pussy against his face. Trying to stuff him with more than enough to eat. André was more than willing and up to the task. His tongue found the entrance to her vaginal cavity. Where he began an extensive search. Swirling in deep and fast circles. His tongued touched every centimeter of her walls. After he removed his tongue. He quickly replaced it with two of his fingers. He fingered her deeper and deeper. While his tongue licked her clit with an erratic pace. Her breathing became more and more intense. André had no intention of stopping. At least, not until he heard her make that magic sound.

"Sllllsssss ooooooh fuck. André." She moaned. "You're going to make me cum." He paused briefly from licking her to respond. "That's the idea." He said. He then dove his head back into her pussy. He began sucking her clitoris. He switched hands and inserted two fingers from his left hand into her. He began slowly running his tongue up and down her slit. He had to maneuver around his fingers. Yet his tongue never lost contact with her. He pumped her pussy intently with his fingers. While sucking, licking and kissing her pussy. Soon, her breathing became audible moans. She grabbed the back of his head. To make sure he would complete the job.

André removed his fingers. Continuing to lick her up and down. All over her pussy. Every few licks, his tongue would find its way inside of her. Where he'd swirl it around. Sabrina was grinding her pussy forcefully against his face. With a determination to cum. "I'm not going to stop until you cum." André said. Immediately, Sabrina let out a yell. Her pussy glazed Andrés' face with her juices. Her body convulsed and shook. The intensity of her orgasm was strong. She now pushed André's head away. However, he fought her off. He kept up his licking and kissing her. As he drank all the moisture he found pouring out of her.

Her body was so sensitive. His oral attack rushed her to another powerful orgasm. "Stop, stop, I can't take any more." She said. He gave her a few more licks but finally relented. She was still panting and breathing heavily. "Come up here so I can please you." She said. "No baby." He replied. "With those sexy full lips you've got. I want you to come this way." He turned her body. So that it lay across the bed. With her head hanging over the side. He then stood over her. Lowering his dick over her face. Her mouth opened. He pushed it inside. She quickly moved her head so that his dick came out wet. Her pursed juicy lips stroked him. Like she was playing the flute. Giving special attention to the tip.

"Oh my God, Sabrina that feels so good." He moaned. She took her hands pulling him closer over her face. He looked down. To make sure he didn't step on her or anything. She gave him a look. That look that said you haven't felt what good is yet. With him standing over her, she began to lick his balls. Sucking them gently into her mouth. Her hands held his thighs apart. Like she was Sampson at the temple. The pleasure he was feeling. Almost made him crumble to the floor. Sabrina licked and sucked his balls. Before putting his dick back into her mouth. He began fucking her beautiful face. While his hands played with her breast.

Sabrina took his strokes in her mouth like a champ. Before letting his soaking wet dick slide across her face. She sucked his balls some more. André climbed onto the bed with his dick still in her mouth. He lowered his head once again between her legs. He began devouring her pussy. His dick was still fucking her mouth. They began having a contest. To see who could make the other feel the best. In this 69 position. He spread her pussy lips open. Inserting his finger and tongue. She ran her juicy lips from the tip of his shaft to his balls. She held it so that she could pretend to play the flute with it again.

Sabrina opened her legs wider. So that he could have greater access. André accepted the challenge. His tongue went wild licking her over and over. Up and down, around and around her clitoris. Then deep inside of her pussy. Sabrina put his dick back into her mouth. She wrapped her right leg around the back of his head. To keep him eating her luscious pussy. She was grinding into his face. As he pumped his dick into hers. Their slurping and smacking sounds filled the air. Almost as if their minds had locked in sync, they both yelled. "Oh Fuck!" They both began a rapid climax. They both began to shake. Each one was climaxing into the other's mouth. They both eagerly accepted the deposits. Sabrina pulled her right leg tighter around his head. To make sure his mouth did not leave. Until her explosion was over.

He pumped his dick deep into her mouth. Cumming on her tonsils. His balls rested over her nose. He slowly rolled off of her. Moving to turn her to the head of the bed. He then lay next to her with his shiny face. Their minds slowly returned to reality. They both uttered, at the same time. "Damn, that was good". "Get out of my head." Sabrina said. "Oh, I'm definitely going back in your head again." André joked. "Oh, do you think you've got it like that?" Sabrina asked. "I haven't gotten it but I'm about to get it." André replied. He motioned her to turn onto her side. He raised her right leg into the air.

He then slid his dick inside of her pussy. Beginning to stroke her softly. His mouth started kissing her shoulder. While his right hand reached around and caressed her breast. "Oooh, your dick feels so good André." She said. But let's stop playing around." She quickly got up onto all fours. Inviting him to do it doggie style. He immediately got behind her. Spreading her legs a bit farther with his knees. He kissed her ass cheeks. Then he lay under her body. Like an automobile mechanic. She lowered her pussy onto his face. She then began fucking him with it. She quickly got herself off. He pushed her back into doggie position. He smacked his dick on her anus. Before shoving it inside of her pussy. At this point. They were both too excited for a slow build up.

He started out fucking her wildly. Sabrina clutched the sheets with her hands. She asked for more. "Oh, Yes, Fuck, Me!" She uttered between each of his thrusts. He banged her harder and harder. His dick plowed into her wet pussy with a fury. He basked in her sweet scent. That seemed to permeate the room. Her natural hair looked so sexy at that moment. So he grabbed a handful of her curls. Then pulled her head back. Sabrina gasped as his pounding intensified. His left hand held her hair. He smacked her ass cheeks with his right hand. "Oh fuck! Spank me daddy." She uttered. He smacked her again and again. He continued to fuck her like there was no tomorrow. She shuttered each time his balls tapped on her clitoris. With each thrust. "Cum for me baby!" She screeched out of her mouth.

She then quickly followed up her statement. "Oh fuck! I'm going to cum." She said. "Yes, Fuck Me, Oh, Yes, Fuck Me! She ripped the fitted sheet off the mattress. Her orgasm took over her body. She squirted her juices onto André's testicles. Seeing her cum that hard was all that he could take. He then began to pump into her with a vengeance. His own body erupted. She could feel the wave after wave of hot cum. Pulsing into her body as he crashed into her. Releasing his flow. Sweating profusely, they crashed onto the bed. Trying to catch their breath.

"Damn woman." He said. "You come over here tearing the sheets off my bed. What kind of home training do you have?" "Shut up, I was caught up in the moment." She replied. "Well, I'm about to get caught up in the shower." André replied. "After I change these sheets." "Oh, do you have to get up early or something?" Sabrina asked. "No, I'm off tomorrow." He said. I'll just be here relaxing. So if you want to stay you know you're good." "Well, I may have to run out for a quick errand in the morning." She said. "But I'd love to spend the rest of my day with you. Do you mind giving me a key? So I don't have to wake you up to get back in?" "That's a good idea." André said.

"Can you get that set on the dresser by my gun?" He continued. "Now don't come back in here acting crazy either. Like you're breaking in. I wouldn't want to mistake you for a burglar." "I see your big gun Mr. Officer." Sabrina replied. "I don't want any problems." I'll be real quiet when I leave and come back." They got up and changed the sheets on the bed. Before going to shower together. Sabrina got out of the shower first. After drying off, she went into the bedroom. Where she is soon joined by André. "Wow, it is 1:19 in the morning." André said. "How did it get so late so quickly?" "Do you have any tea here André?" She asked. "Yeah, I have some." He responded. "I have Peach, Sleepy time and Chai tea in the kitchen."

"Would you like me to make you some?" "No, I'll make you some André." She said. "Then I'm going to suck your dick again." She said. "Well, both of those sound good to me." André replied. "I'm going to check out Sports real quick. While you make the tea." Sabrina soon came back with two cups of piping hot tea. She gave André his cup. She tapped her cup to his. "Cheers." She said. "To a wonderful night." He said. They both sipped their tea. Sabrina stared at his dick. "Why are you staring at me down there?" André asked. "Hurry up and finish your tea so I can suck it again." She said. "I don't want you spilling hot tea all on me. Have me looking like 50 Cent. When Ghost tried to burn him up on 'Power'."

"The only thing I will spill on you are these nuts." André said. Sabrina's mouth opened like she was shocked. Then she smiled at André. "Oh, I told you woman, I'm a freak." André said. "Oh, you don't know what freak is." Sabrina teased. "I may take you to where I play one day. If I think you can handle it." "What?" André replied. "I can handle whatever you've got to show me." "We'll see about that." She said. "Now finish your tea so I can suck you off again." They finished sipping their tea. Sabrina took the cups and saucers back to the kitchen. André yells; "You don't have to wash them. Just leave them in the sink and I'll get them in the morning."

"It will only take me a minute to wash them." Sabrina yells back. "I don't mind." She returned to the bedroom to find André laying naked in the bed. "Oh, somebody is ready I see." She said. "That's right." Andre answered. "You promised me a blowjob. Don't make me take you to court." "Well, I don't want to be sued." Sabrina said. So I guess I better get to work." "She climbed onto the bed and took his dick into her hands. Her head lowered and she kissed his dick gently. Before taking it into her mouth. She flickered her tongue like a snake up and down his shaft. She soon worked her tongue down to his balls. She kissed them with those succulent lips. That sent shivers through his body. Without warning, she took his dick into her mouth.

She worked those magical lips up and down his rod. Each time she took him in deep. Her tongue extended to lick his balls. André could only fight this exquisite feeling but for so long. He was now ripping the fitted sheet off the bed. Sabrina was giving him pleasures. Every man dreams of. André grabbed the back of her head. To force it further down as he erupted into her mouth. Sabrina didn't flinch. She waited for every burst of cream and drained him empty. "Damn, you're trying to make a nigga fall in love with you." André said. "No, I'm not the kind of girl you fall in love with." She said. "I'm the kind that's here today. Tomorrow I may decide I want to live across country. Or out of the country."

"So, I shouldn't get too attached is what you're telling me?" André asked. "Why don't we just see how things go?" Sabrina replied. "That sounds good." André said. "Now, I think you've worn me out because I'm getting sleepy." "Well, let's go to sleep. I'm kind of tired too." Sabrina said. André woke up to find Sabrina's head laying on his chest. "What time is it?" He asked. "It's almost noon." Sabrina said. "Damn, I slept that long?" André asked. "I don't think I've ever done that. I'm usually up no later than 7:30am even if I don't set the alarm. Damn, you must have put it on me Sabrina. Or did you drug me with something?" He asked. "Silly, why would I drug you?" She asked.

"There is nothing missing from your old lil funky house." "Wait a minute." André said. "I had two pennies on that night stand. Are you sure you didn't take them?" He joked. "Yeah, I've got your two pennies." Sabrina replied. "Now I'm on my way to the Bahamas with my man." "Damn, I'm hungry too. What kind of cooking skills do you have woman?" André asked. "I think I have enough eggs, pancake mix and turkey bacon in there. For you to cook if you'd like to." "Oh, now you think you're just going to domesticate me?" Sabrina asked. "To serve you like I'm your woman or something? I'll cook this time, but don't get used to this buddy."

"Can you grab that remote?" André asked. "Since you're by it. Turn on the television for me please?" Sabrina gave him a look and then turned on the television. The announcer said. Police are on the scene, at the North Linthicum Light Rail station. Where a vehicle was found, with a murdered male passenger inside. Several bullet holes poured into the car. Police believe the driver of this vehicle, was also gravely wounded. At this time, they have no clue. As to what happened to him or her. The body is simply nowhere to be found. This investigation is clearly in the early stages. Stay tuned to WBMR. We will update you as soon as we get additional information."

André paused the television. "Damn, that kind of looks like the car. That stopped behind you." He said. "When we had that accident on the I-83." "I'm sure there are a few thousand cars that look like that around here." Sabrina said. "All these Government agencies around here. That car is on almost every street." "Yeah, you're right about that." André said. "The one that was stopped behind you had a DC tag. Which is not at all uncommon here in Maryland." "They didn't show the tag number on the news, did they?" Sabrina asked. "No, they wouldn't do that." André responded. "That's not how you would want a loved one to find out. That their husband, son, brother or friend died."

"Yeah, I didn't think about that." Sabrina said. "You need to be thinking about finishing my breakfast woman." André said. "Look at you." Sabrina said. "I give you a little bit of my Nana. Now you think you can boss me around. Don't make me jump back in that bed. Show you who's really boss around here." "Shit, show me!" André pleaded. "Let me put on my glasses so I can see very well. Whatever it is you have to show me." "You're lucky I'm hungry too." Sabrina said. "We'll do round two after we eat."

Over at St. Mary Church. A few patrons were leaving the midday prayer services. Pastor Kingsley was talking to a couple of parishioners. Sister Chandler Dawns was speaking to Ms. Parsons. "That was really a powerful prayer, sister Parsons." Chandler said. "I only hope my faith and spirit gets as strong in the Lord as yours." "Why thank you, young lady." Ms. Parsons said. "I know the Lord, has some great blessings in store for you. How are those lil babies doing?" "They're doing fine." Chandler said. "Other than driving me up a wall. With all the fighting and yelling at each other." Ms. Parsons laughed. "Well, that's what brothers and sisters do." She said. "When they grow up, they'll be each other's biggest protectors."

"I hope you're right Ms. Parsons." Chandler said. "I hope they get there before they kill each other." "You just tell them. Ms. Parsons says to stop all that fighting. Or I'm coming over there with a switch. I'll tear both of them to pieces." "I wish you would come over and do that." Chandler said. "They need something." "Just read to them." Ms. Parsons said. "One of my favorite stories in the Bible. The story of Joseph. Show them how his brothers plotted against him. How he overcame to become so great. Tell them they don't want to plot against each other. They want to help each other become great. They want to be like Joseph. "That's a great lesson Ms. Parsons." Chandler said. "No wonder you are the Mother of this church."

"I'm sure going to read that to them. Do you want me to walk you back across the street to your house? To make sure you get home safe?" "No, I'll be fine." Ms. Parsons said. "I need to speak to Reverend Kingsley. "So I'll be here a while. My son will be on the porch. Watching for me when I leave here. So I'll be fine." "Well, alright then." Chandler said. "I'll see you on Sunday for morning service." "Yes, you will child." Ms. Parsons said. "I'll be right here on the front row. Praising His name." "Hey, how are two of my favorite ladies doing?" Pastor Kingsley said as he walked up to them. "I'm doing fine, Reverend." Chandler said. "I was just leaving but I really enjoyed the service. The Prayer Ms. Parsons prayed. I really needed to hear. Yours was great too, Reverend."

"Well, compared to Mother Parsons." Pastor Kingsley said. "Few prayers can live up to the bar she sets. Let me walk you to the door and lock up. Ms. Parsons and I will be back in my office. There'll be nobody here to greet any visitors that may wander in." "Well, thank you Pastor." Chandler said. "I look forward to Sunday service." She walked out the door. "I look forward to seeing you here." Pastor replied. He closed and locked the door. "Ms. Parsons, you're looking lovely today." He said. "What can I do for you?" "Don't play with me Reverend." Ms. Parsons said. "You know why I'm here."

"Have you found that money for my building fund yet?" She asked. "No ma'am, I haven't located the funds yet." He said. "I think I'm getting close to finding out where it may be." "Pastor, now that's too much money." Ms. Parsons said. "To have just up and ascended to heaven. You probably want to hurry up and find it. Before my son, Ronnie James is healed." "There is no need to send your son over here Ms. Parsons." He said. "I'm doing everything I can. To try and find that twenty-five million dollars. As far as I know. Nobody has another connect to wash it in the blood of Jesus. If they did, we would hear about a church suddenly expanding."

Or building a new facility." He continued. "All I know is the money gets washed in this church." Ms. Parsons said. "Now we've exchanged twenty-five million dollars-worth of heroin. To our distributors in Bel Air, Maryland. The only people who'd know to bring that money here. Are standing in this office. Along with Drexler, my son Ronnie James and those two bitches. I told Drexler those hoes were up to no good. When he started letting them hang around two years ago. They must have had some real good pussy. To get Drexler to relax around them so easily. I heard one of them doesn't have good pussy any more.

I heard her pussy likes Baltimore so much. It got caught up on The Wire. That other one I saw over here visiting you the other day. I would have sent Ronnie James over here to see her. If that case worker wasn't at my damn house. For your sake. I hope Ronnie James wouldn't have found you. Offering her some type of protection or help getting away with my money. I'm supposed to be at my estate in Hilton Head. Pretending to be out of town visiting my sister. Instead, I'm here looking for my fucking money. That you may be hiding for that bitch." "Now, you know." Pastor Kingsley said. "I wouldn't do anything like that Ms. Parsons. The church needs to wash that money just as much as you need it. I was simply telling Ms. Morgan. That if she knows who has that money. She would be wise to tell us so that nobody gets hurt."

"Too late for that shit." Ms. Parsons said. "Her girlfriend is fucking dead already." "I should have figured you and a shady bitch like that. Would find each other. For something criminal I'm sure. I tried to get Count Drexler over here before she left. Lucky for you. She left before he got here. Or the blood of Jesus wouldn't be the only blood in this church. Drexler's brother. Captain Save a hoe. Doesn't have a clue of who he's having breakfast with. I'd hate for Drexler to have to kill him too. If that bitch puts him too close to our business though. They'll be playing bagpipes in Baltimore." "You can't be serious about killing a cop Ms. Parsons." Pastor replied. "Do you know what kind of heat? That will bring upon everything and everyone?"

"Motherfucker!" Ms. Parsons replied. "I'm missing twenty-five million dollars. You need to be worried about the heat I'm going to bring. Hell has no fury! Like I will reign down on you and this fucking church if need be. That bitch will be next. Your ass is third on the list Reverend Kingsley. So I suggest you pray. To the slave ship Jesus. You have all these niggas in your congregation pray to. Pray to Moses, Abraham, Ralph, Bobby, Ricky and Mike too. By the time you are praying to my son Ronnie James. It would be too late." "Ms. Parsons please." Pastor Kingsley plead. "You know I am on your side. I would never do anything. To jeopardize my relationship with you."

"Cut the shit Reverend." Ms. Parsons said. "Seeing you down there. On your knees during Prayer service today. Made me think of the last time you were on your knees." "Ms. Parsons." Pastor Kingsley said. "I thought we agreed that we wouldn't do this in the church." "Nigga we didn't agree to shit." Ms. Parsons said. "Or maybe we did. We agreed that I wouldn't call the cops. To tell them about your admirable affection. You had for my son when he was a teenager. Or the other boys. Oh, and we agreed. I wouldn't have your stupid ass killed. As long as you don't get on my bad side."

"Now get your ass on your knees." She ordered. "So you can eat this nice seasoned pussy. Then let me feel that little thing you call a dick. "Ms. Parsons please." Pastor Kingsley said. "I need to go pray with sister Bradford. Her husband is really ill." "Nigga, shut the fuck up!" Ms. Parsons said. "Get down on your knees to pray to this wrinkled pussy." She sat and spread her legs. Revealing that she was not wearing any panties. Pastor Kingsley got down on his knees. He did what he was told to do. "Yes, that's it Reverend." Ms. Parsons said. "Lick it like your life depends on it. Ummm, that's a good man. Mama P. likes how you do that. Oh yeah, Kitty likes that a lot. You really know how to speak in tongues Reverend."

Back at Andrés house. "Are you sure you don't want to do something outside the house?" André asked. "No, I just want to stay here with you if that's alright." Sabrina replied. "Well, the State forced us to take time off." André said. "So they don't have to pay us Comp time. I planned to do some work around the house. Maybe drive up to Atlantic City to donate money to charity. I never win so saying I'm donating makes me feel better." "Why don't we just go to the grocery store? Sabrina asked. "Grab a few things." "We can watch some movies. I'll cook us something good to eat later." "That sounds like a plan." André said. "We can chill." She said. "Maybe Friday night, I'll take you someplace."

"Then you can find out if you're really ready." She continued. "For my level of kinkiness." "Where are we going?" An adult toy store?" André asked. "If I think you're ready." Sabrina said. "Then you'll find out this weekend." "I'm a man." André said. "There is no level of sex with a woman. That I'm afraid of. Now you better not be talking about no gay shit. I'm not on that kind of time. That's cool for those that are. That's not my type of hype. You take me to some gay place and you might get shot." "No silly, it's not a gay place." She said. "It's probably something different from what you're used to."

"Now, if you're a little scared." Sabrina continued. "You don't have to go André. This is just my type of hype. What I do to get myself off. I'm one of those women that has found her freedom. To be pleased. Not worry about what anyone else thinks." "Is that right?" André asked. "Well, I'm not trying to stop you from having your fun. I just want to fit in where I can get in. "That's the perfect attitude to have for this place." Sabrina said. André's mind was racing. Trying to figure out what Sabrina was talking about. She interrupted his thoughts. "Come on, let's go get some food." She said. "So we can enjoy this day together."

"Can I borrow one of your baseball caps André?" "Oh, you're trying to be an around-the-way girl?" André asked. "Yeah, you can borrow my Harlem, NY hat." Sabrina put on the baseball hat and some sun shades. They walked into the garage. "Damn, I can barely see your face." André remarked. "Well, when I'm not dressed up." She said. "I don't like everybody looking at me. Call it O.C.D." They drove out to a local grocery store. They filled their shopping cart with plenty of food. A few snacks and toiletry items. To keep them comfortable while they stay in. "Do we need to pick up any movies to watch?" Sabrina asked. "Or do you have all the good stuff there?"

"I have every movie channel that the satellite company offers." André said. Plus I have those jailbroken Fire sticks. Netflix and a big black dick. I also have a camera to make our own film. If you want." "Hell no!" Sabrina snapped. "I can't be on no damn film!" "I was just joking." André said. "Calm down." "Oh, I'm sorry André." She said. "It's just that I don't need. I mean I don't like to be filmed or photographed. Do we need any wine?" Sabrina asked. "Woman, I have enough wine." André said. "To last the next two years. You haven't been down to my wine cellar in my basement yet. I've got some of everything down there." "Okay. Well let's check out of here." Sabrina said. "Get back home to enjoy some movies."

They got in line to check out. Sabrina noticed a man. He had come in the store when they got there. He was just standing by the doorway. With no cart or items in his hand. She grabbed André's arm and clung to him. They pushed their cart outside. Once they loaded the car, they headed back to André's home. Quickly bringing the items inside. "Let me wash up." Sabrina said. "I'll get you some dinner started Dr. Dré." Sabrina said. "Oh, Dr. Dré, I like that." André replied. "I'll wash up too and help you cook." "Oh, you can actually cook André?" She asked. "Of course I can woman." He replied. "I'm a bachelor and I can't be eating fast food every day." "Oh what were you going to make for us, Sir?" She inquired. "I was going to make some jerk chicken wings." He answered. "With some baked potatoes and a little side salad."

"Well then. I can go sit my black ass down." She said. "If you're doing all that." "No, you can sit your black ass on this black dick." André said. "Oh no." Sabrina countered. "No nookie for you tonight. We both need to save some energy for Friday." "Woman I can fuck tonight." He said. "Tomorrow night, Friday night and the night after that. Until the cows come home. Whatever the fuck that means." "I know you can baby." She said. "Trust me, you'll want to save up for this. Let's just cuddle tonight. Enjoy some movies. Some good wine and snacks." "Whatever you say woman." He replied. "In that case, you can get your ass in this kitchen and cook or something."

Ms. Parsons was home watching television when her phone rang. "Hey Ms. Kitty this is Reverend Kingsley. I've got some news for you." "What kind of news at this hour?" Ms. Parsons asked. "One of my Deacons spotted our friend." Pastor Kingsley said. Out at a grocery store with some guy." "She was trying to be incognito. My Deacon stared at her ass long enough to know it was her. He was able to follow them to a house. Which is not far from where my Deacon lives.

"I have the address for you." Ms. Parsons wrote down the address. Then immediately called Drexler. Drexler answered the phone and was given the news. "Yo, Deer Dog. We need to be out. Drive to this address. We need to go see somebody." He and Deer Dog picked up their guns. They then headed out the door to the Yukon truck. They headed east on Pulaski Hwy into Harford County. The GPS advised that they were getting close to the address. Drexler spoke. "Yo, slow down nigga." "I got this Drexler." Deer Dog replied. "That's the house right there. Let's go knock and enter." "No, we're not doing that." Drexler said. "Then what are we doing?" Deer Dog asked.

"Drive the fuck home." Drexler demanded. "Drive home, nigga are you crazy?" Deer Dog asked. "This bitch has our money. And you're not going to go see her." "Motherfucker, this is my brother's house." Drexler said. "What?" Deer Dog said. "This bitch is laying up with your fucking brother?" Deer Dog began to laugh. "She was laying in your bed and now she's in your brother's bed? Oh, this bitch is brilliant. She must be trying to use him. To protect her from you." "Well, clearly she doesn't know." Drexler said. "I don't give a fuck about my brother or her. I'll kill both of those motherfuckers. Now is not the time." "So, when is the time?" Deer Dog asked. "Nigga, didn't I just tell you to drive the fuck home?" Drexler commanded. Deer Dog made a U-turn. They headed back out of the development. As they drove home, Drexler's cell phone rang.

"What?" He answered. "Are you serious? He'd just gotten on the Ambassador Bridge in a U-Haul? Did he have the money in the truck when they got him? Then the money must still be in Detroit. He was making a test run. I'm going to send Rashaad and Kenny to BWI right now. They're on their way out to Detroit. To help you find that fucking cash. None of you niggas better not come back to Charm city without my cash. Or this will be Harm city for your sorry asses." He hung up and dialed another number. "Hello." A voice said. "Kenny grab Rashaad." Drexler ordered. Pack your shit and get to Detroit."

"Meet up with Marcus and go find my cash." Drexler continued. "Oh and in case you niggas get any ideas. About being so close to the Canadian border. Maybe crossing over with my money. Remember it's a dead motherfucker. In a U-Haul who thought about the same shit. I've got friends in Canada too. They will help me protect my interest in every way. I'd hate for us to have a family feud and your asses end up in jeopardy." "We would never think about taking from you boss man." Kenny said. We're not that stupid." "I didn't think you were." Drexler said. "I just thought I'd remind you. Not to take any stupid pills on your trip. Now get the fuck out there."

Later the next day at André's house. He and Sabrina were having lunch. "So, tell me more about Captain André Nichols." Sabrina said. "What do you want to know?" André replied. "Well, tell me about your relationship with your brother." Sabrina said. "That must be incredibly frustrating to you. Being on opposite sides of the law." "I don't talk about my brother." André replied. That motherfucker has thrown his life completely away. The only hard part for me is every time my phone rings. I'm always afraid it will be that call. Saying he's just been killed. Or he's going to prison for life." "That has to be an uneasy feeling." Sabrina said.

I know that would be hard should that call ever come." "It won't be hard." André said. "That nigga made his choices. He will have to deal with the consequences. I won't have any feelings about it." "Fuck him." "He's still your brother." Sabrina said. "There has to be some love there." "Like I just said, Fuck him." André repeated. "Damn, there must really be some bad blood between you two." Sabrina said. "Okay, do you want to talk about anything else?" André asked. Besides my stupid ass brother?" "I mean, since you're not giving me none tonight. If you don't have anything else you want to know. We can go watch a movie."

Just then, André's phone rang. "See, that might be that call about him right now." He said. "Who else would be calling me this late?" Sabrina looked concerned as André went to answer his phone. "Hello." He answered. "What!" Sabrina wondered what news André just got. That made him so upset. André continued, "First, they force us into time off for budget reasons. Now they're calling me in on short notice. For some stupid meeting in the morning?" Sabrina looked relieved. Then upset as she learned what the call was about. "Who was that baby?" She asked. André hung up the phone. "That was the Major. Telling me about some Intel meeting, they're having in the morning.

I have to attend. Some major money and drug shipment is missing. It may be here in Baltimore. Furthermore. They think my brother may be mixed up in this bullshit somehow. I swear if he is. I'm going to lock his ass up my damn self. Like I did when I first became a cop." "You locked up your own brother?" Sabrina asked incredibly. "You damn right." André replied. "He was small time then. He only had minor drugs on him. So he didn't get much time for it. I just had to let him know. Since he chose the streets. I chose my side. I didn't want him to have any misunderstandings, about where I stood." "Wow, that's some cold shit." Sabrina said.

"To lock up your own brother. I'm sure many cops have had family members who got arrested. I'd think they would let other cops do that." "I didn't need no other cops to do my job." André said. "He was selling drugs in my patrol sector. He got locked up for it. End of story." André said. "Now, let's go watch a movie. So I can get some sleep. Then go to this stupid ass meeting in the morning."

Chapter 3

Duty Calls

Andrés' alarm went off at 6:00am. He slowly awoke to turn it off. He looked over at Sabrina. She was also awakened by the noise. She reached her hand to rub his shoulder. "Do you want me to cook a quick breakfast? She asked. While you get ready?" "Yeah, that sounds better, than what they'll have at the office." He replied. "Those folks don't ever wash out that coffee pot. Doughnuts are not my thing. Unless it's Krispy Kreme when the hot light is on." "Yeah, at my job I didn't know too many black folks." Sabrina laughed. "That would drink out the coffee pot in the break room. Go get in the shower."

"I'll wash my hands and get you some breakfast started." She continued. André stumbled into the bathroom and turned on the shower. After brushing his teeth, he called out to Sabrina. She rushed to the bathroom to see what was going on. When she opened the door, she saw him standing there naked. "Are you sure? He asked. "You don't want to kiss it good morning? Before I go?" "Man, I thought something was wrong with you." She replied. "Now I see there's just something wrong with you. I told you no sex. Until we get to the spot tonight. From what I see about you, I think you'll like it." "I'd like it more. André complained. If I knew where the hell we're going."

"Finish your shower, Sir." Sabrina ordered. "Then come eat your breakfast." "I'd like to finish my shower and come eat your pussy." André responded. "We'll see if you have that appetite tonight." She countered. "We'll see if your freak level is indeed level 10. Or if you're still on level 3." "Whatever." André said. "Let me finish and get out of here." After getting dressed, he quickly went to the table. He gulped down his breakfast.

"What are you going to do? André asked. "While I'm at this meeting?" "I'm just going to clean up a bit." Sabrina answered. "Then I'll get back in the bed and wait for you. To come cuddle with me." "Cuddling is all fun and games." André said. Until somebody gets a hard on or wet pussy. Then somebody could get poked. I'm not talking that Facebook bullshit either." André said. "You're so silly man." She said. She gave him a kiss and a patted his behind. He walked out the door. She watched him as he opened the garage door. Until he backed out into the driveway. Once the garage door was closed, she closed the kitchen door. She made a call on her cell phone. "Hey, how are you?" She asked. "No, tonight I'm taking André to the spot. So you do what you normally do. I'll enjoy myself tonight. I have to clean up and get some rest. I'll talk to you later."

André arrived near the Central District Headquarters. As he parked, one of his informants approached him. She works as a stripper. In one of the clubs a block away. "Hey Candy, how are you doing girl?" He asked. "I'm doing well Captain Nichols." She responded. "Just staying out of trouble like you told me. I just wanted to thank you for everything you did. To help me when I was in trouble. Now I'm just dancing at the club. No drugs, no drinking. Just dancing and going home when my shift is over. I've saved up some money. I'm going to hopefully buy a house soon. Out in Owings Mills or Pikesville." "Owings Mills or Pikesville?" Captain Nichols repeated.

"You must have saved quite a bit. Those tips must be real good over there." "Your brother Drexler comes by the club sometimes." Candy said. "Oh, he does." Captain Nichols replied. "Well, I have to go into this meeting now. When I come out. I'll think of some way to say fuck him. Then you can pass it on for me. If you're out here." "Damn, you've always been so cold to your own brother." Candy said. "You know, no matter what he does or who he is. That's still your family."

"I don't need a lecture from you Candy." Captain Nichols said. "About that low life Motherfucker. I'll talk to you later." Inside Central District. Captain Nichols went into the meeting room. The only person he saw. Was Lieutenant Alfred McDavid. "The meeting has been moved. Over to Headquarters building." Lieutenant McDavid said. "Oh, they moved it?" Captain Nichols asked. "Did they say why they moved it Lieutenant Mac?" "All I know was I'm supposed to wait here." Lieutenant McDavid said. "Until everybody gets here and tell you the new location."

Captain Byron McLaughlin of the Western District. Then walked in. Along with Acting Captain Kenneth Young of the Eastern District. "Well, that looks like everybody that's supposed to be here." Lieutenant McDavid said. "Follow me over to Headquarters. Be advised that the Feds are also attending this meeting." "What the fuck are the Feds doing here?" Captain Nichols asked. "I don't know." Captain McLaughlin said. "I'm sure it has something to do with a case we're working. That they are also working. Or want to take from us." "Basically, they're here to fuck us." Captain Young said. "We better listen carefully." Captain Nichols said. "So we can read between the lines."

"Whenever these motherfuckers show up." He continued. "They always have an agenda." "I know that's right." Captain McLaughlin said. "I remember they stole the credit for the Tree Tops Bloods. We infiltrated and busted them. Down on Howard and Fayette. Thirteen homicides we cleared. These fucking Feds swoop in. Then act like their Agents did all the work." They were greeted at the door by Sergeant Marcus White. "Gentlemen, welcome to the Baltimore City Comp Stat room." Lieutenant McDavid said. "Please read the sign off and sign your names. Before you go in. Whatever you hear in this room today. Is strictly confidential. Under no circumstances is to be shared outside of this room. Even if the person is in this room now. You do not talk with him/her about it. Outside of this room. This is the only place. We can assure is not being bugged."

"With that said." Lieutenant McDavid continued. "Everyone pass up all of your cell phones. Both work and personal phones to Sergeant White. Do not turn them off. Just pass them to him. Sergeant White, take the phones to different rooms. In this building and next door please. Everybody take a seat. We're about to begin shortly." Inside were 5 uniformed officers. From various Police Departments in the region. "Were we supposed to Compile Crime Statistics for this meeting?" Captain Nichols asked. "Why are we in the CompStat room today?" Sergeant White moved close to the door and suddenly yelled, "SQUAD! ATTEN-HUT!"

Immediately, walking through the door. Was the Baltimore City Police Commissioner. He was followed by the Deputy Commissioner. The Chief of Police for the Maryland Transit Police. The Superintendent for the Maryland State Police. Along with several individuals wearing suits. The Commissioner stepped to the podium and began to speak. "Good morning, everyone. I am Commissioner Daniel Riggs. I know you're all wondering why this meeting has been called. Before I get into the explanations. Let me introduce a few people to you. To my left is FBI Acting Deputy Director, Carl Tolbert. Special Agent Ryland Johnson. They are currently assigned to the Criminal and Financial Investigative Division.

The Superintendent of Maryland State Police, Colonel Franklin Scales. The Chief of Police for the Maryland Transit Administration Police. Colonel Douglas Delaney. Seated in the back are NSA Deputy Director, Jonathan Baker. Lastly Mr. Vailati. He is here on a classified observation position. Now, let's get down to business as to why we're all here. Director Tolbert, the floor is yours." "Good morning, everyone." Director Tolbert began. "Special Agent Johnson and I. Are part of the career professionals at the Bureau. As you know, our agency has been under constant assault. Since the current Administration moved into the White House. Prior to those barrages of assaults. We were investigating Russia's involvement in the previous election.

"We, along with the NSA and other career Intelligence Agencies." Director Tolbert continued. "Had already discovered some very alarming things. Now, I know you're wondering. What any of that has to do with the local law enforcement? Namely here in the Baltimore area. Well, the truth is. We've found a lot more personnel. Than just this Administration. That have been compromised by the Russians. Those persons include. Many members of the United States Congress. The U.S. Senate. Even some local officials. In the Washington DC Police hierarchy. I'm sure you all find it strange. That so many in Congress, would go out of their way. To protect potential treasonous acts by the President. Unless exposing those treasonous acts. Would also expose them as well.

The NSA has picked up critical conversation. By the Chairman. Of the House Ways and Means Committee. As well as the Judiciary Committee. Which directly connects them. To conspiracy against the United States. With all the moles we have infecting the Federal Government. Installed by this current Administration. There is nowhere safe. Within the confines of the District of Columbia that we can meet. At least, not meet and be sure. Someone will not report that meeting. To a compromised Senator, Congressperson or Administration official." "Okay, but I'm still not sure?" Captain Nichols asked. "What that has to do with local law enforcement here in Baltimore?" "I'm glad you asked that." Special Agent Johnson said. "Your brother, Drexler Nichols. Whom the Bureau is very familiar with. Is why you're all here.

The bureau is very aware of your strained relationship. You've both chosen different sides of the law. Drexler is a major heroin distributor in this city. Try as we might. We have not been able. To make a case against him that will stick. His organization is so large. That he's pretty well insulated. From any personal involvement in crime." "Large is not even the word." Director Baker added. "Your brother took a contingency of his crew. Down to Mexico. Pretending to be on Vacation."

"They went into Juarez city. Then murdered the entire Sarlinos Cartel. The Cartel was trying to establish their Cocaine. As the primary drug in Baltimore City." "That's where they messed up." Lieutenant McDavid said. Baltimore junkies have always been loyal to heroin. No matter what drug is hot. In every other city in America. Be it Crack, PCP, Crystal Meth or whatever. Baltimore junkies have never abandoned Heroin. They never will. The Cartel should have been murdered. For not doing their homework." The room erupted with laughter. "That's pretty much the attitude." Agent Johnson said. "The Mexican Government took. Our Justice Department as well."

"The Mexican Government felt. "Count Drexler did them a favor. They had no interest in having him extradited. Our side had no interest in prosecuting him, for this crime either. Of course. This is the one crime that we could prove his involvement in." "Lucky motherfucker." Captain Nichols uttered. "Well, his luck may have just run out." Director Tolbert said. "Drexler's organization had been getting their heroin. From a distributor in New York City. By the name of Anthony Carlistino. Aka Fat Tony C. Two days after the Presidential inauguration. Fat Tony was found floating. In the Hudson River near 126th street."

"He had just been observed an hour earlier. At the Red Lobster a block over. With this guy. Nicholas Kinstov. A reputed Russian Mafia guy. He works directly for our President's favorite BFF. As an enforcer. After Fat Tony died, from a severe case of lead poisoning to the head and chest. Several other members of his clan. Met with similar fates. We assume the Russians, didn't want them getting any ideas. About taking over the family business. These murders escalated. In normal times. Protocol would be to inform the U.S. Attorney General. The A.G. would then advise the President. The President would then move. To expel these Russian nationalists. Out of the country. So that they don't get a stronghold. Dominating criminal territories in New York City and L.A."

"Right, because once they establish." Agent Johnson said. "In these two territories unchecked. They will look to expand. However, these are not normal times. Reporting them to this Attorney General. Will only bring the Bureau and possibly other intelligence Agencies. Under increased scrutiny. In any case. Drexler's organization here, along with others in Charlotte. Detroit and New Orleans. Suddenly found new suppliers with Russian accents. Interestingly unique about these four cities. Is their drug trade. It's pretty much run by one large entity in each city. In Baltimore, it's Drexler's Black Gangsta Family. "The leaders of these gangs are all women chasers." Special Agent Johnson continued.

"So, it was easy. To have female agents infiltrate their organizations. We actually had two female agents, infiltrate each gang. To kind of watch each other's back. They were supposed to entice the leaders. Into an easy armored truck robbery. That the FBI sanctioned. The agent's story was they used to work as drivers. They knew the routes and weak points. Of course, the gangs wanted to commit the robberies. They're criminals and that's what they do. The bills were supposed to be marked. When the gangs bought drugs from their new suppliers. Aka the Russians. We could trace that money. When that money showed up in the hands of Russian Nationals. Ones we have documented. With ties to this current Administration. Congress would have no choice but to impeach.

However, when it was time to mark the bills. The current Treasury Secretary. Did not want to spend 100 thousand dollars. To protect $100 million dollars." "You mean $100 million dollars, are out there unmarked on the street?" Superintendent Scales asked incredulously. "No Sir." Director Tolbert interrupted. "$600 million dollars is out there. Unmarked on the streets. You see, each gang took $25 million dollars in cash. Ensuring it spread as deep into the Kremlin as possible. That way, no one could deny. That the Russians this Administration is involved with. Is clearly tied to criminal activity.

"Any Congressperson who would risk." Director Tolbert continued. "Protecting this President after that proof. Would risk being caught up in Rico Statutes. $500 million dollars of the money. Was supposed to be transferred electronically by our agents. Straight to Russia. It was to be digitally marked. That money had a 27 digit access code. That only the Treasury Secretary, Director Johnson and I knew. Then the Treasury Secretary called our undercover agents. Gave them a new code advising he changed it. The reason he changed it is still unclear. We have our suspicions which are unverified." "So only the undercover agents, know how to access the money is what you're saying?" Captain McLaughlin asked. "That's correct." Director Tolbert replied. "Apparently, the Treasury Secretary forgot what he changed it to. Or he won't tell us."

"This shit is like a comedy show." Colonel Delaney said. "I've never seen anything. This ridiculous in Government before." "Then you must not watch the news Colonel." Director Tolbert said. "As crazy as this sounds, it gets worse. Someone above us. Put the names of our agents on an unsecure computer. This was far more reckless. Than the unmasking of Valarie Plame. Done two administrations ago. We suspect it was the A.G. but we can't prove it. Of course, since we've done nothing to improve our Cyber security. The Russians walked right in the door and took that information. All of our agents are dead. Except one who was working here in the Baltimore area.

The second one working here in Baltimore was found dead. With a wire brush shoved up her vaginal canal. Over in Westport. She may have been trying to take the money and run. We believe she hid the cash portion for Drexler. When he got word. That one of his warehouses was about to be raided. We don't know how he stays one step ahead of us. Whenever we or local law enforcement. Have tried to raid his property. Anyway word is. She tried to claim amnesia. When Drexler wanted to get his money. Allegedly, she was having an affair. With one of our FBI Agents in Detroit. Whom she went to Quantico with.

"They figured out. They were working different ends of the same case. A case that is so screwed up. They figured they could take the $500 million plus. Then just flee the country. Since it's all untraceable, it was a pretty smart plan. Except Agent Williams was found. On the Ambassador Bridge in Detroit. Trying to flee into Windsor, Canada. We don't know if it was the Russians. Or the Band Crew Street gang. He was shot over 20 times in a U-Haul. No trace of the cash. So we believe he was making a trial run. Or a decoy for another vehicle carrying the cash. Before he died. We think he alerted the agents in Baltimore. About their names being compromised. We won't disclose the name of the remaining agent. Her life is already in grave danger."

"Why isn't she in Wit Sec?" Lieutenant McDavid asked. With the Federal Marshalls?" "The same reason we're not meeting in D.C." Director Tolbert said. We don't know how deep this Russian influence goes. Within ALL Federal Agencies. We do know. Our Agent is not staying at her house. Which is smart of her. We know the Russians are not aware. Of the $500 million dollars. We also know someone, is trying to centrally locate all the cash money. There is some minor form of Security. On the electronic funds. No one can transfer the money by any WiFi device. She has to be at a terminal. That is hardwired to the internet. Whenever that happens. The location of transfer will be transmitted to us. Anywhere in or out the U.S. We can have law enforcement there within 15 minutes. Unless it's in Russia.

It's very doubtful, she'd get out of that location. Before we have her in custody. We also have TSA and Border Patrol on alert. Bus stations, Amtrak and Highway Patrol. In all 50 States on high alert. With facial recognition software. Vetted Federal Agents are also posted. At every possible mode of transportation out of the country. So far, she hasn't even attempted. To make arrangements to leave. We do know she's here in the Baltimore area. We know of some public locations she's been. We just don't want to alert the Russians to her activities.

"The gangs in New Orleans, Detroit and Charlotte. Really don't have a connection to the electronic money. The Russians or somebody. Eliminated our undercover agents. In each of those cities. If they knew about the code. They would have used it by now. If we don't get the access code, from our one remaining agent. That $500 million is lost forever." "So why aren't you tailing her to get it?" Captain McLaughlin asked. "We tried that with an undercover officer." Agent Johnson said. "From the Metropolitan Police in DC on loan to DEA. They were following her here in the Baltimore. His last report was that he had an informant with him. An informant that could tie the Black Gangsta Family. To some Federal personnel. Possibly even local law enforcement.

That informant was found shot to death. On a Maryland Transit Light Rail parking lot. Our Agent hasn't been heard from since. His body was not recovered at the scene." "That was all over the news." Captain Young said. "At this time, we don't know who killed the informant." Director Tolbert said. "Or where our Agent is. Again, these are not normal times. If we tail her and the bosses above us. Disclose that information. The Russians will probably kidnap and kill her. All our vehicles have GPS on them. Even if we go buy a car right now from Carmax. They have a list of every Agent working for the Bureau. They could easily make sure every car we drive is tracked. They can bug our homes, phones and anything they want."

"Some agent is bound to tell his wife. He's going out to track one of our own. In casual conversation. We just can't risk that. The FBI is now the target. Of the Government we were sworn to protect." "That's what happens." Captain McLaughlin said. "When you white folks elect a racist criminal as President. Along with Klan members to Congress." "I didn't vote for that bastard." Superintendent Scales said. "Regardless, we have too many unknowns." Director Tolbert continued. "Are there those within our own Government? Who would try to get that information out of her?"

"Once acquired, would they discard her? Then use the money for their own personal gain? We can't put anything past our Government these days." "So, what's the plan to retrieve this money?" Captain Young asked. "Well, right now, we really aren't sure." Director Tolbert said. "Of what our undercover agent is waiting on? We understand why she may be apprehensive. About coming in with the access code. She probably doesn't know, who she can trust within our agency either. If she gives it to someone. Working for the current administration. They may kill her and take the money. We don't put anything past this Administration. She probably doesn't either."

"Then there's also a possibility. That she may be trying to run with the money as well. We simply don't know. We just don't want to risk her dying. In case she's looking for a safe passage back home. So that part is basically on her time. The other parts we can tell you the plan. We know Drexler Nichols has a stash house on Haven St. We're going to hit tomorrow. All of us will muster around 11:45pm. We have good Intel. That says he'll have a shipment of drugs. From his new Russian suppliers come in about 9pm. That area is pretty deserted at night. So there shouldn't be any casualties of civilians. Our esteemed colleagues in Congress. Many of them ride the Amtrak and Marc trains. To and from work.

Some have been observed having unofficial contacts. With the Russians on those conveyances. Those transportation modes. Fall under the jurisdiction of the Maryland Transit Police. Colonel Delaney has agreed to offer us undercover officers. They will pose as passengers on these trains. They will sit as close to the lawmakers as possible. Pretending to be listening to music on their phones. In actuality, they would be recording conversations." "Do we really think? Captain Nichols asked. "That a Congressman, will actually be talking criminal activity? On a public train. While they're going home to their family?" "We don't need them to talk criminal activity." Director Tolbert said.

"We just need to prove a familiar relationship." Director Tolbert continued. "With murdering drug dealing criminals. From an enemy country of the United States. Once we do that, we can maybe save our country. In reference to the raid. The Police Command vehicles. Will stage at the MTA Eastern Division. For Security Purposes. MTA Police will control strict access onto the property. BCPD will control access to Eastern Ave and Lombard streets. Between Ponca and Oldham streets. State Police will control Eastern Ave and Lombard from the Bayview Hospital Area out to Eastpoint Mall. Foxtrot helicopter will lend air support. By hovering over Martins Airport. It can get to Haven St. in about two minutes.

We'd love to provide more Federal support. But we simply don't know who we can trust right now." "May I say something?" Captain Nichols asked. "Of course Sir." Director Tolbert responded. "Hey, we all know my brother is no good." Captain Nichols said. "I don't want anybody. Going in there and relaxing your guard. If he doesn't comply. Then tell your officers to do what they have to do." "Well, there you have it." Agent Johnson said. "If there are no more questions." Director Tolbert said. "I'm going to let you all get back. To your agencies. So you can prepare for tomorrow."

"Remember, nothing leaves this room." Director Baker said. "Don't talk to your wives or your mothers. Not your colleagues, nobody!" "Sergeant White will take you all to locate your phones." Agent Johnson said. "We just couldn't have it looking like. We were all pinging off the same location. Just in case somebody was looking for us. "Chief Delaney." Agent Johnson called. "Would you stay a minute please? Along with Director Baker and Mr. Vailati? Commissioner Riggs, you too please. Director Tolbert and I have a few questions?" The rooms quickly cleared out. Left are the requested personnel. "Are we sure it's a good idea?" Director Tolbert asked. "To have Captain Nichols in on these meetings?"

"I mean. It is his brother that we're targeting for arrest. If things go bad. One of his own personnel. Could end up killing his brother." "Hey, I've expressed my concern." Chief Delaney said. "Of him being Police with the Governor. The Governor did authorize us. To tap his cell and his home. In fact, his phones have been tapped since he made Sergeant. Eleven years ago. Although no one has officially notified him. I'm sure Captain Nichols, understands law enforcement enough. To expect that we would." "We've also scoured his phone conversations." Director Baker said. "Over at the NSA. We can't find one time he's called his brother. In the last 12 years. Or one time his brother has called him."

"No Thanksgivings together. No Christmases, birthdays or anything." "They have run into each other briefly." Chief Delaney said. "On the street. Because they both work in the same city. From all our eyewitness accounts. They haven't had any pleasantries, to exchange with each other." "Work? Agent Johnson asked. "Is that what you call what Count Drexler does? The man is a cold-blooded killer." "We're all aware of what he is." Chief Delaney replied. "We just haven't been able to prove it in a court of law. That doesn't change the fact. That those two brothers, have no love lost between them." "Alright, as long as we're certain." Director Tolbert said. "Captain Nichols will not do anything. To jeopardize the integrity of our operation."

Chief Delaney walked over to the door. He checked to make sure no one was standing outside. He turned back to the Federal Agents. "Look, truth be told." Chief Delaney said. "I never liked Captain Nichols. I never believed two birds from the same feather. Can be all that different. However, when he arrested his brother. Several years ago. That convinced many in the State Legislature. And the previous Governor's office. This Governor was in the State Legislature back then. He's protected the Captain. However, when the election comes around. Once we get a new Governor. My priority will be to run Captain Nichols, out of this department.

"For now." Chief Delaney continued. "I've been prohibited. From conducting any serious investigation. Of him and his brother's connection. If I can find anything after the election. I will strip him of his pension and if possible. Put his ass in prison. Where he and his brother belong. My gut has always told me something is not right. Otherwise, he's a hell of a Cop." "Commissioner Riggs." Director Tolbert called. "We're going to need the file on one of your people too. We understand there is no love lost. Between you and Major Carver." "No, there is not." Commissioner Riggs replied. "He lied on me. Back when we were both in patrol. He said I skipped court. Over at North Ave. District court. He said I was trying to leave early for vacation."

"I was actually testifying on the stand at Calvert St. In Circuit Court on a murder trial. We had both taken the test for Sergeant. His lie launched an investigation. That got me passed over for promotion that time. It got straightened out. By the time it did, they had promoted his ass. When his score was lower than mine." "Damn, that's some low life shit." Mr. Vailati said. "Well, you know what they say." Commissioner Riggs said. "What goes around comes around. Who are you again?" "Who I am is the Deputy of my department." Mr. Vailati replied. "You probably don't want to ask too many questions. About my department Commissioner. We like to operate in the shadows."

"Can I at least ask?" Commissioner Riggs asked. "Which congressional committee you answer to?" "We don't answer to Congress." Mr. Vailati said. "Not to The President or the Judiciary branch. The men and women in my department. Only answer to the Director and me. My job is to keep the country from being transformed. Into a one group power-controlled entity." "Isn't that what you're saying? Chief Delaney inquired. "Your shadow organization does?" "You gentlemen are asking too many questions." Mr. Vailati said. "Trust you don't want to know the answers. Now Commissioner Riggs. I need you to get that file. On the Major and keep it with you."

"The next time we meet, I will need it." Mr. Vailati continued. "All you gentlemen need to know is. That we are working with you. To rid you of thorns in your sides. You're working with us. To help save the republic. So you both should feel very patriotic." "We're only concerned." Chief Delaney said. "With crime in and around Baltimore City. It's not our job to help with whatever you're doing." "I see." Mr. Vailati said. "I hope the next time we meet. You both will feel more patriotic than you do today." "Commissioner and Chief." Director Tolbert said. "We'll see you both tomorrow night. We have to catch that train at Penn Station. Back down the road. I left my car at the Deanwood Metro in DC. Agent Johnson parked at the New Carrollton station. In P.G. County."

"We can't be too careful. About who may be tracking our movements." "Alright gentlemen, have a safe trip back." Chief Delaney said. "Give the President my regards. I'll give him my regards soon enough." Mr. Vailati said. "Oh, by the way gentlemen. I need you to keep your phones on. We may need to reach you, real early tomorrow morning." Outside on Baltimore St. Captain Nichols walked over to the strip club where Candy works. "Hey, you're awake from your meeting?" Candy said. How did it go?" "It was a dumb boring typical meeting." Captain Nichols replied.

"Your brother Drexler was just here." Candy said. "Now why did you have to ruin a nice conversation? Captain Nichols asked. "By bringing that fool up? Tell him I said fuck him 3 times. I've got to go now. I thought we were going to have a nice conversation. About you quitting this business. Maybe being my girlfriend. You have made me mad now. I'll catch you next time. When I'm summoned downtown by the brass." "Alright sugar." Candy said. "It was good seeing you again Captain. Can I get a hug before you go?" "That depends." Captain Nichols said. "Depends on what?" Candy asked. "You haven't just finished sucking a dick have you? He asked. Or giving lap dances?" She punched him lightly in the chest.

"Nigga, fuck you." She replied. "We can't fuck right here. Captain Nichols said. Too many people looking." "Let them look." She said. "I'm not ashamed of my body. It doesn't look like you should be ashamed either." "As fine as you are woman." Captain Nichols said. "You better not be ashamed of that body." He opened his arms to hug her. She held him extra tight before letting go. Captain Nichols walked out to his car. He then headed home. He turned left onto President Street. He then entered I-83. He voice-dialed Sabrina. "Hey babe, what are you doing?" He asked. "I'm washing clothes." Sabrina replied. "I'm dusting in this raggedy house you have."

"Oh, well, if my house is raggedy." André said. "Then your ass tore it up. That means I'm going to have to bang, $250,000 worth of equity. Out of your ass when I get home." "You're so nasty, you little freak." Sabrina said. "No sex until tonight. If you can handle it. You can bang half a mill out this pussy." "I can't wait." André said. "To see what type of shit you're into tonight. Do you need me to pick up anything on the way home?" "No." Sabrina replied. "Just bring your fine chocolate ass on up in here. So I can go to sleep in your arms. Once we wake up, it'll be time for your introduction."

"I'll give you the rules of the game." She continued. "You can decide if you want to play or not." "Introduction, rules to the game?" André prodded. "What the hell? Are you into that BDSM or crazy white people shit? I told you if somebody tries to stab me. Or poke me in any kind of way. They will be shot until my clip is empty." "Just come on home babe." Sabrina said. "So I can lay in your arms." "I'm on my way." He replied. Soon he merged onto the beltway. Then traveled up to I-95 into Harford County. Arriving home, he entered and closed the garage door. Sabrina opened the kitchen door. With an excited look on her face. "There you are, you sexy chocolate man." She said. "Come give me some sugar." She wrapped her arms around him. Kissing him passionately. "Damn girl." André said. "You're trying to start something up in here. I'm ready to give it to you."

"Umm, umm, down boy." She said playfully. She softly touched his groin. "Stay down boy. I'll make sure you're taken care of tonight." "Man, I wish I knew." André said. "What this tonight shit was all about. I'm going to hurt somebody. If this turns out to be a trip. To get in touch with our feelings. Or some other bullshit." "Will you stop tripping?" She said. "I told you, I'll tell you the rules later. You can decide, if it's what you want to do. If you don't want to do any part of it? Or the whole thing all together. That's fine." Sabrina assured. "For now. I need you to take off those clothes and get in the bed. So you can hold me while I sleep." "Alright baby." André said. "I'm getting in the bed. You could give it just a little kiss. Before I go to sleep, right?" André pleaded. Sabrina unsnapped his belt and then his pants.

She then tugged on the waistline. Of his pants and underwear. She lowered herself to her knees. She then kissed the head of his rapidly growing penis. André closed his eyes in excited anticipation. "That's all you get for now." Sabrina said. "What! This is some bullshit!" André exclaimed. "I'm about to jerk off in this moarfugger." "Man, get yourself in this bed." Sabrina demanded. Let's get some rest." André cuddled up next to her. Pulling her close to him. "You know when you kiss it like that." André said. "Then don't finish. Doctors say my balls will explode. I'll be in a lot of pain." "Oh no you didn't." Sabrina laughed. "Try to use the trick boys use. When they're 15 dealing with 15 year-old girls." "How about I fall for that tomorrow?"

"Oh, I won't be here tomorrow night." André said. "We have an operation to do." "What kind of operation?" Sabrina asked. "I really can't talk about it." André said. "Will you be in any kind of danger?" Sabrina asked. "Oh no, I won't be doing any of the action work." André said. "I'll be safe in one of the Command vehicles. That's what these Captain bars are for." "Alright. Well you better not let anything happen to you?" Sabrina said. "I wish something was happening." André said. "In this bed right now."

"Man, please go to sleep." Sabrina ordered. Shortly into the midday. They both began to fall asleep. To the soothing sounds of contemporary Jazz. They woke around 6:30pm. André turned the television to the evening news. He then staggered into the bathroom. To brush his teeth. Sabrina quickly joined him at the other sink. "Now, what is this damn secret?" André demanded. "The one you've been hiding from me all this time?" "Can a sister finish brushing her teeth first?" Sabrina complained. They both swished some mouthwash and returned to the bedroom. "Alright now." André said. "Where are we going? What are you trying to get me into?"

"We're going to a Swinger's Club." Sabrina said. "If you must know." "A Swingers club?" André repeated. "Yes, a Swinger's club." Sabrina answered. "Don't worry, we'll have mask on. Nobody will know. There's an upstanding Police Captain. Getting his freak on. In fact, most of the people there. Are Bankers and Lawyers. Doctors and Police. Mostly professional people. Now guys can't just walk in and join. You can only get in. If a female member brings you." "Now, why in the world?" André asked. "Would I want to go to a damn Swingers club?" "Because you can have me and another beautiful woman." Sabrina replied. "Of your choice licking you all over. Then you can take turns fucking both of us. Even decide which one of us, you will come inside of."

"Oh, well." André said. "Maybe I shouldn't be too hasty in judging this Swinger's club. So, you mean I can go in there? Pick any woman? And she's going to have sex with me?" "Yes, that's basically it." Sabrina answered. "I will get to pick any man who will have sex with me." "There's a club like that in Baltimore!" André exclaimed. "How did I not know anything about it?" "Well, this one is in Baltimore County." Sabrina replied. Down in Catonsville. There are clubs like this all over America and around the world." "So, do you know any of these people?' André asked. "The ones you're having sex with? Or setting me up to have sex with?"

"No, I don't know them." Sabrina replied. "They're all wearing masks. Some people just come out to watch. Some come out to participate. If you just want to be a spectator tonight. Then we can do that. If you want to get your dick sucked. By two beautiful women. Then you can do that too." "Is this the kind of stuff that turns you on?" André asked. "It absolutely does." Sabrina said. "I told you, I'm a free spirit. I love to be pleased to the ultimate degree. I also love to please to the ultimate degree. So trust if you indulge, you will have fun." "So, besides the masks." André asked. "What are the rules of this joint?" "The only rules." Sabrina said. "You pick someone. If they want to have sex, you go ahead."

"If they are just there to watch or don't want you." She continued. "Then you move on to the next one. Now because this is your first time. It is your first time, isn't it?" Sabrina asked. "I booked us into the theater floor upstairs." "What the hell is the theater floor?" André asked. "There is someone there, sort of like an MC." Sabrina said. "They give us a script which is just a general outline. Of what we're supposed to be doing. You don't have to remember the lines verbatim. Just the general idea of the story given. For instance, if they gave you a script of being a cop. You would find some reason to stop and arrest me. Unless I did you a favor. You make up your own words. As long as you play along with the story line."

"The rooms have huge windows. So anyone can stop by and watch. Whatever we are doing. As long as you keep your mask on. They won't know exactly who they are watching. The script may have another woman. Or another man in it. No guys ever interact with each other. They are just there to please the female." "I know no motherfucking man better not." André said. "Try to interact with me. That motherfucker will die right there in that fucking club." "You don't have to worry about that André." Sabrina said. "These are guys just there taking advantage of free pussy. With no commitment. Just like we women are there. Taking advantage of free dick with no commitment."

"Well, you have sparked my curiosity." André said. "What time are we rolling?" "Well, the club doesn't open until 10:00pm." Sabrina replied. "So we can have a lite bite to eat. Then we can shower and get dressed to go." They showered together. Sabrina teased him. By pressing her body against his. "You better stop that woman." André warned. Before I catch a rape charge in this damn shower." "How about we do the rape fantasy on Sunday?" Sabrina suggested. "Damn, you're all kinds of freaky." André said. "You might be on level 20. With this freak shit. I'm about to catch the elevator. Up to your floor tonight." André promised. They get out of the shower. Sabrina began her regiment. Becoming as beautiful as possible.

André picked out a black suit for the formal affair. He sprayed on some cologne. He then promptly got dressed. Sabrina put on her red strapless evening gown. They headed out. Driving down I-695 in Sabrina's car. They listened to John Legend's "The best you ever had." Both sang along. "Are you nervous?" Sabrina asked. "A little." André responded. "I'm anxious to see what the environment is like." "Like I said, if you're not feeling it." Sabrina said. "We can just watch, or we can leave. Just because this is my thing. Doesn't mean it has to be yours." They finally arrived at Club Tabu2. They could see several couples in black tie attire. All of them were wearing masks that covered their eyes and nose.

"Wait, we have to walk in and get masks?" André asked. "No silly, look on the back seat." Sabrina said. André grabbed the masks from the rear seat. He handed Sabrina hers. "We put them on here." Sabrina said. "Within the confines of the tinted windows. Then we go inside and have a good time. We can sit here and talk for a moment. If you want to think about this André." He quickly opened his door. Walking around to the driver's side. He then opened Sabrina's door. "What are we doing?" Sabrina asked. "We came here to play woman." André said. "Now get out of the car." They walked to the door. Sabrina showed her I.D. to get them in.

Upon entry, they were handed two drinks. They began to observe the room. André took Sabrina's hand and they walked around. Looking at the scantily clad and naked people. They stopped to watch a couple having sex. The woman's legs were over the man's shoulders. André said; "That's a good position right there." Sabrina' replied; "Oh you, like that huh?" Just then, a masked guy with no clothes on. Walked up to them. He said hello to Sabrina. André said; "What up?" Sabrina replied; "Hi." Sabrina didn't really show interest in him. So he walked away. "Do you see any women in here you like?" Sabrina asked. "I see a lot of good-looking women." André replied. "I may be ready to go talk to one" "Look at that guy over there." Sabrina said.

They walked a little closer, to the guy Sabrina pointed out. André noticed the tattoo on his neck. It read; "Kings get better." André noticed Sabrina was fixated on this man's nakedness. So he told her she could shake his dick hello. Sabrina looked at André. As if to ask are you sure? André told her to not be rude and shake the man's dick. Sabrina slowly reached for the masked man's dick. It was semi-erect and she stroked it gently. Causing it to become firm. "That's enough." André said. "Nice meeting you brother." Sabrina turned to André and said; "Oh my God. You don't have a problem with that?" André replied; "We're here, aren't we?" "I wouldn't mind seeing what he can do with that thing." Sabrina said.

A well-built, naked woman walked over to them. She had beautiful brown skin. She wore a gold and shiny mask. She stopped to say hello. André asked her if he could touch her beautiful ass. She said yes. André asked Sabrina if it was okay. Sabrina said; "I guess fair is fair." André grabbed and caressed the mystery lady on her ass. Sabrina said; "That is enough." André lingered another few seconds, before the lady walked away. "Were you cool with that?" André asked. "I guess I have to be since we're here." Sabrina said. A waitress came by with drinks and they both took another glass.

André sipped his drink. He let it sit on his lips and then kissed Sabrina. They ventured up the stairs and came across a room. There a light skin woman with a beautiful body. She was in the doggy position. There was a man fucking her from behind. Another man in front of her. With his dick in her mouth. "Oooh, now that's what I'm talking about." Sabrina said. "I wish I was being dominated like that." "Oh, you want to be dominated I see." André said. "Let me finish my drink. See what we can get started up in here." He then led her to an empty viewing room. He asked her to undress him. As she removed his clothing, he helped her out of hers. They were standing in the room naked. With about two people watching them.

André placed his hands on Sabrina's shoulders. Pushing her down to her knees. He told her to suck his dick. Sabrina did as she was told. A few more people stopped to watch. "Lick my balls for me baby." He moaned. Sabrina complied. André was loving the pure pleasure Sabrina was giving him. He told her how much he loved the way, she sucked his dick. He took his dick and rubbed it across her face. Before sticking it back into her mouth. The viewers were growing in number. André was holding Sabrina's head steady. So he could fuck her mouth like her pussy. His balls were pressed against her chin. As he drove his dick down her throat. She gagged a little.

André grabbed her head a bit firmer. He began to shoot his hot cum in her mouth. Sabrina took it all in. André spoke to her. "You better not spit that out." He said. "In front of all these people. Swallow it woman. He ordered. Sabrina readily did as she was told. André soon stood her to her feet. He kissed her passionately. He then told her to get on the bed on all fours. It was his turn to please her. André walked behind her and spread her ass cheeks. Exposing the most beautiful view in the universe. He began to lick her all over. As he marveled at the beauty of her pussy and ass.

His tongue flickered all over her in quick flashes. Before he pulled her apart further. So he could stick his tongue inside her pussy. More people were now watching. Neither of them cared. André knelt down. So that he could have better access to her pussy. He began pushing his finger inside of her. Then took it out and sucked her juice off. Before pushing it back inside. This time, he walked around to her face. He offered his finger to Sabrina to suck. She happily did. André was walking back to her ass. When he saw the man. That Sabrina was fascinated with moments earlier. Sabrina saw him too. She asked André if the man could come over to play.

André was reluctant at first. Then he thought. "She told me not to get attached. So we can dog this bitch." André called the man into the room and spoke to him. "You are here as a guest." André said. "These are the rules. Don't touch me in any way, shape, form or fashion. You are here to worship her and only her, got it? You only do what I tell you to do. Or you have to leave." The masked stranger nodded yes. André told him to lick her from behind. The stranger pulled apart Sabrina's ass cheeks. He began to lick her all over. His rhythm was slightly different from André's. It felt so damn good to Sabrina. Meanwhile, André lowered himself under Sabrina's upper body. Positioned like an auto mechanic. He began to suck her breast. André's tongue flickered all over her nipples. While this stranger was licking her ass cheeks. Like it was chocolate pudding.

They both took a finger. Jamming them into Sabrina's sloppy, wet pussy. They began to finger-fuck her. While the stranger was licking her pussy. André continued sucking her breast. Sabrina grabbed the sheets with both hands. Clenching them tightly. As the two mouths worked on her body. Their fingers pumped in unison. So that when one got tired, the other was working her pussy. They did this until she could take no more. She let out a scream of pleasure and released her honey. The stranger moved his mouth. Down to Sabrina's treasure. He began to lick her juices from the source.

André stood and walked to her face. He kissed her like they were long lost lovers. Reunited after years apart. Meanwhile, the stranger kept kissing her pussy. André then told the stranger to stop. So she could be put on her back. They laid her down. André told the stranger he could have her left foot. André would take the right. They began sucking her toes with affection. André sucked her big toe, so the stranger did the same with her left one. Each and every toe on Sabrina's feet, was bathed with kisses. They kissed the top of her feet. Licking the bottom and sucking her toes. Sabrina twisted with pleasure.

Sabrina waited in eager anticipation for each kiss. Suddenly André grabbed both her legs. He spread them wide. He walked up to her pussy. Rubbing his dick up and down her wet Slit. He told the stranger to go stand by her face. The strange man stood on Sabrina's left side. André walked to the right. He told Sabrina to keep her mouth closed. He then told the strange man to rub his dick across her left side. André rubbed his dick over the right side of her face. Sabrina had dicks rubbing her entire face. André could tell she wanted to suck them. He told the stranger to wait. André ran his dick across her mouth. While the stranger rubbed across her breast. "Open your mouth woman." André said. He pressed his dick that was dripping pre-cum, into her waiting mouth.

She turned her head to him for easier access. He pushed in and out. Going deeper with each stroke. The strange man was rubbing his dick. All over her breast. André asked him to try. Sabrina turned to the stranger with an open mouth. He gladly pushed his dick into it. Sabrina's hands were touching herself. As she sucked on the dick of this masked man. While André rubbed his dick across her neck and shoulder. Then Sabrina turned back to André and took him in her mouth. André made sure to rub his balls. All over her cheeks and mouth. Especially when his dick came out of her mouth. He asked the strange man to rub his balls on her other shoulder.

Sabrina turned to the stranger. Sucking his dick some more. André began fondling on her right breast. The stranger positioned himself. So that he could keep his dick in her mouth. Then bend to suck her left breast. Both mouths worked on her Sun-kissed breast. They sucked them like two newborns. The stranger pumped faster in and out of Sabrina's mouth. Sabrina moaned. As she embraced the smell and taste of this strange man. The sensations being worked on her tits by two men. Made her delirious. She turned again to take André in her mouth. He shuttered. André then told her to suck him. She turned to take the stranger in her mouth.

After a few seconds he said; "Now suck me." Sabrina turned back to suck André. "Him, me, now him, me, him, me." André ordered. Sabrina had to keep turning. To keep up sucking both men. They were stroking their dicks. In between her oral pleasures. As she turned to the stranger. He released a blast of sticky goo. All over his side of her face. She helped him by sucking the rest of it out of his dick. She then turned to André. He quickly put his dick into her waiting mouth. Then he began to cum. He jammed his dick down her throat. Then coated her face on his side. Leaving creamy cum in all the places the stranger missed. Both men were trying to catch their breath. Sabrina traded men. Cleaning any remaining cum off of their dicks. Her sexy juicy lips worked pure magic on them. "Damn!" André said. "You even look sexy covered in cum."

I'm just not kissing you right now." The stranger handed Sabrina a towel. There was a sink in the room with warm water. Some facial cleanser and body wash. Sabrina washed her face and body. The men cleansed themselves as well. André asked her what she wanted. "I want to be fucked." Sabrina said. "By who?" André asked. "Me or him?" Before Sabrina could answer. A woman was at the door. The one André had fondled earlier. "Or by her?" André said. André invited her in. He put Sabrina on all fours on the bed. Then the woman next to her. "You two may kiss." André said. We'll work on your pussies." André began to eat the masked woman. The strange man licked Sabrina's pussy.

Sabrina and the woman, kneeling next to each other began to kiss. The men relentlessly sucked and licked their pussies. André shoved his finger into the woman's warm and wet pussy. The unknown man finger-fucked Sabrina. "Now, you ladies turn around and suck our dicks." André commanded. Sabrina and the woman turned to face the men. Sabrina took the stranger back in her mouth. She began caressing his balls. The woman took André into her mouth. Licking his balls. The men held the women's heads. Fucking them deep in their mouths. Slapping their balls against the women's chins. Then André took his dick out of the woman's mouth. Letting her help Sabrina suck the stranger's dick.

Sabrina and the woman's mouth kissed. As they sought position. On sucking the man's hardened dick. Then the man stepped back. Sabrina and the woman took time. Sharing André's dick in their mouths. Sabrina licked André's balls, while the woman sucked his dick. Then they switched. André was in pure heaven. These two sexy ladies worked their magic on him. André found delight in rubbing his dick all across their faces. While each one sucked on one of his balls. Then André asked the lady to lay on her back. He then had Sabrina straddle her face in a 69 position. The two women began eating each other's pussy. Like experts. With Sabrina on top. André directed the stranger to go stand behind her.

The man put his dick in the woman's mouth. When it wasn't on Sabrina's pussy. When Sabrina lifted her head. André's dick was waiting for her. André nodded. The stranger took his dick out of the woman's mouth. Then slammed it into Sabrina's pussy. Fucking her like a mad man. André pulled the lady's legs from under Sabrina. He lifted them onto his shoulders. He pulled her pussy close to the edge of the bed. He started fucking her. From his vantage point. He could watch this strange masked man fucking Sabrina. He could see the expressions on her face. Her vantage point allowed her to see André. Fucking this mystery woman. André took his dick out of the woman's pussy. Then put it in Sabrina's mouth. He told her to suck it clean.

The stranger offered the woman his dick. She sucked off Sabrina's juices. Both men began fucking them some more. The stranger held firm to Sabrina's hips. He rammed in and out of her. The sound of her wetness seeping onto him, told André she liked it. André was also enjoying, the softness of the pussy he was in. He lowered the woman's legs from his shoulders. He told her to slide up by the head of the bed. As she did, he told her to lay on her side. He had the strange man, lay across the top of the bed. With his dick near her face. Then he laid Sabrina. With her pussy to the man's face. André laid across the foot of the bed. With his dick in Sabrina's face. The mystery woman's pussy was in André's face.

"Okay everyone." André said. "Start licking and sucking." Each of them had a mouth. Eating their pussy or sucking their dick. They were all delirious with pleasure. Sabrina sucked André's dick with passion. While the stranger ate her pussy and licked her ass cheeks. André ate the mystery woman's pussy. Licking it and sucking her clit. He could look up and see. How this woman masterfully sucked the stranger's dick. As if they were long lost lovers. They stayed in this position. Until Sabrina began to breathe harder and faster. As if her tension was building uncontrollably. Her sucking pace quickened. Her hips began to grind in the stranger's face.

The woman André was eating. Also began grinding her pussy faster and harder. André felt his balls tighten to push out his semen. He looked to see the stranger. Release his load into the woman's face and mouth. Immediately Sabrina let out a yell. She clamped her legs on the man's head. As she forced him to drink all of her juice. Sabrina was convulsing in spasms. She let the stranger have access to all of her glory. Her last spasm caused André to release his cum. Once again into her pretty mouth. Finally, the woman grabbed André's head. To hold it steady. As she poured out her juices into his face and mouth. After climaxing and floating back to earth. They all got up from the bed. To the roaring applaud of the viewers.

They walked over to the sink to grab fresh towels. Using the body wash and facial cleanser. To clean themselves up. After they were all cleaned they stood smiling at each other. "Ummmm, is everybody happy?" The woman asked. "No," André replied. "I think my lady wants to be fucked in her ass. I may need both you ladies. To help in getting hard again. With those nice asses you ladies have. I bet you both like dick in them." The ladies knelt down. Presenting their mouths to the two waiting dicks. André stroked his dick and put it in the woman's mouth. While Sabrina took her mystery lover's dick into hers. The women were side by side. Sucking their respective partner's dicks. All while playing with their increasingly wet pussies.

"Oh, this feels so good." André moaned. "I want the both of you to together." The ladies quickly turned to each other. Then started to kiss. They took each other to the floor. Sabrina quickly kissed her way down the woman's body. She began devouring her pussy. She spread the woman's legs. Pushing her knees to her chest. Sabrina gave her a severe tongue lashing. The woman was tortured. With the delight of Sabrina's tongue. She was licked, sucked, kissed and made love to. By Sabrina's sweet mouth. Sabrina's nice ass was bent upward. So her mystery lover, began to give her another oral tease. Kissing her pussy as if it were her mouth. André knelt down over the mystery woman. Rubbing his dick across her face. Then he entered her mouth.

Sabrina then abandoned her female lover. She turned to suck on the unknown man's dick. Soon both men's dicks were rising hard again. The women then got back on their knees. Kneeling side by side again. They sucked their lovers off almost as if in a contest. Each lady showing the other. How she pleases her lover. The other coming up with different techniques. Sabrina licked the underside of her lover's dick. The woman licked André's balls. Sabrina took her lover's balls. Sucking them whole into her mouth. The mystery woman began to hum on André's balls.

The viewers were cheering the ladies on. The ladies were delighted to put on a show. Soon the men are hard again. André pulled Sabrina from her lover. He sat down on the bed. "Sabrina, I want you." He said. "To sit down and stick my dick in your ass." Ride this dick baby." The stranger took the mystery woman. Laying her down. He pulled her legs over his shoulders. He gently pushed his moisten dick, into her ass. They began a slow grind. André moistened his penis, with Sabrina's juices and his saliva. Sabrina carefully, lowered her dark hole over André's chocolate dick. They both moaned in ecstasy. Her warm anal walls. Gripped and surrounded his throbbing dick.

She fucked him slowly at first. Until her ass adjusted to his rod. Then she began to hump him up and down. As if she was on a bouncing ball. The other woman was yelling loudly. As her lover was fucking her unyieldingly. Sabrina could feel the tip of Andrés dick. As it stroked her G-spot. She quickly obtained a massive orgasm. Grabbing André's knee, to steady herself with her left hand. While fingering her pussy with her right. She was reeling. With the explosion of her orgasm. André was caressing her breasts. While kissing her back repeatedly. Sabrina was out of breath. Her orgasm was body-shattering. André was not done fucking her. He put her on all fours. Then guided his dick right back into her ass. He began slamming it deep inside.

His balls were knocking on her labia. He held her hips with a vice grip. So that she could not pull her ass away from him. "Oh, God baby!" He said. "You feel so damn good. You've had me dreaming. About fucking you in your ass all week. I know you love having this dick in your ass. I know what you really want. A dick in your ass and one in your pussy. You're a fucking nasty girl, aren't you woman?" Sabrina could only squeak out, "Yes. I'm a nasty fucking girl." She moaned. "I love that dick in my ass." André continue, "You loved sucking his dick too, didn't you?" "Yes, I loved sucking his dick." Sabrina said.

"Did you love eating that pussy over there?" André asked. He pulled his dick all the way out of her ass. Before shoving it in again. "Yes, I loved eating her pussy." Sabrina squealed. "I loved it, I loved it!!!" "You'll do it again?" André asked. "Because you're my freak?" André playfully asked. "Yes, I'm your nasty freak big daddy." Sabrina replied. "I'll do whatever to turn you on." "Then fuck me with your ass freak!" André ordered. "Ram that dark chocolate hole on this dick! I'm about to cum in your ass woman! You sexy, hot freaky slut. Oooooooooooooooooooh FFFFFuuuuucccccK! Wooooooommaaaaaannnn!!!!"

"I'm cummmmming in your ass baby…Hot sticky cummmmmmmmm in your ass." The feel of his dick. Massaging Sabrina's G-spot to perfection was overwhelming. Sabrina began bucking wildly. Her own orgasm was boiling over again. "Draaaaaaaa…" She almost called his name. In front of company but caught herself. "Oh, my god. I'm fucking cummmmmming." He rammed into her and held his position. Until Sabrina was done. They both collapsed onto the bed. They were completely spent. They labored to catch their breaths. André began to kiss Sabrina. On the back of her neck and on her shoulders. Seemingly, in the distance. They could hear the other two people in the room. To Sabrina and André. They were in their own world and no one else was there. André massaged her back. He told her how beautiful she was.

Sabrina got their wine glasses. That a waitress apparently brought. They sipped their glasses and rested. Then cleaned at the sink and got dressed. They thanked the other two persons for their services. "Maybe we will meet again." Sabrina said to the strange man and woman. The masked woman kissed the strange man. André boldly held Sabrina's hand and led her out the room. They walked around a little to watch others before heading out. Sabrina asked, "Did you have a good time?" André replied, "Hell yes, I did. Let's take off these masks now that we're in the car." "Thank you baby." Sabrina said. "For what?" André asked.

"For letting me have my fantasy." Sabrina answered. "Just as long baby." André said. "As you don't make any arrangements. With this or any other dude. Unless I'm with you." "Yes Master." Sabrina said. "I wouldn't invite anyone between my legs. Without your permission." André took Sabrina's hand and they smiled at each other. "You're not going to think less of me are you?" Sabrina asked. André looked into her eyes. "Sabrina, I've long understood." He said. "That many women have sexual desires. Outside of what society calls norm. You're just one that is honest about yours. I like the same things you like. This can be a nice little bit of excitement. Every now and then."

She leaned over to kiss him. André pulled away. "You still have to brush your teeth first." He said. "I don't want that dude's dick on my mouth. Matter of fact. The way you was sucking his dick. You need to brush, floss and gargle twice. You damn freak!" "Oh, listen at you." Sabrina replied. "After you licked that woman's pussy until it turned red?" Sabrina teased. "Okay, we'll both brush and gargle." André said. "Your ass might need to use Clorox." He joked. Sabrina pulled her red dress up over her thighs. André could see her panties. "Damn, you're still horny?" André asked. "I'll pull this car over into one of these parking lots. Put you on the back seat. If you don't stop playing." He warned.

"I'm just teasing you." Sabrina said. "I'm ready to go take a hot shower. Get myself in bed." "Now that sounds like a good idea." André said. They made their way home. Beginning to peel off their clothes at the door. Sabrina turned on the shower. Grabbing two towels and wash cloths. They went to their sinks and began brushing their teeth. André then grabbed the mouthwash and poured some. Before passing the bottle to Sabrina. They both gargled and after about 60 seconds. They smiled at each other. André followed her into the shower. Sabrina let the warm water wash over her body.

She then allowed André to do the same. She began to soap his body with body wash. He reciprocated. Sabrina asked André to shampoo her hair. He was happy to comply. They made sure they were both squeaky clean. Then enjoyed sometime playing together in the water. After they were done, they left the shower. Drying each other off. Sabrina wrapped her hair. "I'm going to have a fruit salad before bed." She said. "Would you like one?" "Yeah, that sounds good." André said. "I want mostly watermelon. That's natural Viagara I can use with you Sabrina." Sabrina went to the kitchen to prepare the fruit salads. André turned on the television in the bedroom.

She soon joined him and they started a movie. They finished their fruit salads. André took the bowls into the kitchen to wash them. Sabrina was laying comfortably when he returned. She raised the covers for André to enter. He cuddled next to her. She kissed him softly on his shoulders. He turned to kiss her. "What time is it?" She asked. "It's about 4:30am." André replied. They made efforts to watch the movie on television. However they were both fading fast. André turned the television off. He soon fell asleep. Sabrina watched him breathe for a few moments. She then grabbed her cell phone. She typed and sent a text. Before shutting her phone off. She checked on André again. To make sure he was still asleep. She too also succumbed to exhaustion.

Chapter 4

The Black House

At a non-descript warehouse in Laurel Maryland. Colonel Delaney and Commissioner Riggs meet. They have been summoned at 5:00am. "Good morning Commissioner." Colonel Delaney said. "I didn't know you were going to be here. I thought the Feds were just fucking with me." "No, they called my motherfucking phone." Commissioner Riggs said. "At four this morning too. Told me I had an hour to get down here. Good thing I had those lights and Siren. I know the Capitol Police would have stopped me on I-295. "Did they tell you what the fuck this is all about?" Chief Delaney asked. "I'm the Goddamn Chief of Police. I don't like being summoned no Goddamn where."

"No, I don't know what the hell this is about." Commissioner Riggs replied. Director Tolbert and Director Baker soon entered the room. They were followed by Mr. Vailati and two other men in black suits. One of them, an African-American male. The other, apparently Italian. "Who the fuck are these guys, the Men in Black?" Commissioner Riggs joked. "Yes, they are actually." Director Tolbert responded. "So what do they do?" Chief Delaney asked. "Do they kill aliens or some shit?" "You could say that." Mr. Vailati replied.

"They kill anything that is alien. To the fundamental principles of our democracy." "What does that mean?" Chief Delaney asked. "It means the American people." Mr. Vailati replied. "Have always believed that this is a country for the people. By the people. If they don't like something. They can simply change it by their votes. The men and women who work at The Black House. Work diligently behind the scenes. To ensure that belief is passed on from generation to generation."

"The Black House?" Commissioner Riggs inquired. "Is that some racist name? You guys gave the White House, when President Obama got elected?" "No, not at all." Director Tolbert injected. "President Obama was great for our perception. However, this current administration. Is destroying any semblance of the ideology. That this country was founded on. The Black House is called what it is for other reasons. Our powers operate in the shadows of darkness. The White House administrations prior to this. Operated in the light of the public eye. We operate in the dark, behind closed doors. When Presidential administrations were caught in lies. As most of them would be. They didn't go through extensive lengths to cover up.

Nor were they able to get, a large segment of the population. To believe they were being unfairly targeted. For their criminal activity. However, this administration. Has tried to operate a shadow Government. In concert with our biggest enemy threat. Shadow Government is our territory. The men and women of the Black House. Don't appreciate the intrusion." "So why don't you help the Congress?" Commissioner Riggs asked. "Find incriminating evidence? Then indict this criminal motherfucker?" "We're not in the business of building cases." Mr. Vailati said. "For courts or Congress." "So, what exactly is your business?' Chief Delaney asked.

"Well, as stated earlier." Mr. Vailati replied. "The men and women at the Black House kill aliens. We have a liaison with the FBI, CIA and NSA. Homeland Security, State Department and the Secret Service. We also have a liaison with the Commanders of the U.S. Military branches. Including the Coast Guard. This way, we can never be seen in direct communications. With anyone from those agencies. Yet we can communicate with them. As easily as I'm talking to you now." "Thank you for that brief history." Commissioner Riggs said. "On your shadow organization. Many of us always suspected it existed anyway. What does that have to do with Colonel Delaney and me?"

"Why did you drag us out of bed at 4:00am? For a damn history lesson?" "Not a history lesson Commissioner." Mr. Vailati said. "You and Colonel Delaney will help make history. You see this week. The President is going to visit the Inner Harbor, here in Baltimore. The Inner Harbor being the crown jewel of Baltimore. It's always crawling. With tourists and visitors. It's also not far from the Federal Building. Where our Deputy A.G. came from. The Deputy who is now, in the cross hairs of this administration. It wouldn't be hard to see. How some here in Baltimore. May want to stand up for one of their own." "So, you want us to lead a protest against the President." Chief Delaney asked. "When he visits Baltimore?"

"No Colonel, you're thinking too small." Mr. Vailati said. "The men and women of Black House don't lead protests. They kill aliens. One could argue that this Presidency. Is alien to our democratic process." "Are you fuckers talking about killing the President?" Commissioner Riggs asked. "Now, you're thinking too small, Commissioner Riggs." Director Baker said. "We're not just going to kill the President. We're going to kill every member of Congress. That has been compromised by the Russian Government. It's essential to saving the very fabric of our society." "Oh, hell no!" Chief Delaney said. "You can count me the fuck out of this kind of crazy talk." "I'll resign my position as chief immediately. Before I let you muscle me. Into participating in a suicide mission like this."

"That's for damn sure." Commissioner Riggs echoed. "I'll resign too." They both got up to leave. "Gentlemen, please sit down." Mr. Vailati said. "Your value to us isn't in your positions. As Chief and Commissioner. Well, a small part of it is. Yet we value family so much more. Commissioner, you live at 98 Shawan Road in Hunt Valley, Maryland, correct? You and that beautiful wife of yours. Those two gorgeous teen children." Commissioner Riggs and Colonel Delaney looked stunned. "Your wife visits her mother. Who still lives in West Baltimore. Over in Bolton Hills.

"It would be a shame." Mr. Vailati continued. "If some of that violence from North Ave. Were to bleed over into that quiet neighborhood. Leaving your wife bleeding out from a gunshot wound. Or two. Hell, we'll shoot the bitch as many times as necessary. To make you understand. We're asking for your help. Don't make us beg you for your help. There are too many kids. That die from violence in this city as it is. Oh, and Colonel Delaney." Mr. Vailati continued. "You live at 5018 Painters Mill Rd. In Owings Mills correct? Your lovely wife Sheila and you. Often caring for your lovely grand kids. At your residence. You have such a lovely view in your back yard. That leads into the woods. Maybe you should get bulletproof vest. Issued for your grand kids."

"Who knows? Some nut case in a black suit. Could be in those woods one day. With an M-16 assault rifle." Colonel Delaney stood, as if he would attack Mr. Vailati. "I'm just kidding, Colonel." Mr. Vailati said. Chief Delaney returned to his seat. "We both know." Mr. Vailati continued. "A bulletproof vest won't help those babies against an M-16. Gentlemen, the men and women of the Black House. Don't like to kill innocent women and kids. However, in shadow Government. You don't always get to do, what you like to do. You do what you must do." "Now, before you both go thinking. You'll call your families. Have them pack up and go somewhere safe."

"Commissioner Riggs, your 92 year-old grandma. Lives at 1000 N. 23rd St. in Baton Rouge, Louisiana. Your sister lives 235 Marina Way. In San Francisco, California. You have a brother in Rockaway Park, New York. What are the chances? You'll get everybody moved to a safe home? Before we move them to a funeral home? Of course Colonel Delaney. We know where every member of your family is too. Now, all we're asking is for you to help us. Then we'll help you too." "How in the hell are you helping us?" Colonel Delaney demanded. "By threatening our families?" Director Tolbert answered, "Well, Colonel. You've expressed concerns about your Captain Nichols.

"How you'd have long moved to get rid of him. If it were not for the protection he has in Annapolis. At the Governor's Mansion. Commissioner, the Major of your Northeast District. Has been a pain in your side as well. When the President comes to town. There's going to be Secret Service everywhere. The only people who can possibly get close to the President. Will be Law Enforcement. Of course Commissioner. You're being asked to be there. We want you to invite Chief Delaney. Along with Major Carver.

Chief Delaney will invite Captain Nichols. As part of his detail. Captain Nichols is going to kill the President. He won't actually kill the President. One of our men in black will. He's highly trained in causing death. He'll make sure the President dies. Reliable Intel is The President refuses. To wear a bullet proof vest. At these public outings. He discards the advice. Of trained Secret Service staff around him. Once our Agent takes the shot. We will take advantage of your Captain's natural instinct. Which will be to grab his weapon. Immediately he'll remove his weapon from his holster. Our Agent will give him a shot of gamma-hydroxybutyric acid. Which will make him appear to collapse. From the terrible deed he's done.

Another agent will take his weapon. Then replace it with the one that fired the shot. Of course, Secret Service will move in. To arrest him at that point." "You're going to inject a Captain of a Police Department?" Chief Delaney asked. "With a date rape drug?" "Yes, we are Colonel." Director Baker replied. "After a few hours in custody. Captain Nichols' Police Union Attorney, is going to show up. We both know he or she will not be a Public Defender. Or some kid just out of Law School. They are going to demand the results. Of any blood or urine test. Law Enforcement takes from the Captain. We don't need any drug we give him. Hanging around in his system too long. Gamma-hydroxybutyric acid gets in and gets out. Like a thief in the night. We can stall the blood test for 12 hours."

"Under the pretense of processing someone. That just murdered the President. After that. His attorneys can have the results to any test they want." "Why Captain Nichols?" Colonel Delaney demanded. "It's simple." Mr. Vailati replied. "If a sniper kills the President. Then it will confirm for those who believe. That the President was killed by a deep state system. One out to get him. They will mobilize. We'll have a Civil War on our hands. If a disgruntled black cop kills him. The white trash that supports the President. Will just think it was a rogue nigger. That should have never, been given a badge and gun to begin with. They'll still be mad. But we'll avoid having to turn Military power. On Willie, Cooter and white power.

Blasting them in the fucking woods. Of Kentucky and Montana. Showing them how many guns they have. Never mattered to the Federal Government. Not when we have helicopters. With .50 caliber machine guns. Not to mention Predator Drones. As well as other firepower. We can use to light their asses up. Like a fucking Christmas tree." "There may be an increase in hate crimes." Director Tolbert added. "Against blacks for a moment. We can stomp that out in a year or so. So, you see gentlemen. You're helping to save the country. You get rid of your thorns. We avoid a National crisis. Of our Government openly killing its citizens. Citizens who will certainly try to overthrow. If they believe we're behind this murder."

On Bentalou St. Ms. Parsons came out of her home. As she saw a young man walking down the street. "Hey son, let me use your cell phone!" She yelled. The young man brought her his phone. Just as he handed it to her. Her home telephone in her house rang. "Go get that for me." She said. Tell them I will call them back." The young man did as he was told. Ms. Parsons dialed a number on the cell phone. She waited for an answer. "Hey, tell Drexler. I need a Lyftee up to Mondawmin. I need to get some lingerie from Victoria's secret.

The young man came out of her house. With her son Ronnie James. He told her the call. Was from Pastor Kingsley across the street. "He wants you to come over and see him." The man said. "When you get a minute." "Doesn't he know today is not Sunday?" Ms. Parsons asked. "Here's your phone, sugar. Thank you." "Yes ma'am." The young man said. "Do you need me to do anything else?" He asked. "Yes, you can do me one small favor." Ms. Parsons said. "Go over to Pulaski and Smallwood. Tell Skeeter I heard about some young man. One he was close to being killed. Up in Edmondson Village. Let him know that I will referee the game. For him and his boss Count Drexler. So there's no need for him to call a play."

"Ms. Parsons doesn't need all that violence." She said. "Going on in her district. Let him know that whomever did it. Has a girlfriend down in the Village. Mama Parsons will throw the flag. Then assess the penalty. I'm going to pray. That everything turns out alright. Hopefully that young man, Dirty Red. Can learn the playbook." "Yes ma'am, I'll make sure I tell Skeet." The man said. "Anything else you need Ms. Parsons?" He asked. "No son, Ronnie James will see me across the street." She replied. "You have a blessed day. Mama Parsons loves you." "I love you too Ms. Parsons." He replied.

"Ronnie James, go get your Poncho." She said. Sit out here and watch mama go across the street." Also, I have a Lyftee ride coming to get me. Send him over to the church." "Deasssam ma,ma,ma, mama." He uttered. She walked across the street. There she pushed the intercom button. The door buzzed open and she walked in. "Good afternoon, Ms. Parsons." Pastor Kingsley said. "What do you want nigga?" Ms. Parsons asked. I have a ride coming to take me up to Mondawmin." "It's good to see you too." Pastor Kingsley replied. "I've got word. That the young lady you and Drexler are looking for. Is staying over at Drexler's brother's house. The cop dude that grew up around here." "Okay, I know you didn't call me over here." Ms. Parsons said. To tell me something that I already knew."

"We're just waiting on the right time. To go there and pay her a visit." "Yes, I figured you did know that." Pastor continued. "But did you know she was Fed working undercover?" "What? Ms. Parsons gasped. "A God damn Fed?" "Yes, but word is" Pastor Kingsley said. "She may have gone rogue. She may be trying to figure out a way. To leave the country with the money. I have reliable information. From one of the President's spiritual advisors. That she has an access code. To about half a billion dollars. The money is completely untraceable. Because the Feds didn't want to put an encryption tracer on it. My friend was not supposed to see this information. Except our current President is an idiot."

"He routinely has people in his office. With classified information just laying around. My friend goes in there to pray. The idiot and chief closes his eyes. So, my friend and all the other Pastors. See some really mind-blowing stuff." "Half a billion dollars?" Ms. Parsons repeated. "So that cash money Drexler and I are chasing. Is nothing compared to this electronic stuff? We're going to have to move up the timetable. On paying a visit to this bitch. I'll speak to Drexler soon. See what we can do about this. Thanks Reverend. You actually were useful today." "Well, the Reverend is hoping." Pastor Kingsley said. That once you get the electronic transfer. You wouldn't mind letting the church. Have a nice piece of the cash portion?"

"If this works out Reverend." Ms. Parsons said. "The church will never have to ask. For donations again. I know your greedy ass will anyway." "I can't let the flock think they're not needed." Pastor Kingsley said. "To help the Lord do His work." Just then, the buzzer rang. Alerting that someone was at the door. "That's my ride up the block to Mondawmin." Ms. Parsons said. I'll be back later, Reverend." "I may need you to lay hands on me. Speak in tongues to this pussy again." She walked and opened the door. At the door was Deer Dog. They embraced in a brief hug. He escorted her to his blue Yukon SUV.

She then looked over across the street. To see her son Ronnie James. Sitting on the steps with his poncho. She nodded to her son. He got up to go back into the house. The shotgun he was holding under the poncho. Was briefly exposed. Before he covered it and took it inside. He turned to his mother. As she got in the vehicle. "Ba,ba,ba,ba, bye mmmmama." She waved to him as Deer Dog closed her door. Ronnie James dragged his limp left leg. Along with the poncho inside the house. "So how have you been Otacilius?" Ms. Parsons asked. "I've been good Mama P." Deer Dog replied. "How have you been? "You know you and family are the only ones. That call me Octacilius."

"Boy I've known your daddy and mama." Ms. Parsons said. "Since we were in elementary school together. I was there when Myrtle Crawford brought you home. From being born. I remember when your friend Butch. Gave you the name Deer Dog. He said you were so ugly. You looked like a cross between a deer and a dog. That name just stuck with you. Since way back then." "Yeah but nobody would be cracking jokes on me these days." Deer Dog said. "These are strange days out here, Deer Dog." Ms. Parsons said. "God damn Russians seem. To have taken over the United States Government. Now they're about to take over the drug game."

"If that shit happens. You know who will be getting squeezed out? Right now. The Russians are giving us Grade A. heroin. They need us to get into the game. Who knows how this game will play out? When they figure out the logistics of Baltimore. Plus everywhere else they're moving into. If we want to win the game. We have to be black chameleons Deer Dog. When I got started in this game. I was a dancer at the only black-owned club. Over on the block many years ago. I used to bring in the most fellas. Earn the club the most money. The owner of the club was this guy named Jarvis Gaston. He was the cousin of Nicky Barnes. Out of New York. He didn't really like drugs. But he loved all the money it made him. The crowd I brought in. Would buy drinks all night. Just to stay and watch me dance."

"It wasn't long before Nicky told Jarvis. That if they would buy drinks. They would buy drugs. Especially if they thought. That would get them some alone time with me. So, Jarvis offered me a position. Of being his point person. For all the heroin he flowed into Baltimore. Being that Nicky absolutely ran the game. In Harlem and beyond. We had the best product. I had the muscle of The Council behind me. Once Nicky killed that Italian mafia guy. Their authority went unchallenged. All I needed was crew to distribute for me. Next thing you know. I was a millionaire. After The Council was arrested. Jarvis couldn't get the good product any more. Without his cousin Nicky, breastfeeding and protecting him. He became weak."

"By this time. I understood the game. I took a trip up to New York. I brokered a deal with the Carlistino family. Johnny Carlistino, ran that family back then. I met young Fat Tony. When he was visiting here a few months later. Once again. Heroin was flowing into Baltimore. I stayed under the radar of law enforcement. By staying close to Reverend Woods at St. Mary. Until he passed. He let me launder money through the church. For a fee, of course. Then he set me up with other Pastors. All over the DMV. I set up my own non-profit organization. I would give a million dollars drug money to a church. That church would then turn around and give $900 thousand back. To my non-profit.

Because of the tax exempt bullshit with churches. The Government will never ask. Where they get their money from. Nor will they ask how they spend it. The members never ask either. I raised my son as if he was mentally handicapped. To keep the government even further away. There is nothing for the Feds to connect. Me to drug money. After all. I'm the Mother of St. Mary Baptist Church. Who would suspect? I'd blow your motherfucking head off? At 7:00p.m. Saturday evening. Then be in church at 7:00am Sunday morning. Getting my praise on. My son, Ronnie James is a sharpshooter and a black belt. He can go from crazy to killer real quick. He's pretty much all the muscle I need. Of course, I have other killers at my disposal."

"Your man, Drexler was one of my prized protégés." She continued. "I'm just not sure where his loyalty lies these days. I've been thinking it may be time to make some changes. To the leadership of your crew Deer Dog. Do you think you'd be ready to step up? Be mama's point person for over East side?" "You want me to run the East side, mama P?" Deer Dog asked. "What happens to Drexler?" "If you have to ask that question." Ms. Parsons said. "Then you're not ready Octacilius." "Oh, I'm ready." Deer Dog said. "So, are you going to have Ronnie James kill him? How are we doing this?" "To be the man, you have to beat the man." Ms. Parsons said. "Nobody is going to follow you. When you farm out your dirty work."

"Mama can't breastfeed you with these old tits. You either sit down with the grown folks. Or go sit at the kids table." "I'm ready to sit at the grown folks table." Deer Dog said. "Consider it done. Just let me come up with a plan." "No need for that." Ms. Parsons said. "I already have one. There was a foul committed by Dirty Red's team. Against Drexler. I'm calling a review of the play. I'm assessing a 15-yard penalty on Dirty Red. Every yard is $10,000. So this motherfucker owes me $150,000. $75,000 to make amends to Count Drexler. $75,000 for Mama P. I want you and Drexler to be there. So this young cat can get to know the players. I'll introduce Drexler as the #1. You as the #2. So he knows you're in line for the throne. Once I secure the funds. He and Drexler will shake hands. You'll be standing behind Drexler. I want you to blow his brains out."

"This serves two purposes. It will get Drexler out of the way. So you can run things. Two, it will send a clear message. To Dirty Red. That I'm not to be fucked with." "Okay, if that's the plan." Deer Dog said. "Then that's what I'm rolling with. What the fuck man?" "What's wrong?" Ms. Parsons asked. "This damn lady Transit cop." Deer Dog replied. "Has been following us. Since we left the church." "Well, there is a subway station at Mondawmin." Ms. Parsons said. "She's probably just going up there like so many other people do."

"Yeah, I know that." Deer Dog said. "She has been riding awfully close on my ass. Like she wants to pull us over." "You don't have any drugs in the truck, do you?" Ms. Parsons asked. "No, I don't have any drugs." Deer Dog replied. "I do have this .45 on me." "Well, you're not speeding." Ms. Parsons said. "Don't give her any reason. If she stops us. Let the old church lady talk for you." "Oh, she just made a turn." Deer Dog said. "Going towards Dru Hill Park." "See, you were getting all nervous for nothing." Ms. Parsons said. "A number one can't crack under pressure." "I wasn't cracking." Deer Dog responded. "I was just wondering. Why she had to be all close? To my truck like she was running my tags or something."

"Well, your tags are legit." Ms. Parsons said. "So nothing to worry about there either." They arrived at Mondawmin mall and Deer Dog parked. He went to open the door for Ms. Parsons. He walked her inside the mall. His head was on a swivel. Looking for any danger that may approach. Ms. Parsons turned to Deer Dog. "Here, take my phone and walk around the mall." She said. "You never know who may be tracking my movements." They made their way to the Victoria's Secret store. Ms. Parsons walked up to the register. The woman at the register was about mid-twenties. She appeared to recognize Ms. Parsons. "What do you have in a retro style from say, 1944?" Ms. Parsons asked. "I'll take you back to the back and let you look around." The cashier said. They walked back into the employee area. The cashier unlocked the door.

Inside the room was Count Drexler. Also his bodyguard Fats. Ms. Parsons nodded to Deer Dog. He left to walk around. While walking through the mall. Deer Dog saw the stripper named Candy. She was walking towards him. "Hey, what's up sexy lady, how are you?" Deer Dog asked. "Heeeeey, how are you Deer Dog?" Candy replied. "You're not out with that damn Drexler today? I thought you two fools were inseparable. I'm glad you're not. He irks my last nerve." "Is that right?" Deer Dog asked. "Well, he's not here right now."

"Between you and me." Deer Dog continued. "I may be the only one you have to deal with. In the near future." "Well, I would love that." Candy replied. "If you come to the club without him. I can't stand Drexler's dirty ass hands touching me. Now you Deer Dog. I'd let you touch me everywhere. If he wasn't there being so jealous." "I know right?" Deer Dog said. "Don't worry Candy. Mama P. and I are about to make some changes." Back in the storage room of the Victoria's Secret store. Ms. Parsons and Drexler were talking. "What the fuck is going on Drexler?" She asked. Why haven't you dealt with this bitch? I heard she is hiding out at your damn brother's house."

"That shit is of no consequence to me. You still need to handle this." Ms. Parsons demanded. "Trust me, I've got something for her ass." Drexler replied. "Do you, really?" Ms. Parsons asked. "What exactly did you show that bitch? I just found out she is a motherfucking Fed bitch. Working undercover." "A fucking Fed bitch?" Drexler repeated. "Are you serious?" "Yes, I'm serious." Ms. Parsons replied. "Although they think she has gone rogue. Wait until I tell you why. It seems little Ms. Actress has an access code. To about half a billion dollars in untraceable funds. The Government is usually pretty good. With keeping tabs on this kind of money. The way things are now. There is very little oversight on this. Probably other operations as well."

"By the time someone gets in to look over something. They've had to resign. Apparently, the idiot at the top. Never heard of background checks. Speaking of background checks. How did you meet this want-to-be academy award winning bitch? "I met her and Cynthia out at Arundel Mills." Drexler said. One day when I was buying some art pieces for my house. They came in the art store. Buying something and we got talking." "Cynthia? That was the bitch that you wired up?" Ms. Parsons asked. With a damn scrub brush right? "Yeah, the wire was the last show she watched." Drexler said. "I got word that one of my stash houses was about to be raided."

"So, I had those two bitches move the money. They were supposed to move it. To this spot on Rogers Ave. In Northwest. Next thing I know. One of my boys spots Cynthia. Sleeping in the parking lot of Home Depot. On Patterson and Reisterstown. The other bitch Jasmine and our money. Were gone in the wind. Cynthia told me some man carjacked them. Up on Park Heights Ave. She said he drove up Garrison. Turning on Chalgrove." "You didn't believe her?" Ms. Parsons asked. "I won't believe shit nobody says." Drexler replies. "Until I get that fucking money back. Now, this half a billion you're telling me. Jasmine has the code to."

"That's going to be some we're leaving the country money. If we can get our hands on that." "You mean WHEN we get our hands on that?" Ms. Parsons interjected. "You need to go grab that bitch. From your brother's house where she's laying up. Then we can get that damn code from her. Hell, the way I hear it. We may be able to use your brother as bait. To make her talk. I can get Ronnie James to talk to your brother. Since you probably have a soft spot." She continued. "Soft spot!" Drexler said. "For that sell out, bitch made motherfucker. If that nigga gets in the way. I will personally. Put two bullets in his fucking chest. And one in his fucking forehead." Drexler said. "I don't want Ronnie James to touch my brother. I'll take care of him my damn self."

"Well, you better take care of that damn girl." Ms. Parsons said. "If need be, your brother too. You better not let this opportunity slip away. I know of at least a dozen murders you've done. That I could let the Police know about." "I'll take care of my end." Drexler said. "You just make sure you have the safe houses set up overseas. We're not going to be anywhere. That this Government is going to be able to extradite us from." "The houses are already set up." Ms. Parsons said. "The keys to them are in a P.O. Box in Randallstown. Satellite television, Internet and all the luxuries of home. Are up and running in each house. Hell, I'm ready to leave this country at 67 years old.

"Since that damn Devil got in the White House. It hasn't felt like this since the 1960s. With that kind of money, I want to enjoy life a little. Before I get to where I need to be taken care of." "When the time comes." Drexler said. "I'll make sure you are taken care of Ms. Parsons." "You may have to take care of your brother André." She replied. "Long before you take care of me. I told you to kill him a long time ago. You see he has gone in there. Climbed all the way up to Captain. He has completely bought into working with our enemies. They cut us off from decent paying jobs. Flood our neighborhoods with drugs. Then try to lock us up. When we're just trying to make enough money to be comfortable."

"My punk ass brother, knows better than to fuck with me." Drexler said. "I knew he was soft when we were growing up. Mama always encouraged him. To go to school and read. While I had to be out on the streets. Hustling to feed his little ass. I always knew he would grow up to be a nerd. He never had the heart for these streets." "Well, when we grab that bitch he's shacking up with." Ms. Parsons said. "His little heart may get broken and a bullet in it on the same day." "I told you already." Drexler said. "If anybody is killing my brother. It will be me." "That's all fine and good." Ms. Parsons said. "If you don't. Then I will have him killed. Before you can say, I believe it."

"I'll give you a few days." She continued. "To get that bitch out to the church basement. So we can find out what that code is. That should give you time. To figure out how to deal with your brother too. Next week. I want to be on a plane headed to Cape Town. Then I can watch on satellite T.V. This damn Devil in the White House wreck this country. I don't want my money tied up. Anywhere near what's about to happen. This market is about to go down. Like a French whore on a payday weekend." "With half a billion plus to split." Drexler said. "We can ride way above the crash. Without even smelling the smoke."

At an undisclosed location. Director Tolbert and Baker were seated at a table. Across from one another. "Did you hear that bitch ass Senate Majority leader?" Director Baker asked. Talking about cutting FBI funding. To pay for those rich Bastards tax cuts?" "Those motherfuckers are too stupid to know. The FBI generates its own funding. By asset seizures. Along with good old fashioned helping a Senator or Congressperson. To cover up their fuck ups. For a good price of course. "Those idiots have fucked up seriously before." Director Tolbert said. "But how in the world? Did so many in Congress and the Senate. Allow themselves to be compromised? By the Russians? This doing anything to win and keep power. Has gotten way out of hand."

"I can't figure that shit out my damn self." Director Baker said. "Their head was so far up. This shit for brains President's ass. That they followed him into treason. These motherfuckers literally are in a position. Where they have to give up National secrets to Russia. Just to keep Russia from exposing them. As the treasonous pieces of shit they are. The only way we can save people's idea. Of the ideal America. Is to kill every one of these bitches, who sold this country out." "Yes, but don't you think a Signal-13 alarm would be raised?" Director Tolbert asked. "When so many prominent politicians. Are all being murdered at the same time?" "Of course it will." Mr. Vailati said. He stepped into the room.

"We'll just drop some documents to the press." He continued. To show these bastards in Congress, all grew balls or tits. Around the same time. They decided they were no longer, going to allow Russia to pull their strings. They were going to confess. The names of their Russian Puppet masters. The Russians got wind, and started killing these bastards. With the cuts to the State Department. We had no advanced Intel to warn us. That the Russians would make such a bold move. By the time we get a grip on what's happening. The President's horses and The President's men. Will be dead.

"We'll blame the President's death." Director Tolbert said. "On that poor sap of a Transit cop in Baltimore. Major Carver will be blamed. For killing the Senate Majority leader. The others, we'll go find some Russians. Working at a sandwich shop or somewhere. Then tell the world they are assassins. They had a ladder taller than that stupid wall. Oops they hatched a plan to attack our government at its core. Who's not going to believe that story? Since these dummies in Congress. Didn't do anything to protect the country. From the last Russian attack." "Yeah, that is a very plausible story." Director Baker replied.

"Alpha West team should already be in Nebraska." Mr. Vailati continued. Getting ready to take care of the Speaker. Bravo East team is in New York. Awaiting the arrival of the Senate Majority leader. Charlie East team is in Pittsburg. To wash away the Senate Minority leader. Now Delta West team has the biggest assignment. Seven Congressmen are all flying out to Las Vegas. For a fundraiser when the session closes. They're all flying commercial. On the same jet. So they don't look like the greedy bastards they really are."

"According to the airline manifest we hacked. There are going to be 321 passengers on that plane. It's a shame they all have to die. In order to rid our government of these seven treasonous bastards." "That reminds me." Director Baker said. "I have to check with my family and friends. Inconspicuously find out if they are planning any flights that day." "Well, you better get them to miss that shit if they are." Director Tolbert said. "Let's make sure we have everything and everyone in place." Mr. Vailati said. "We only have days before Congress is out of session. Before dumb ass takes the podium in Baltimore. Make sure all team leaders are studying their assigned areas." "They need to know what looks normal. In their assigned cities or towns. Who the locals are? What the local routines are? The best way to execute the plan and get out undetected."

"If any of these traitor bitches survive." Director Baker said. "It won't be long. Before Moscow traces those deaths to us. Then they'll launch a campaign to expose The Black House." "That's never good for business." Mr. Vailati replied. "If we kill them all. Then Moscow no longer has a listening ear. At least not in our government. The Republic will be saved. The other idiot becomes President. We'll begin pulling his strings. "If that's not the damn truth." Director Tolbert said. "With regards to pulling strings. We have to make sure. Nothing happens to this Captain Nichols. Until we can pin this murder on him." "Speaking of Captain Nichols." Director Baker said. "We have to start getting ready for this raid tonight. On his brother's stash house."

"Man that is going to be fucked up." Director Tolbert said. "If we get into a fire fight? With his brother and end up killing him. I just don't believe. That he won't be mad at whomever pulls the trigger." "He can be mad." Director Baker said. "But he absolutely cannot be a part of the raid." If he fires one shot from his weapon. He's on administrative duty for six months. We'll miss our window of opportunity to kill the President." "I'll personally babysit his ass in the command vehicle." Director Tolbert said. "I'll make sure he gets nowhere near the scene. I've been wondering since we met him. How the State of Maryland, even hired him to begin with. I mean his brother is no small time average drug dealer."

"I guess if they judged any of us." Director Baker replied. "By every member of our family. None of us would ever have made it in law enforcement." "Yeah, that's true." Director Tolbert said. "But something seems to be way out of place with this one." "I hear he has friends down in Annapolis." Director Baker said. With the State legislature. Although I'm not sure how they came to like him. He doesn't exactly play the political game. Nor is he affiliated with any of them. On any personal level. As far as we could dig up." "I know how he came to be there." Mr. Vailati said. "That's irrelevant to you gentlemen at this time."

"Whatever connection they have with him." Director Tolbert said. "I'm sure they'll be denying it in a few days. They will drop his ass like sin on judgement day. When he's accused of killing The President. "Look, I'm going to go get me a few hours of sleep." Director Baker said. "Before we do this raid tonight." "Yeah, some sleep sounds like a good idea." Director Tolbert replied. "I'll see you tonight." "Hey look, since you're going to be sleeping Jonathan. Why don't you send your wife over to my place?" Director Tolbert said. She'll have something exciting to do for a change." "She told me she went over to your place once before. Director Baker said. "She didn't like downsizing."

André and Sabrina were seated at the bar in his basement. "Uno Dammit!" André yelled. "Draw four dammit!" Sabrina yelled back. "Did I ever tell you I don't think I like you no more?" André asked. "You may not like me." Sabrina replied. But you want me." "Yes, I do want you." André said. "Give me that luscious kiss with those lips." He ordered. Sabrina sat her cards on the bar face down. She leaned in to kiss him. André wrapped his right arm around her. Trying to lift her cards with his left hand. She smacked his hand. "Look at you, Mr. Cheater." She said.

"I can't take my eyes off of you for one second." She continued. Before you try to cheat." "I wasn't cheating." André protested. "I thought I saw a leprechaun crawl under your cards. I didn't want him to bite your fingers. "No you didn't say a leprechaun?" Sabrina questioned. "You just make up a lie that quick. "Okay, it was a roach." André said. "You don't have roaches." Sabrina countered. "I was going to give you some. Before you went to work tonight. Now it seems like you wanted to lie and look at my cards. More than my naked body." "Ummmm, that sounds so good." André responded. "If you do. I will not get out of the bed until Monday. So I should pass."

"Speaking of bed." André said. "I better carry my ass in there. Can you wake me up? If I'm not up by seven, Breen?" "Of course I will darling." She replied. "You go get you some rest. I'll cook up something nice for you to eat before you leave." "Damn." André said. "I know you said, I shouldn't get attached to you. If you keep treating me like this. I may need some treatment. For feelings prevention." "Oh, I haven't treated you yet." Sabrina replied. "Wait until tomorrow night. I'm going to take you to the next episode." "Is that a club like the last one?" André asked. "No, it's not a club. Sabrina replied. "We're not going anywhere. It'll just be you and me. Along with my directing debut."

"Directing debut?" André questioned. "Are we making a movie?" "I told you film or pictures are not in the plan." Sabrina responded. "What is the plan?" André asked. "The plan is for you to go get some sleep." Sabrina responded. So you can be alert tonight." "Fuck tonight." André said. "I want to know. What's going down tomorrow night?" "Well, if you go get some rest." Sabrina said. Get done what you need to at work. I'll be going down tomorrow night." She teased. "Okay, then let me take my ass to bed right now." André said. Sabrina then closed the blinds. She turned out the lamps on the nightstand. She left André to sleep. While going to watch television in the basement.

Later that evening in Greek town. The command vehicles were motoring up Eastern Ave. The streets were quite crowded with folks. As usually seen on Saturdays. The command vehicles were big and cumbersome. So they had to move slowly through the streets. MTA Police Command 1 halted at Eastern Bus Division. BCPD Command 2 halted a few blocks away. At Johns Hopkins Bayview Hospital. On board MTAPD Command 1. Was Chief Colonel Doug Delaney. Along with Captain André Nichols and Lieutenant McDavid. Also NSA Deputy Director Baker.

Along with FBI Deputy Director Tolbert. Sergeant White was driving the vehicle. "Damn! Our vehicles aren't this nice at the Bureau." Director Tolbert joked. "You motherfuckers have Satellite T.V. in this bitch. A kitchen and a goddamn switchboard. That makes the phone companies jealous. All you need is a damn transporter. To beam a motherfucker up to the Enterprise." "That's in the back." Chief Delaney joked. "I'm just looking for a bottle of water." Lieutenant McDavid said. "Could you hand me one." Director Tolbert asked. "Out of that refrigerator. When you go back there please?" "Anybody else?" Lieutenant McDavid asked. "I'll take one." Sergeant White said.

Over at Bayview, onboard Command 2. Were Baltimore City Commissioner Riggs and Major Carver. Captain Young, Captain McLaughlin and Special Agent Johnson. Mr. Vailati was also there. Sergeant Kindall was their driver. "Are all units in place Major?" Commissioner Riggs asked. "Yes Sir. We have mobile units posted at Pulaski and Haven. Lombard and Haven and units N,E.S.W. In case subjects try to run. Also, Foxtrot is on standby at Martins Airport for air support." "Okay, let me check with MTAPD Command." Commissioner Riggs said. Make sure we're a go. BCP01 to 9Adam01. What's your status?"

"9Adam01 to BCP01. Chief Delaney answered. "We are 10-8 and awaiting confirmation on your end." "10-4, 9Adam01 we are 10-8 as well." Advise all MTAPD units to keep the air clear. Unless an extreme emergency." Chief Delaney picked up his Police radio. "9Adam01 to KMT. Please open channel 4 for this operation. Monitor for us BCPD channel 7." Commissioner Riggs also picked up his Police radio. "BCP01 to KG8, please open channel 7 for this operation. Monitor for us MTAPD channel 4. Also advise all assigned units on this detail. To meet me on that channel at 2301 hours." "Why do we pick some off the wall time like 11:01pm to start this? Why not 11 on the dot?" asked Sergeant Kindall. "Because I said so." Commissioner Riggs responded. "That's all you need to know, Sergeant."

"Okay, we're going live in 9,8,7,6,5,4,3,2,1." Chief Delaney said. KMT Operation Crossray has begun." All assigned MTAPD units. Should be live on channel 4 at this time. KMT please conduct a roll call. To ensure compliance and officer safety. "KMT to all units assigned to Crossray." The dispatcher said. KMT will be conducting roll call at this time. Starting with 9David10. Then to all units in stationary and mobile posts." Simultaneously, Commissioner Riggs began his radio transmission. "BCP01 to KG8, we are now live for Operation Crossray. All assigned BCPD personnel assigned to this detail. Should be on channel 7 at this time. Please conduct a roll call to ensure compliance and officer safety."

After several moments of officers calling and acknowledging. That they had made the switch and are present on the correct channel. The Police Dispatchers reported. "KMT to 9Adam01. All units are present and accounted for." "KG8 to BCP01. All units also are present and accounted for." Onboard MTAPD Command 1. Sergeant White compared the radio roll call. With his list of officers assigned on his operations sheet. "I'm going to head around with one of my officers out there." Captain Nichols said. "As a support unit." "No, you stay here, Captain." Director Tolbert said. "We'll give Director Baker a break. From listening in on everybody's phone calls. Give him a chance to see what real Police work is like." "You're going to send the Deputy Director for the NSA?" Captain Nichols asked. On a raid for some drug dealer?"

"We do what we have to do." Director Baker said. "To keep the country safe. Besides, you're very valuable to the country too, Captain." "We all are important to the country in this day and age." Director Tolbert said. "9David10 to command." The radio transmission blasted into the conversation. The two Directors stared at each other. "Command 1 to 9David10." Chief Delaney responded. "Thermal imaging of the target location." 9David10 continued. Shows approximately 15 to 17 subjects inside."

"We're also able to detect. At least four canines within the premises. Subjects seem to be moving. Boxed packaging into a central location." "Command 1 to Command 2, did you copy?" Chief Delaney asked. "10-4, Command 1." Commissioner Riggs replied. "That has to be that big drug shipment. Okay, ladies and gentlemen. It's show time. Let's do this by the book. So that we all go home safely. So we don't lose this in court over some technicality. Command 1 to 9David10. I want your units to secure any and all drugs found on the premises.

Baltimore City PD will secure any weapons. After all subjects have been disarmed or neutralized. Command 1 to all units. Be advised that the Feds will have to process every scene. Prior to our departure. So please ensure. You protect the integrity of each location you enter. "That's a 10-4." 9David10 replied. Multiple others on the radio also acknowledged the instructions. "Give me a minute Commands 1 and 2." Director Tolbert asked. He then stepped out of the Command vehicle. He went to one of the marked patrol cars. Inside, he pulled out his cell phone and called Director Baker. "Hey, it's me Carl. Did Captain Nichols make any phone calls? To his brother or anyone who could have gotten word to his brother?"

"No, we've recorded every call he's made." Director Baker said. From his cell and home phones which were minimal. He only called a Jasmine and work. We monitored her phone calls as well. She didn't call anyone connected with his brother. As far as we could find. We even surveilled their travels. They only left the house to go to the store. They made no contacts with anyone that we observed. They've been locked up in his home touching each other. For the most part. I can send you the video of their interactions. Including them fucking if you like." "No, you go ahead and keep that." Director Tolbert said. "The FBI is only interested. If they're having sex with little kids or some other illegal shit. You people at the NSA. We let you do the listening in on the other stuff."

"There aren't enough people." Director Baker replied. "Working in the Government to listen to every phone call. Our computers listen. They're only looking for potential terrorist acts. We don't care what kind of freaky shit people are into. Or if they call their dealer to bring them some coke. "Well, that's good." Director Tolbert said. "I'm glad nobody was listening. To all that freaky shit your wife was saying to me. On the phone last night." "Oh, I did listen to that." Director Baker said. "It was hard not to hear. I was lying in bed next to her. While she talked to you." "I knew you were a sick bastard." Director Tolbert laughed.

"I have to go." He continued. "Now that I know the Captain, hasn't compromised this joint operation. I wouldn't want us walking in there. With the bad guys expecting then greeting us. With more firepower than we have." "Yes, that would not be good." Director Baker replied. "Let's go catch these motherfuckers in the act. Then connect these Russian dots." "Alright, I'll talk to you." Director Tolbert said. "Once we secure the scene. Try to figure out what we have." "Sounds like a plan." Director Baker said. I love it when a plan comes together."

At the Walmart on Route 40 in Aberdeen Maryland. Sabrina pulled into the parking lot. She parked in an area somewhat secluded. She then turned off her engine and looked around. Off to her left, she saw a car flash its headlights briefly. She then exited her vehicle. She walked over to the black BMW with heavily tinted windows. She opened the passenger door and stepped inside. "Why are you risking us being seen together Michael?" She asked. "I'm risking going crazy every minute I'm not with you." Michael replied. "Not kissing on this luscious dark skin?" He then pulled her close and kissed her passionately on the lips.

Chapter 5

Brotherly Love

"I'm missing you too." Sabrina said. She pulled herself away. "Soon, we'll be together. We'll have all the money we need. To live the life of a fairytale." She continued. "Yes, but we need to hurry." Michael said. "It won't be long before the office in Detroit figures out. I've been sabotaging the investigation. I was able to get most of the cash. By setting up the agents to be killed. In Detroit, Charlotte and New Orleans. How dare those greedy bastards? Try to take advantage of the disarray in our Government?" Cutting themselves a slice of the pie. "You've got the twenty-five mill from here in Baltimore right?" Sabrina asked.

"Yeah, that money is in a safe place." Michael replied. "At a storage unit in Bel Air." "I still feel bad." Sabrina said. "I had to make Drexler think Cynthia hid his money. I knew he was going to kill her. He did it in such a sick ass way. I'd love to go and arrest his ass. Or better yet, put a bullet in it." "Let the Feds deal with that fool." Michael said. "We've got to get out the country. With a hundred million in cash. Then make sure we get the encrypted transfer completed. Before someone shuts that faucet off. You should give me that code babe. In case you lose it, then we'll have a backup copy."

"Hell no brother." Sabrina said. "If I give you the code. You may decide to take off without me. Leave me facing charges. I've got the access code for the $500 million. That we'll transfer to an offshore account. As soon as we're safe out of the country." "Woman, I just rode in a truck." Michael said. "With a smelly redneck from New Orleans to here. In a tractor trailer. Had to pay him $200,000 in cash. To drive the crates with the 25 million inside. And not ask any damn questions. About what's in the crates. I had to help him unload the truck. So he could put our crates in the back. Then load the truck again. With that smelly ass swine meat he was hauling."

"Worst of all." Michael continued. "I had to listen to that fucking country music. Plus his stupid stories. Had to do the same thing from Detroit and Charlotte. So our friend down at the docks in South Baltimore. Can take us and the cash money safely out of the U.S. He will get us and our crates safely in Morocco. Traveling by freight ship. To spend the rest of my life with you. Now, if I'm doing all that? Do you really think I would take off without you? For a few hundred million dollars?" "Negro you're a black man." Sabrina says. "You speak multiple languages. You just orchestrated the killings of these undercover agents. Even the Russians knew full well. When they reached out to you. That you'd draw very little suspicion. Because of your race."

"That's right." Michael said. "If we just start thinking. We can make white people's racism. Work in our favor. I'm fluent in Yoruba, Hausa and English. Also Russian, French, German and Hungarian. Yet these bastards kept assigning me. To gang task forces in New Orleans and Detroit. Or other U.S. places. They never took me serious enough. To do international assignments. I bet they'll take me serious. When I'm the six hundred million dollar man. When they find out I helped the Russians. To find and eliminate the Carlistino family. The Feds didn't even think to look in my direction. As possibly working with the Russians. They probably think I'm too stupid. To pull off something like that. Or the Russians are too racist to work with me. The Russians are some racist motherfuckers. No doubt about that."

"Yet, right now, they are on the verge of taking over the American drug game. Plus getting U.S. military defense codes. Once they have that, they will destroy U.S. missile sites. The Pentagon will scramble to put up defense barriers. Only to learn then. That the Russians have changed the codes. Vladimir will have the master codes. That he got from dumb ass. Russia will pound this country's Military into submission. Then march to take over Europe. Thankfully, we'll be in South Africa, Saudi Arabia or somewhere far from the madness."

"Yeah, that will be funny to watch." Sabrina said. "The dumb ass white trash that voted for this idiot. They wanted to Take America to Greatness. They'll be sitting there with stunned looks on their faces. Asking 'How did this happen?' Stupid motherfuckers. There was a ton of evidence. That you idiots ignored. Telling you he was in bed with your enemy. Now, they'll be singing the Russian National anthem. Karma is a bitch ain't it baby?" "Yes, it is." Michael replied. "Once the Russians take over here. I doubt anyone will come looking for us. Or our money. So we can live out in the open."

"I wish your legs were open right now Jasmine. Why don't you let me get inside that pussy?" "I am not fucking you in the back seat." Sabrina replied. "Of a BMW in a Walmart parking lot. You're just going to have to wait. Until we're on a plane out of here. Maybe, I'll introduce you to the mile-high club. "Well, at least let me stick my finger in it." Michael begged. "Let me suck the juice off. Damn, you look good tonight." "Oh, I don't look good every night?" Sabrina teased. "You probably do." Michael replied. "It's just now you're fucking that Transit cop. I don't want to think about how good you're looking. While you're with him." "You're right baby." Sabrina said. "I'll let you finger it real quick. Then I'm going in this store. To buy a few items. Just in case André is home. When I get back."

Sabrina pulled down her pants and panties. He tried mightily to arouse her. Enough to want to jump in the back seat. Her mind was set. After several minutes of him rubbing her clitoris, he gave in. "Damn, you could at least give me a blowjob." He said. To hold me over until we leave." He complained. "Look, I have to go fuck this damn Transit cop." Sabrina said. "A few more times. I can't be all tired and sore. I need to wear him out. Make him think I'm all about him. I'll get him defenseless in bed. Then you can come in through the entrance I told you about. When the time is right. You can kill him." "Why are we killing a cop anyway?" Michael asked.

"Why can't you just up and leave his ass?" He asked. "Because that motherfucker ruined my family." Sabrina replied. "What family?" Michael asked. "You've never been married or had children." "Yes, but I have a brother." Sabrina said. "A brother who was very successful. He and I were the first in my family to go to college. My brother graduated Med-school with honors. He went on to gain a very prestigious position. At Johns Hopkins Hospital. One of the top Spinal Surgeons. On the East coast." "So what happened?" Michael asked. "Did your transit cop friend pull him over? Gave him a speeding ticket or something?" "No." Sabrina replied. "My brother had an issue. With liking the women too much. After he became a successful Doctor. He reconnected with the woman we knew. When we were at City College."

"Unbeknownst to him. She had gotten into some shady business. Of dealing prescription medicines." "Wait." Michael said. "Your brother was married. With the two children, right?" "Yes, he was married." Sabrina asserted. "Like I said, he liked women. So, this bitch he was screwing. Started to blackmail him about telling his wife. If he didn't do something for her." "Okay, I'm confused." Michael said. "I thought you said the cop ruined your brother's life. Sounds like his dick and some side bitch did that." "Well, the bitch put things in motion." Sabrina said. "André was the one who finished him. You see the whore. Made him give her access to his prescription pads. Along with his signature stamp."

"She would then write out prescriptions. To low life scum in the city. They would go get them filled. Then they would turn around and sell the drugs. In front of Lexington Market. All over Cherry Hill/Westport and anywhere they could. My brother wasn't the only Doctor. This whore was fucking. With no cost to buy her supply. Other than pussy. She was making more than many Doctors combined. Two stooges she had working for her. Get stopped by André. Stopped for loitering of all things. They were standing in a bus stop and never got on a bus."

"André goes and asks them. What they were waiting on? You know they didn't have a straight story. André wrote in his report he was going to let them go. Until their lies made him suspicious. That they were up to something. He calls for backup. Threatens to lock them up for false statements. That's when these dummies start trying to win a Grammy. Singing like Michael Jackson and Prince. Hitting high notes and everything. They tell André that they work for this lady. That she supplies them with prescription pills. They then tell. How the entire operation goes down. They agree, of course. To tell the Police. When the next meet with this woman is."

"Transit Police go in plain clothes. To Mondawmin Mall. Which was where the meeting took place. She hands those idiots the prescriptions. The Police arrest them all. She, of course to save her ass rolls over. Gives up all the Doctors she uses to write prescriptions. The Transit Police then go to all these hospitals. Where these Doctors work and arrest them. My brother loses his license to practice. His wife divorced him. He lost the nice home and life he worked so hard to get." "That's messed up." Michael said. "But it kind of sounds like. Your brother got himself into that jam." "My brother was a professional." Sabrina said. Making a difference. André could have had a great case. With just the woman."

"He was greedy and wanted a bigger case. He went after my brother and the other Doctors. So, you see, André has to die. To pay for ruining my family. Once we have all the money. We're going to get our families out of this country. Before it burns. I can make sure. That my brother never has to work. Any degrading job ever again. My brother will have the money. To maybe practice again. In another country. Or at least do research. Besides, we need to get out of the country. Without André or anybody else looking for me. He will alert law enforcement. If they start looking for me. Then our entire plan is fucked. Right now. They think I'm trying to find a soft landing back home."

"If they think I'm running." Sabrina continued. "When they don't have the money. It will take the Feds all of two seconds. To try to bring me in. André has to die. To give us time to leave. We couldn't ask for a better opportunity. With so much distrust sown throughout the Government. Very few people even know. That I and this money are out here. If André reports me missing. The people who do know about the money. Are going to issue an A.P.B. I don't know about you. I'm not trying to do any Federal time or be tried for treason." "So, you're staying in homeboy's house." Michael said. "Yet you don't have any feelings about killing him?"

"My feelings are with my brother." Sabrina said. "He now works at a clinic drawing blood. Unable to make ends meet." "I thought we'd just use the insurance policy." Michael said. "You took out on the Captain to keep him quiet." "Yeah, I put him in a real jam." Sabrina said. "Then I thought about it. Why just ruin his life? When I can ruin his after-life too? We need the time to get out of the country. We can't leave until our ship is set to leave. His death gives us ample time. To get far enough away. You just come in like a burglar. Make sure you put two bullets in his fucking head. He's single. Nobody will be looking for him until Thursday. By the time they piece everything together. We would have landed in Morocco. Beyond the reach of the Feds."

"I must admit." Michael said. "You've put together a very good plan. When you found out about André. Being Drexler's brother. You said he'd be the perfect cover. Then you literally bumped into him. On purpose on the highway. To get yourself acquainted with him. He has no idea you've been playing him. This entire time." "He won't either." Sabrina replied. Not before we gather up all the money. Headed to the other side of the world." "Look, I'm tired as hell." Michael said. "From having to sleep in those damn trucks. Instead of a nice bed all this week. I'm going to my hotel. To get some real rest. So I won't be sleepy. When I come to see your temporary lover."

"No, you better not be sleeping." Sabrina said. "André keeps a gun on the side of his bed. One in his nightstand. A few in the dresser. If I try to hide all of them. He will know I'm up to something. He would kill me before you can get to our room. He's a light sleeper. So you'll have to come in while we're having sex. That's the only time. He's not in tune with every noise. Outside the bedroom. I'll get him defenseless, but you need to be quick." "Oh, don't worry." Michael said. "I'll be quick baby. I'm going to blow his damn brains out. All over that nice Harford County home of his. Oh, and I'm taking all those guns too. Except the one you used as insurance."

"By the time he's dead. Our money will be loaded onto the ship. We can give James his $500,000 for helping us out. Then a few hours later. We'll be floating on a freighter ship. Headed to Morocco. Then we can talk. About our beautiful life together." "Ummm, that's sounds wonderful baby." Sabrina said. "Now, let me get in this store. Pick up a few items. I have no idea what time André will be back home. If he's there and I'm just coming in the house. He's going to want to know where I've been. Walmart is always a good cover story. You can be in here forever. Then leave out with pretty much anything you may need. I'll pick up a few food items. So I can make him breakfast in the morning."

"I might even get him some flowers. Since I won't be able to attend his funeral services. It's the least I can do for the man." "Damn, I'm glad you're on my side." Michael said. "You're one cold Dirty Diva. When you want to be. I know if I ever get flowers from you. I better watch my back." "I would never hurt my man." Sabrina said. "It's going to be you and me forever. Nothing or no one will ever come between you and me." "I've heard that line in some movie before." Michael said. "Well, now you're hearing it from me." Sabrina said. So you know it's true." She leaned in and kissed him passionately. While rubbing his crotch. "I can't wait to feel you inside of me once again." She said.

"The other night with you." She continued. "Felt so damn good." "Yeah, that felt good to me too." Michael said. "Be careful out here this time of night girl. Make sure you get back to his house safely. I wouldn't want anything to happen to you. Or that access code."

Back on Haven Street in East Baltimore. The Joint Task Force prepared to move in on the warehouse. "Alpha4 are all units in place?" Chief Delaney asked. "10-4 BCP01, 9Adam01. We're waiting on your command." A41 replied. "Two large trucks did drop off multiple crates. Within the last four hours. That has to be our shipment." "BCP01 to Alpha4, Bravo1 and Charlie6 teams." Commissioner Riggs said. Commence Operation Crossray. Ladies and gentlemen. Please be careful. Subjects are armed and dangerous. Alpha4 team was set on the left side of the warehouse. Bravo1 team on the opposite side. They began to launch, tear gas canisters through the windows.

Immediately, Charlie6 team rammed the front door. Units began to scramble inside. They began a frantic search for the occupants. None of whom appeared to be on the ground floor. Units rushed upstairs and kicked in a door. Where they heard voices coming from. Inside the room was Drexler Nichols. Sitting at a card table playing spades. With members of his crew. They were all wearing a gas mask. "Officers." Count Drexler said. "You don't need all those guns. To get in on this card game." He then removed his mask. "We're just playing for chocolate chip cookies. There are plenty of cookies for everybody. I just had two truckloads of cookies delivered here. So help yourself please."

"Oh, by the way. These two gentlemen in suits. Are my Attorneys. They know what's in each crate. So hopefully, you don't drop anything in there. By accident and say it's ours." Officers began checking the crates. They found in fact. That all the crates contained were chocolate chip cookies.

Multiple officers began shaking their head no. As they looked at their team leaders. "Fortunately, I had a feeling that you cops." Drexler said. "Didn't like Famous cookies. That you would come in here. With all this damn noise and smoke. What's the matter? You only eat girl-scout cookies? Or is it just doughnuts officers? Look there is a 7-11 around the corner. I can have someone go get you guys some doughnuts. If you like. Otherwise, you're interrupting my card game. You're trespassing on my property. Now, my dogs you hear barking back there. We didn't give them any cookies. So they are pretty hungry."

"They don't eat humans. However they will bite the fuck out of pigs. Or other disgusting Animals. "Alpha4 team leader to Command 1 and 2." A41 said on his radio. "That's a negative on contraband and inventory at this location. You can reopen the air for all communications. Call this operation 10-7 at this time." "This motherfucker had to know we were coming." Captain Nichols said. "Nobody can be this fucking lucky this many times." "9Adam01 to all units." Chief Delaney said on his radio. Return to your staging areas. Prepare for debriefing by me and BCP01. Before you end your assignments. Team leaders make sure all units and equipment. Is accounted for prior to our arrival."

Within minutes, BCP01 arrived and boards Command 1. Along with Mr. Vailati. He was soon joined by Director Tolbert and Baker. Along with the Maryland State Police Superintendent. "What the hell happened?" Superintendent Scales asked. "How did he know we were coming? I mean this motherfucker had gas masks on. Just waiting on us." "Nobody here reached out to him." Director Baker said. "That I can tell you. We're monitoring everybody's phone in real time. That was in any way connected to this operation. We also tracked your movements as well. As an extra layer of protection. We monitored the calls of anyone you talked to. In the event anyone was using codes."

"So, if nobody here spooked him?" Commissioner Riggs asked. "How in the hell did he know?" "That's what we need to find out. I'll contact Citi-watch and get video footage. Of anyone who was in or around this block. In the last 24 hours. I want the tags off of those cookie delivery trucks. The faces of who was driving. Director Baker, do you mind giving to Chief Delaney and me? The records of phone calls made by any BCPD and MTAPD personnel? Related to this task force?" "Not at all." Director Baker said. "The Chief and I would like to go over them with fresh eyes." Commissioner Riggs continued. Check against all the numbers in our system."

"Don't look at me." Captain Nichols said. "I will personally go lock my brother up right now. For jaywalking if I thought I could make it stick." "I'm sure it's not a surprise to you Captain Nichols." Director Baker said. That we did monitor your calls. We tracked your movements as well. We don't think it was you. That could have given the heads up. We will find out who it was eventually." "Well when you do." Captain Nichols said. "Let me do the honors. "Of putting them in handcuffs too." "Why don't we just tear down this tent?" Director Tolbert said. "Get home to our families. Enjoy what's left of our Sunday morning." "I'll just need the Chief, the Commissioner and the two Directors." Mr. Vailati said. To stay behind for a few minutes."

"That is if you don't mind." He continued. "Obliging me for a few minutes." The other personnel cleared off the Command vehicle. Sergeant White was the last to leave. As he was stepping outside. An older black male in a suit approached the vehicle. Sergeant White began to stop him. "If you want to live. To see your wife and your family again Sergeant. I suggest you get out of my way." The man said. Sergeant White immediately took a defensive stance. "That wouldn't be a wise move on your part Sergeant." Mr. Vailati yelled. "You are very much near death and don't realize it." "Who the fuck is that?" Chief Delaney asked.

"Why he is The Progenitor 1491." Mr. Vailati said. "The Director of the Black House. That is my boss. The only person I answer to. Mr. C. or Cecil A. Blackmon is his name. If you want to be formal. He is the power. That actually powers this thing called America." "Good morning gentlemen." Mr. C. said. He boarded the vehicle and nodded. Mr. Vailati closed the door behind him. "I wanted to come and speak to you." Mr. C. continued. "Before you go to do some soul-searching. On this little tactical snafu you conducted. Mr. Vailati advised me that you've all been briefed. On what we must do to save the republic. I just wanted to come and meet, some real American heroes. As they have been in short supply lately."

"So, you're behind the wanting us to kill the President?" Commissioner Riggs asked. "And prominent members of Congress?" "Don't look at it as killing anyone." Mr. C. replied. "Look at it as your patriotic duty. If this imbecile is not neutralized. The Russians will know more, about our Security systems than we do. Right now, the United States, is the only Country able to stop the Russians. From expanding their dominance to take over the world. The way they took Crimea. Will be the way they will march to take Europe. They've long wanted to get Alaska back. From there, it will be a short assault on mainland United States. We will be defenseless to save ourselves. Due to the idiot in the oval. He had two of Russia's top spies in the office."

"Of course, they planted listening and video devices. Wouldn't you? The only reason they don't know everything. Shared by the Intelligence agencies. Is because this fool is watching Faux news. Instead of actually reading and discussing Presidential Daily Briefing. How much longer can we wait? Before the Kremlin convinces him. To open one of those daily Intel envelopes. Then give them some harmless information. Like OUR FUCKING SECURITY CODES!" "So, you're telling me a black man." Chief Delaney asked. "Has the ability to get to the President of the United States?"

"Sir, we are The Black House." Mr. C. replied. "We can get to anybody, anytime, anywhere. On God's green earth. If they can be seen, they can be hit. If they can be hit, they can be killed. When Candidate Reagan was running for President. Back in 1980. He promised to eliminate. The budget for the Department of Education. Something our agency took very personally. At the time, our budget was supported from various sources. The biggest piece came from the education budget. Then not many would dare argue. To take money from the children. Where most believed the money was going. Reagan pledged to come in. Then eliminate the bulk of our budget. That could not be tolerated."

"Now, Reagan wasn't a traditional politician. In the sense that he actually came from Hollywood. He truly didn't understand. The power of Washington D.C. Or he wouldn't have tested us. We warned him and his campaign. To cease with that ridiculous promise. To kill the education budget. One of our men spoke directly into his ear. The night he gave his first State of the Union address. In February 1981. Still, he took the podium and spoke of slashing budgets. As if to say fuck us. He's President and we're nobody. So, on March 30th, 1981. We reached out and touched his ass. Through Mr. Hinckley Jr." "So, you're telling me?" Commissioner Riggs asked. "You guys had that nut shoot Reagan?" "Sometimes, tragedies happen." Mr. C. replied.

"Sometimes, we make them happen. That poor young boy who is driving down the road. When a big rig comes across the yellow line. Obliterating him to ground meat. Sometimes, that's not because the driver was texting. Or tired nor drunk. It's because the young boy's father, wouldn't do whatever we asked of him. Like with Reagan. We have to show people sometimes. We are not to be toyed with. Reagan believed the Secret Service could keep him safe from us. Imagine the look in his eyes, when we showed him they couldn't." "So, you'll ruin people's lives just to get your way?" Chief Delaney asked.

"You'll kill the young boy? The driver of the big rig what about him? He probably suffers no serious injury. But goes to prison in order for you to make a point?" "Oh, my dear Chief." Mr. C. replied. "You are so naïve. As to how justice works in America. Yes, the driver is likely to be arrested. Yes, he will go to trial. Most likely he'll be convicted. That's what the public sees. Once people who do our bidding are sentenced. The press and you the public, forget about them. We simply go to the prison. Flash our Black Access Cards and presto. We transfer the prisoner to a home in Montana. Wyoming or someplace nobody will look for them."

"If there is an appeal or parole hearing. A medical situation or any good reason. We just transfer them back into prison. When we know the press or public may be looking." "So, what happens if they like being free?" Commissioner Riggs asked. "In Montana or wherever and don't want to come back to prison?" "Then we transfer them back anyway." Mr. C. replied. "Because we can. Then they probably die in a prison. Stabbed about 15 minutes after we drop them off. You find out in the news that they were killed. You think they were in prison the entire time." "You people are sick." Chief Delaney said. "No, not at all Chief." Mr. C. replied. "I admit the first school shooting I took part in. Out in Colorado took me a day or two to get over."

"Yet, now. It's one of our most effective tools. Imagine identifying one of these loner kids. You show him pictures of his mom. She's usually his only friend and source of support. Show her talking to whom the kid believes is the FBI. You then tell that kid his mom is about to go away. For a long time to prison. Now offer him a way to save her. All the kid has to do is take this AR-15. Go into the school making sure he gets a specific person. A specific student whose mom or dad. Didn't follow our instructions. The other kids and teachers. Well, they're just casualties of the situation. Victims of circumstances. Next time that happens and you see the crying parents. Note the parent crying the hardest."

"They know their child would still be here." Mr. C. continued. "If they just complied. We send them an untraceable text message. That deletes from their phone. Within 25 seconds of them reading it. Usually, it's a video from the camera our shooter was wearing. As he pulled the trigger and shattered their world. I can assure you. They don't refuse any other requests we make. Neither will you. Yet, we don't like to involve the children. Unless it's absolutely necessary." "So, is this what the government does?" Commissioner Riggs asked. "Just sit around and figure out ways to kill people?"

"Actually, you people." Mr. C. replied. "The citizens are the ones who teaches the government how to kill. Think about it. Someone invents a remote-controlled plane. Or helicopter. They have to get it patented. So that no one steals their idea. Naturally, they have to submit the idea. With meticulous detail to whom? The Government. Now, we can steal their idea and improve it. We add Cameras, (that someone patented). Weapons of Mass Destruction, (that someone patented). Artificial Intelligence, (that somebody else patented). Along with the ability for the aircraft. To have self-renewable energy. Then we just call the remote-controlled aircraft a Predator Drone. Some lady in a trailer home in Cleveland, North Carolina. Is arrested for killing her husband.

"Turns out she poisoned her husband. With a concoction of plants and/or household chemicals. The Police then have to write a detailed report. For the murder investigation. Where do you think that report ultimately ends up? In the hands of the government. We read that over the course of six months or however long. She fed her husband substance X. Eventually he died of a heart attack. We just increase the dosage of whatever she used. Now we have a biological weapon that causes death in minutes. You see, the government is not powerful because. We spend a ton of money on devices and schemes to stay powerful."

"The government is powerful because we created a system. To feed us information. Information gives you knowledge. As the old proverb says; 'knowledge is power." "So, we are really living in the Matrix." Chief Delaney asked. "If the government controls all the flow of information. Then they can determine what information we see or don't see." "Actually, that's not totally true Chief." Mr. C. replied. "I don't see how it's not." Chief Delaney countered. "That's because you're blinded by the Matrix." Mr. C. replied. "Think about it. The government can control internet. Also television and radio by way of the FCC. We can say you can't air this or that. If we deemed it offensive."

"We can control mainstream music. By making a record label add an advisory sticker. If an artist sings or raps something. That we feel may make the public too aware. We'll just single out a lyric. In a completely different song on the album. We'll then create a campaign. That says the lyrics are Anti-Semitic. Anti-LGBT. Anything to embroil the artist in controversy. After that. You'll never listen to the song we didn't want you to hear. We control the internet in much the same way. We can't delete anything from the internet. Once something goes on the internet. It's there forever. However, we can bury information on it very deeply. So deep that your average person. Just isn't going to look that hard for it. Let's say you searched right now for, "The Black House." You of course, can find us on the internet. We hide in plain sight. However, we've added so many dummy links. It would take you serious time to locate us. You'd find The Black House Publishing. The Black House Boxing, Music, Restaurants. Even entities in other countries. You'd grow mentally tired of searching for us. Which is exactly what we want." "So, like the Chief said." Commissioner Riggs replied. "You control all the information." "No, we don't." Mr. C. replied. "Like every system in the world. Our system has a flaw. A weak link. Something that is beyond the Government's control."

"That Vibranium or Kryptonite for the Government." Mr. C. continued. Is called Books. It's the one form of media. That we simply have no say to control. On record, television, radio or movie. We can deem a work offensive to a group and make it disappear. However in books, people can share all types of information. We have no way of stopping it. They can tell the truth about Government conspiracies. The truth about history, religion, pollution. Any knowledge that they've acquired. The Government can only hope. That no one reads the information."

"Other than that. There is nothing that can be done to stop anyone. From publishing enlightening information. That is the public's key to defeating the Matrix. That is your red pill because it can't be stopped. Unfortunately, most of the public. Choose to swallow the blue pill. Because staying unconscious means you don't have to change. Even when people can clearly see something is not right. They swallow the blue pill and hope someone else will fix it. The Black House does not fix, your typical every day, crooked politician. We don't do that because you citizens have voting mechanisms. Already in place to do that yourselves."

"However, when members of your government. Are literally about to make the public incapacitated. We have to act. Recently, you've seen a slew of Congressmen. Just up and announce they are resigning from Congress. Folks with seniority and Chairman Positions. On powerful committees. All of them have been using their position. To summon classified information from our Intelligence agencies. Then turning that information over to the Russians. So, we sent a member of The Black House. To meet with each Congressman. We gave them a choice. To resign or we'll kill them and their families. The smart ones have resigned. The dumb ones think by hiring extra Security. They are safe." Their children can't hide from Wednesday June 6th, 2091. King Kong will return to the top of the world trade. "What the hell does that mean?" Commissioner Riggs asked. "That's after your time Commissioner." Mr. C. replied. "I'll handle that."

"So, you have the ability." Chief Delaney asked. "To get to Congress and the President as a black man? Is that right?" "Yes, I do." Mr. C. replied. "Or should I say, we do." "So, you see black people in this country." Chief Delaney continued. "Getting the short end of the stick. Why haven't you long ago done something? Given black folks more control? Or does your position, not allow you to have any racial pride?" "I would love to do that Chief Delaney." Mr. C. replied. "Then why haven't you?" Chief Delaney asked. "Because you niggas are still infected with that religion. Religion they brainwashed in our heads. You would just give control back to whites. Ever since white folks introduced you to the Slave ship Jesus. Told you a fancy story about him being perfect. You have been looking for a perfect leader. That motherfucker does not exist. No leader is going to be perfect, EVER!"

"I see black Folks every day. Build up some brother or sister who steps up to lead. Then the hood detective with a 10th grade education. Finds out the brother lied to his teacher back in kindergarten. About some candy he ate. Now black people will spend an enormous amount of energy. Trying to convince others that this person is a fraud. You think white people don't know that their President lies? Of course, they do. But they are willing to overlook that. Because their agenda is being done. You Negroes will fallout with a black person who speaks up. For the pettiest of things. "Oooh, he dated a white girl in middle school.' Or he's into that Muslim stuff. I can't stop poisoning myself with pork."

"We don't want to make any sacrifices or struggle. But we can't figure out why we never progress. The Black House can't just turn the country over. To such fickle Negroes. Until you learn to stop nitpicking. Every little wrong thing a black person does. You will never be ready to lead. White folks rally behind their leaders regardless of how imperfect they are. White folks never ask Jesus to fix anything. From whatever threat they perceive. They know better. They fix up Federal Judges, Politicians and Prosecutors to save themselves."

"They're lining up money and power to keep you oppressed. The only time white folks are thanking Jesus. Is to say thanks for making you niggas dumb. Too dumb to realize what's happening right in front of your eyes. You're calling on a Slave ship to come save you. White folks are calling on voter restrictions and guns. To save them from you. When you Negroes wake up from under the Ghost spells. Or what you call Gospels. Then you'll have power. You thinking some man died and is coming back to save you is naïve. Especially when that man didn't lift a finger. For 350 years of Slavery and Jim Crow is beyond naïve."

The very fact that these Pastors endorsed and stand with this President. Should be all the proof you need about their belief in Jesus. Is it possible in your minds? Knowing how some white folks think today. That they could send the very first slave ship name Jesus to Africa? Then kidnap, chain, rape, torture and kill you. While telling you that Jesus, was the best thing to happen to you? You know the same white mindset. That believes you're disrespecting the flag by peacefully kneeling? Their thinking has always been twisted. The descendants of the people, that forced Christianity on your ancestors. Have no fear of Jesus judging them. Because they know the truth."

"You're living by rules and principles. That your oppressors never have and never will. This is why you lose the game every day. Why would I waste my vengeance, on taking out the entire Congress? Only to have you religious niggas. Give control back to their children? It was said that when whites came to Africa. They had nothing in their hand but a newly-written bible. The Africans owned all the land. The whites said, 'let us pray.' So dumb Negroes knelt down. Closed their eyes and prayed. When niggas opened their eyes. The whites owned all the land. Niggas had the bible. 400 years later, you niggas are no smarter. It sickens me every time I hear that Kirk Franklin song. "Silver and Gold," that we learned on the plantation."

"Dumb negros talking about they would rather have Jesus. Than Silver and Gold??? Do you know what a Slave could have bought with Silver and Gold? **HIS FUCKING FREEDOM!** Freedom for themselves and their children. Under those ghost spells they'd rather live and die a slave. In between birth and death. The slave literally had the shit beaten out of him. Numerous times. Watched his wife and kids gang raped. Then had his wife and kids watch him get gang raped. If he was lucky, they killed him. Now, how fucking stupid do you have to be. To not see you're being played? Ask any white person today would they rather go to church. Be baptized and accept Jesus. Or take a bucket full of silver and gold? Not one of them would give up a bird in the hand. For some afterlife bullshit. Not even the Pope."

"Yeah, all of that may be true." Commissioner Riggs said. "Yet whites will pay for what they did. When their soul is burning in hell." "Hello! Earth to dumb nigga." Mr. C. replied. "You do know that based upon the principles of nature. That God set up. Fire can only burn physical matter. Your soul is not physical, so it cannot burn. They told the slaves that lie. To scare them into not rebelling. Hundreds of years later, you sound like Fiddler. You can't process the laws of nature. You're under a ghost spell. I do not understand how black people. Can get college degrees showing intelligence. Then when it comes to religion. You fall for shit that couldn't possibly be true."

"I'm sorry you feel that way Mr. C." Commissioner Riggs said. "I've always believed Jesus died for all of us. So that we could have eternal life." "Okay, let's look at that Commissioner." Mr. C. said. "You say Jesus died for all of us. So that God could forgive us for our sins, right? What stopped God from forgiving us in the first place? He's God. If He wants to forgive us. He doesn't need any special event to take place. To do what He could already do. What kind of sick God would say? 'I'm able to forgive you, but I'll make someone die anyway. Then I'll forgive you. Like I could have done from the start. That's European dumbology that they made up."

"They made up Jesus shedding His blood. So you wouldn't focus on them shedding your blood. All over the Slave ship Jesus. If you break your arm, you're in a lot of pain. However, if you believe someone else had it worse. With a spear in their side. Nails in their hands and feet. You feel more sympathy for them than yourself. Now after that. When white folks convince you that Jesus died for them too. You reflect that sympathy onto them. Next thing you know. Some crazy white boy shoots up a church. Christian niggas are fighting on television to be the first to forgive him. The victims in that church. A husband, mother, brother or sister were shot. Families got on national television. Forgiving the murderer.

You and I both know. Those niggas in that church that forgave that white boy for murder. Have not spoken to somebody black in 20 years over something petty. *'Man, I remember Leroy came over to my house for Christmas in 1999. He drank up all my whiskey. I haven't spoken to that nigga ever since.'* White boy kills your mother? *'Jesus forgives you and I forgive you too.'* Black person stepped on your new Jordans or Tims 15 years ago? *'That nigga did that shit on purpose, I don't fuck with him.'* Can't you Negroes see? How Christianity makes you see yourself? How you see white people?" "With all due respect Mr. C." Chief Delaney said. "The Bible was written by men inspired by God." "White folks may have had a hand in translating it. It's still the word of God."

"See? This is why I can't help you Negroes Chief." Mr. C. countered. "In 1597, King James wrote a book called Demonologie. That is Latin for "The Demon Logs." It was a book of Devil worship. In it, he urged people to worship Satan. To practice sorcery and witchcraft. So here is a man of great power. That openly worships Satan. Which means Satan could tell him. How to deceive the world. Seven years later, in 1604. King James had some of his demons, including William Shakespeare. To begin working on what you call the word of God."

"They finished it in 1610." Mr. C. continued. "1604-1610 is 6 years. When they finished the "Word." From Genesis to Revelation, there are exactly 66 books. 6 years, 66 books. 666 the number of the beast. That is what you're reading. It says it right on the cover. King James '**Version**.' Look up the word sometime. King James didn't feel he was qualified. To ensure the book was all Satan wanted. So he turned to his mentor. Sir Frances Bacon. He was to make sure the words were written just right. See when you line up words correctly. You can tell a woman to stand out in 20 degree weather. Sell her body and bring you the money. It makes no sense to anybody watching that. She heard words just right, it makes sense to her."

"Likewise you can make a race of people. Forget their power. They go looking for someone else to do for them. What they could do for themselves. They become helpless. That is if you line those sixes up just right. Especially if they keep looking to the sixes, designed to lead them astray for answers. In 1611, King James ratified the book. Immediately after the "Word" was completed. The European Slave trade began in 1619. It took them nine years to spread the "Word with no television, radio or internet. They spread the word through savage violence. You cannot run a work place without an employee manual. That book is the manual for making slaves."

"The book was completed in 1610. Slavery began in 1619 which is 9 years. There are 9 innings to a baseball game. Which is called America's pastime. All this information is right in front of your faces. Yet you niggas keep trying to see shit that isn't there. And are blind to what is there. People that control the government have learned an important thing. About controlling people. If you tell people there is a directive from on high. People will follow it. How many times at your job have they told you? Something came from the higher ups and you went along? You never question it. Because you don't want to get in trouble. Just as you never question. Why the children of Israel who were slaves in Egypt? Would have a written word?

Typically, slaves are kept ignorant. Not allowed to read. Then supposedly, they wandered the desert. For 40 years. We know there were no mobile schools. So why would God give a written word to people? WHO COULDN'T READ!!! King James could read. He reigned at the beginning of the European Slave trade. If the King who is a Devil worshipper. Says 'this is the word of God'. How will people who can't read. Be able to know if it's true? People who've been in bondage. People looking for some power to change their condition. A wise man would say. Never let your enemies choose your weapon to fight them. You could be the best shooter. This side of the Mississippi river.

You could shoot the ears off of a fly. From 200 yards away. I just picked up a gun yesterday for the first time. I challenge you to a gun fight. Conventional wisdom says you will win that fight without effort. Yet, if you're dumb enough to let me choose your weapon. I will make sure your gun has no bullets. It may take me 64 shots. However I will kill you and win the battle." "So, you're saying." Commissioner Riggs asked. Black folks have been shooting an empty gun for 400 years?" "I didn't say that." Mr. C. replied. I'm asking you to think. "You niggas pay millions to the building fund. Then your Pastor hires white builders. Then has your black asses praying for jobs he/she just gave away." Whites aren't praying for jobs. Your Pastors keep THEM employed with YOUR money."

The black church has systematically cut off every avenue for black self-sufficiency. It should be creating businesses. You have a building full of customers already. It doesn't matter that you don't trust each other. You all trust the crooked ass Pastor. So he/she should be the glue that brings all the businesses together. The Pastors works for the government. His/her job is to keep you focused on anything. Except self-determination and your independence. Ask yourself what kind of God you are following? That would have you totally dependent on another race? A race that historically has been hostile to you."

"Yet, here you are today." Mr. C. continued. "Totally dependent on those people. That's because you're not following your God. You're following the house Negro Pastors. Any real leader called by God. Would have long asked how to get his people some power. Power, so you can hold someone accountable. When you are being shot down in the streets. You prayed when Yusef Hawkins was murdered in. Decades later you're in no better position to stop it for Trayvon. Has your Pastor asked God how to keep a great many of you. From being trapped in the ghettos? Your Pastor doesn't ask those questions of God. Their only mission is to keep you oppressed. Guess who runs the theology schools? The one your Pastor trains and gets ordained at? Your oppressors!"

"At any minute, dark skin people could rise. To dominate in this country and the world. What stops you are demons that you call Pastors. If your house catches fire and someone calls 911. The fire department will respond. If you're in the house. The fire department personnel are trained to get you out. However, if you have the opportunity to get out? Why wait on the fireman to save you? Just because you know they are supposed to? Why go meet at the White House on Prison reform? With someone who owns stock in Private Prisons? That's proof that these Pastors are idiots. If these Pastors can be so easily manipulated and fooled. It proves they are incapable of thinking.

To believe that man making millions off of private prisons. Wanted Pastors to tell him how to make less money is beyond stupid. Yet people fall for Pastor's dumb lies that makes no sense. As long as you cling to the gun your enemies gave you. To fight them. Then you will be shot again and again and again. They told you your bible, is how you fight the evils of the world. If your enemies are the evils of your world? Why would they give you a weapon to defeat them? Why would they be okay with you reading that book? Would you do something that stupid? Would you give someone you're trying to destroy a weapon?"

"It's time we start thinking." Mr. C. said. "We are behind by four touchdowns in the fourth quarter. Anyway, that's enough history and religion this early morning. I know we're all anxious to get home. I just need to make a real quick phone call. You don't mind, do you Chief?" "No Sir, go right ahead." Chief Delaney said. Mr. C. used one of the phone lines in the Command vehicle. Shielding the number he dialed. The phone rang once. Someone picked up but didn't say anything. "Yes, this is 0841926. This code expires in 19 minutes. Are you in position?" The voice on the other end replied, "Affirmative".

"On your assessment within 17 minutes. You may light the Christmas tree. Blow out the candle on the birthday cake. I'll stand by the airwaves for confirmation. 0841926 authorized." Mr. C. then hung up the phone. He turned only to see everyone staring at him. "You're getting ready for the holidays a little early, aren't you?" Commissioner Riggs asked. "There are no holidays in The Black House Commissioner." Mr. C. replied. "We are always working to save the republic. Every second of the day?" "That's how you work." Commissioner Riggs joked. "Lighting Christmas trees and buying birthday cakes?" "My birthday is coming up. Can I get a birthday cake?" "Sure, I can arrange that for you." Mr. C. replied. "In a few short minutes. You probably wouldn't like it though."

"Wait, no cake from that bakery in Pig town please." Commissioner Riggs said. "I know the Sheriff's Department has shut them down several times. For rats and roaches. I shouldn't be eating cake anyway. I don't want to hear my wife's mouth about my diet. I may be the Police Commissioner of the city. That woman lays down the law at home. I am not trying to get caught violating the law with her. She does not believe in 2nd chances, parole or probation. I thank the Lord she is not a Judge. At one of these court houses here in the city." "HOLY SHIT!" Chief Delaney yelled. "Did you see what just came across our phones?"

"Let me turn on the news real quick." Chief Delaney continued. He grabbed the remote control and turned on the news. "This is a WBAL BREAKING NEWS STORY! The announcer said. We now go live to New York City. On 7th Ave. and 57th street. We want to warn our viewers that this is a graphic story. Some of the content you may find unsettling. "Thanks Stan, we are here." A reporter said. "Outside this active crime scene. Where we're told the Senate Majority leader. Has just been shot by a sniper's rifle. Police will not say at this time. If they believe this is terror-related. Here is what we do know."

"A few hours ago." The reporter continued. "The Senator was here visiting New York City. He was campaigning with Senator Roberts. Roberts is locked in a highly contested race. The two of them had come to the building to my left. Which is Carnegie Hall. They took in a symphony earlier. We understand, that today was the Majority leader's birthday. We have not gotten official word. As to why the two of them were still in the area at this late hour. We do know that the Majority leader, has stated in the past. That he liked to get an early start on his Christmas shopping. New York was a favorite place for him. According to eyewitness accounts. The two men exited the building across the street. Which may have held a private fundraiser."

"Shortly after. They made it down the steps to the sidewalk. Where their driver was waiting. The electricity went out. This entire area was dark for about 21 seconds. No automobile lights, no building lights. It was just pitch dark. People we spoke with in the area. Said their cell phones would not work at that time. What's weird is that the street light, just above the Senator did not go out. It appeared to be the only thing that had power. For several blocks. Everyone appeared to be looking up at the only light. A single shot rang out. From what is believed to be a high-powered rifle. The Majority leader was struck in the head. He fell instantly to the ground. We do not have any confirmation on his condition. Eyewitnesses who were there, told us that his head shattered into pieces."

"We did get unofficial word." The reporter continued. "From a few of the NYPD officers on the scene. They do not believe the Senator is still alive. Of course, those officers are speaking. On condition of anonymity. They are not authorized to speak on behalf of the NYPD. The FBI is on scene. Along with NYPD. They are scouring the area. In search of a suspect or suspects. Suspects are still at large. The FBI was hampered by the fact. That electricity went out in this area. The surveillance cameras also had to transition. From the bright lights of the city to the sudden darkness. Then back to bright lights again. Experts tell us this may have some critical effect. On what the cameras may have picked up. With regards to suspicious activity."

"We're told the Senator has been rushed to Bellevue hospital. We don't have any further word, on his condition at this time. We do know the Senator, had been an adamant supporter of the President. The President is currently embroiled in a Russia scandal. It was also recently revealed. That the Senator himself has had some questionable meetings. With Russian Intelligence Operatives." "And the penalty for Treason is death." Mr. C. interjected. He then turned the television off. "What the fuck just happened?" Commissioner Riggs asked. "Do you still want me to arrange your birthday cake Commissioner?" Mr. C. asked. Have your candles blown out?" "No, I'm good." Commissioner Riggs replied. "I'll just stick to socks and ties for my birthday." "Well, it's been a pleasure, gentlemen." Mr. C. said.

"I look forward to seeing you serve your country in the near future. Now, if you'll excuse me. My driver has to get me over to Hopkins Bayview. Where I have a helicopter waiting." Mr. Vailati opened the door to the Command vehicle. Mr. C. descended down the steps. The Chief and Commissioner followed him out. They watched him and Mr. Vailati walk over to the vehicle. They saw them enter the car and drive off. "Are you thinking what I'm thinking?" Chief Delaney asked. They went back onto the Command vehicle. Chief Delaney picked up the phone Mr. C. had just used.

The Chief called KMT and spoke with the Dispatch Supervisor. "This is 9Adam01." He said. "I need to know phone calls made to and from this phone line. Within the last hour. Contact the State switchboard. Advise them it's an emergency. I need that information ASAP." "You should get the recording too." Commissioner Riggs said. "Since it's a State-owned line, all calls are recorded. "Also, have the on-duty Commander respond to radio dispatch." Chief Delaney said. "Have him pull the tape recording. From all calls to and from this line. In the last 24 hours." The Chief then hung up the phone to await his information.

"What kind of dude is this?" Commissioner Riggs asked. That can cut the lights out in New York City? Killing a sitting Senator?" "Not just any Senator." Chief Delaney added. "The Majority leader." "I don't even know what to do with this number." Commissioner Riggs said. "Once we find out about it Chief. I mean, we can't turn it over to the FBI. Can we? We don't know if whomever we give it to. Will do their job. Or if they're compromised by the Russians too." "Well, we have to try to give it to somebody." Chief Delaney said. "I mean, if it comes out that we knew. Who murdered a sitting Senator and we didn't come forward. We could get caught up in a conspiracy case."

The phone in the Command center rang and Chief Delaney picked it up. "Hey Chief. This is PCO Harrison. I spoke with the State switchboard. They said that there were no phone calls. Made from that phone in the last hour. The only call they have logged is your call to me." "No, that's not right." Chief Delaney said. "There was a call made from this phone. A little less than 20 minutes ago. Has Lieutenant McDavid gotten there to pull the tapes yet?" "He's just got here." Dispatch supervisor replied. "He's gone back to Lieutenant Carson's office. To retrieve the tapes." "Okay have him call me." Chief Delaney said. On this line and play the recordings from this phone." "Hold on Chief!" Dispatch supervisor said. "Lieutenant McDavid is screaming something from back in the office."

"The fire alarm has just been triggered." She continued. There's a fire in Lieutenant's Carson's office." We have to exit the building. "Of course, there is." Chief Delaney said. He hung up. "So much for any recording we may have had." Chief Delaney said. "I'll contact Citi-watch cameras." Commissioner Riggs responded. See if we have any video footage of this mysterious man. Then maybe we can at least show someone who he is. Maybe testify to what we heard him say and what happened." Just then, the phone rang on the Command vehicle. The Chief and Commissioner looked at each other. The Chief picked up the phone. "MTA Police, how may I help you?"

"Good morning again Chief. This is Mr. C. Just a quick note. Before you and the Commissioner. Think about investigating me again. You need to make sure your families has black suits and dresses for your services. Oh, and the Citi-watch cameras were all malfunctioning in your area. You can take my word. Or you can be dying to find out." Mr. C. then hung up the phone. Suddenly, there was a knock at the door. Both men removed their guns from their holsters. They walked towards the door. Chief Delaney opened it but there was no one outside. The two men looked at each other. Instantly, the power went out in the area. "Doesn't this thing run off of a generator?" Commissioner Riggs asked.

"Yes, it does." Chief Delaney replied. "I'm not sure why the power just went out." In this and the entire neighborhood?" Just as he ended his sentence. The street light above the Command vehicle came on. It was the only visible sign of electricity. The Commissioner hurriedly closed the door. Both men moved away from it. "Someone is sending us a message not to mess with them." Chief Delaney said. "I get the message loud and clear." Commissioner Riggs said. "He doesn't have to say anymore. This is one serious cat to do some shit like this. I don't think we can do anything he wouldn't know about. He just killed a Senator. I'm not trying to be next on his list."

Over at Drexler's compound. "Did the city not pay their light bill or something?" Count Drexler asked. "I don't know if they did or not." Deer Dog replied. "We may want to make sure we have full clips. Just in case some fools get the wrong idea. About running up on us in the dark." Suddenly, all the lights and power came back on. "Nobody wants to run up on your ugly ass in the light Deer Dog." Count Drexler joked. So they damn sure don't want to run up on you in the dark." "Man fuck you." Deer Dog replied. "No, thank you." Drexler replied. "Did you see the looks on those Cops faces? When they ran in our spot?"

"They found nothing but chocolate chip cookies?" "Yeah, the look on their faces was priceless." Deer Dog said. "Good thing your intuition told you. Not to have the real stuff delivered here. I don't know how you keep out guessing these cops. All these years." "That's easy." Drexler replied. "Cops are simple-minded." "They think they know this. So their protocol tells them to do that. Cops say all the time. To catch a criminal, you have to think like a criminal. I just apply that in reverse. To outsmart a Cop. You have to think like a Cop." "Well, you outsmarted them tonight." Deer Dog said. "So bad that you hurt their feelings. What time are we going over to the other spot? So, we can make sure. Our real stuff was right in weight and quality?"

"We can head over there right now." Drexler said. "The Police are getting a million calls. About the power being out. Everything from it's dark. To I think somebody is breaking in my house. Or I just saw Bigfoot walking up Eastern Avenue. We could lay our crates out on a city sidewalk. The Cops wouldn't notice being as busy as they are right now." "Shit, we need to figure out." Deer Dog said. "How to turn out the lights around this motherfucker. Every now and then."

André arrived home after his long drive from the city. He opened the garage door. Pulling in next to Sabrina's car. He opened the kitchen door. She was standing at the stove. "Hey babe." She said. She greeted him with a hug and kiss. "How was work?" She asked. "How are you doing?" He replied. "Work was a waste of time. We expended all this manpower. Taxpayer dollars, time, effort and energy. To raid one of my brother's stash houses. My brother was there but nothing else was." "Awww, I'm sorry." Sabrina said. "Can I get some breakfast?" André asked. "Of course, you can sweetie." Sabrina replied. "You go jump in the shower. I'll fix you up something light. So you can go to bed." "What are you going to do while I'm sleeping?" André asked.

"I'm going to sleep beside you." She replied. "I was up all night….ah, wondering if you were okay." "Let me find out you're getting hooked on me." André said. "You're talking all that old, don't catch feelings. Then you're staying up all night waiting on me?" "Nobody is catching feelings." Sabrina said. "So let's just keep it simple." "You're right, I'm going to shower." André said. "I'll be right back for my breakfast." After breakfast, Sabrina cleaned up the kitchen. The two of them retired to the bedroom. "Is there anything good on television?" André asked. "We can satellite-surf and see." Sabrina responded.

She flipped through the channels. She saw the news story of the Senate Majority leader. "Whoa, how in the hell did that happen?" André asked. "Who in the world could get to a sitting Senator?" Sabrina asked. They watched the details of the story. "They've been saying on the news." André continued. "That he and others have had some contacts. With Russian operatives. I wonder if this had anything to do with that?" "I don't know." Sabrina replied. "Nothing would surprise me." She continued satellite-surfing and came across a movie. "Clockers." André said. This is a Spike Lee joint, isn't it?" "Yes, it is." Sabrina replied. It's one of my favorites." "I think I can clock that pussy right now." André said.

"I'll let you do that tonight." Sabrina replied. "You go on and get some sleep André. When we get up this evening. I'll give you your script. We'll see how well you can follow directions. If you do it right, you can make me follow directions. "I have to say." André replied. "You are the weirdest person I have ever had sex with." "Weird can be good for variety." Sabrina replied. "Or would you rather we just did plain old vanilla missionary? Where nobody is really having any fun." "Oh no, I'm good with the weird stuff." André said. "As long as it doesn't get too weird. Then again. I'm agreeing to act out a script for sex tonight. So I may have crossed that line already."

"From the way you were." Sabrina said. "At the swing club the other night. I can almost assure you that you will like it." "Why can't we just go back there again?" André asked. "We can, but just not tonight." Sabrina replied. "I want to live out this fantasy with you." Besides, I worked hard on putting this script together." "Oh, so now you're Spike Lisa or somebody." André joked. Next, you're going to be directing adult films." "No, I have much bigger aspirations than that." Sabrina said.

"Why don't we just watch this movie?" She said. Until we fall asleep. You'll find out everything you need to know. Soon enough." "Okay, okay, Miss secretive, freaky lady." André replied. "I'll play your game. You just better be ready to take a pounding on that pussy." She leaned over and kissed him passionately. "I wouldn't want to be fucked any other way." She said. "Now, lay back and watch the movie." She laid her head on his chest. They relaxed into each other. André played with her curly 'fro. They both tuned into the action on the screen. Soon, they both drifted off to sleep.

Later that Sunday morning at the St. Mary Baptist Church. Services had just ended. Pastor Kingsley was standing on the front steps. Talking and shaking hands with members of the congregation. "That was a really beautiful sermon Rev." Mrs. Langston said. "Thank you very much, Sister Langston." Pastor Kingsley replied. "The book of Job is one of my favorites." "Yet, you haven't created one Job in this neighborhood, go figure." Ms. Parsons said. She walked into the conversation. "Well, that's not what the church is for." Ms. Langston said. "Isn't that right, Pastor?" "You'll have to forgive Ms. Parsons." Reverend Kingsley said. "She's become quite feisty in recent times."

"I might be feisty." Ms. Parsons replied. "I'm just not deaf, dumb and blind. Like some of your members Pastor." She looked at Mrs. Langston as she spoke. "Oh, what am I saying?" Ms. Parsons continued. "This is not a Korean church. A Jewish synagogue or a White Folks church. We didn't form the church under a 501d religious community. So the congregation could profit from businesses. We is just black folks. Pastor formed under a 501c3 Corporation. So only he gets paid. Isn't that right, Pastor?" Ms. Parsons continued. Reverend Kingsley smiled. He told Mrs. Langston he would see her the next Sunday. Mrs. Langston walked away. Toward the few remaining members. "What's the matter Reverend?" Ms. Parsons asked. "The cat got your tongue? I know my cat had your tongue the other day. It felt so good." "Ms. Parsons please." Pastor replied. We've just come out of holy services."

"The only hole-eating-services I'm interested in." She replied. Is you doing mine and it's about that time." Ms. Parsons responded. "Later for that though. Did you get the layout for that Cop's house taken care of?" "Yes ma'am, I did." Pastor Kingsley replied. "I sent Mr. Crawford and Ms. Adams over there. Posing as members trying to recruit people to the church. Mr. Crawford was able to walk around the house. Pretending like he heard someone in the back. He took some photos with his cell phone. I will email you the entire layout."

"The front door is a steel door." Pastor Kingsley continued. "You'd never get that kicked in. Without him hearing and being ready for us. Same thing on the back door. He does have a satellite though. On the back right corner of his roof. It sits right over a window of a guest bedroom. We can watch for whenever they leave home. Have the boys go there pretending to be from the satellite company. They will put a ladder up and one will go inside. Hide out in that guest room. We'll make sure he has a tool belt full of food and drink. A few jars for relief purposes. He can lay out in there as long as need be. The other one will drive the van out of there. Before the Cop comes back home.

When the time comes. The inside man will pop a hole into this Cop. Then grab the broad. You then bring her back here for confessions. Down in the basement. I'm sure Ronnie James can get her to tell it all to Jesus." "That's a good plan Reverend." Ms. Parsons said. "You should have gone into crime instead of ministry." "Then again, I can't tell the difference." "You have such a flattering way with words Ms. Parsons." Reverend Kingsley replied. "I'm not here to flatter you, nigga." She replied. "You serve a purpose for me, that's all. Now let me call Drexler. Let him know how he can get inside his brother's house.

"That's a damn shame." She continued. "This man has never been to his own brother's house." "Well, they did choose opposite sides of the law." Pastor said. "I can imagine it would raise eyebrows in both of their worlds. To be hanging out with each other. Even if they are brothers." "Yeah, that's true." Ms. Parsons said. "I couldn't imagine the first time I go to my brother's house. It was to kill him. "Well, I've done my part." Reverend Kingsley said. Helping you all get inside. The church will be really grateful for the contribution. The one hopefully you're going to make. After you acquire her confession and location of the cash." "We haven't found the cash yet." Ms. Parsons said. "So you get Mr. Crawford and Ms. Adams out there. With those pamphlets and see if they can find out anything.

"That's a brilliant scheme you use Reverend." She continued. "These old people can walk around homes." Businesses and anywhere. Nobody ever suspects what they are doing. Nobody even questions why they're over East Baltimore? Trying to recruit people to a church in West Baltimore? They just think they're two elderly people. They want to hurry and get rid of them. By the time they're gone. Mr. Crawford has taken all the photos. Or assessed how to get back on the property undetected. They never notice what he's doing. Not when Ms. Adams is shoving that bible in their face." "Well, I have to admit." Pastor Kingsley said. "I didn't originate this idea." "We learned this from Pastor Barnette Smith. He is the most corrupt Pastor you will ever meet."

"Takes one to know one." Ms. Parsons said. "Once Drexler gets that broad from his brother's house. We'll get that code and no longer need Drexler. His ass is getting undisciplined. Letting those two broads infiltrate. That's a rookie mistake. Since he can no longer see the angles. I'm going to have Octacilius surprise his ass. With a bullet to his brain. Then we can install Octo to run the East side. He should have less ego. None of these niggas wouldn't be shit. If I hadn't hooked them up. With my Italian connect years ago. I got them connected to a good steady supply. Then I connected them with this church. So they could wash the money."

"On top of that." She said. "I have faithfully refereed the game. Handling problems between their rivals. On the West Side of Baltimore and Over East. Now, I've told this fool Drexler. To go kill his brother and grab that bitch. He's making me wait? Who the fuck does he think he is? These niggas grew into bosses by sucking my tits. Now he thinks I have to wait? For something I want done?" "Well, the Pastor will help you in any way." Reverend Kingsley said. "To wash away this sinful money. That's another fringe benefit. Of being at this church." "Speaking of fringe benefits Pastor." Ms. Parsons said. "Let's go in your office."

"Nana needs you to speak in tongues." She said. "Have your rod or staff comfort me again. All this money and murder. Has got me all worked up." "Sister Parsons." Pastor Kingsley said. "We've just had worship service here. The Lord is still in His Holy temple." "I bet if I were Mrs. Langston." Ms. Parsons said. "You wouldn't be thinking about worship service. You'd be laying hands all over her. Like you did with Mrs. Wallace. Ms. Evans, Ms. Brawley, Mrs. Clarke and Ms. Evans' little boy. Now get your ass inside. Before I have Ronnie James, come over here and put a hole in your temple."

They both looked across the street. Ronnie James was standing in the doorway of the house. Looking at them. "Like I said." Reverend Kingsley replied. "The Pastor is here to serve the community." They walked inside the church. The Pastor locked the doors behind them. Ronnie James looked at his watch and began to track the time. He then came outside with his Poncho and shotgun. He sat on the porch. Staring at the church, scanning the side. Pastor Kingsley's vehicle was parked on the side. If that car were to ever try to leave. Before Ms. Parsons was visible. Ronnie James would know what he had to do.

Over at Andrés' house. He was slowly waking from his sleep. "Good morning, sleepy head." Sabrina said. "Welcome back to planet earth." "Is it still morning?" André uttered. "No, it's almost three o'clock in the afternoon." She replied. "You must have been really tired." "Yeah, I was." André said. "I think I'm still tired. I'm also hungry." "I knew you would be." Sabrina replied. So I made some old fashioned smothered chicken. With rice and gravy. I cooked some yams, collard greens and cornbread. Oh, and I found a bottle of Pinot Noir wine on your rack. I would love to finish with that you." "Damn, you did all of that?" André asked. "Yes, I did." Sabrina replied. "As they used to say. I went in your kitchen and put my foot in it."

"There may be a few toenails in those collards." She joked. You're going to have to watch out for." "It's all good." André said. "You have some pretty feet. I'll just call it seasoning." "Let me brush my teeth so I can eat." "Yes, you do that." Sabrina said. "Maybe after dinner, I can get you to play a game of Scrabble. I found the board in your wine room of all places. I'm guessing since you have it, you know how to play." "Yeah, I can issue out a beat down for you Sabrina." He replied. No problem at all." "You?" Sabrina asked incredulously. "Beat me in Scrabble? André, you're supposed to turn in the drugs. Not smoke them."

"Alright." André replied. "I love it when a woman talks shit. That way, I don't feel guilty, while I'm whipping your ass." "Oh, you clearly don't know." Sabrina said. "I was the spelling bee champ in my middle school. For two years running. I'm not an MC. Talking all that junk. About who could beat who? Sound like a punk. I just throw down, and go for mine. Add up the points. I got 69!" "Oh, you're going to drop some old EPMD on me." André said. "We'll see how dope of an MC you are. After I start raining those triple word scores on that ass." "Go brush your teeth." Sabrina said. "Come on in this kitchen so you can eat." Sabrina said. "I'll let the score do my talking for me." André got up and went to brush his teeth.

Sabrina returned to the kitchen. She began preparing his plate. They sat and ate while savoring the wine. "Don't think I'm going to be too drunk." André said. "To drop some big words on that ass." André remarked. "Do I look scared over here?" Sabrina asked. "I'll clean up the kitchen." André said. "You go set up the board." "I'll pick my own letters. Thank you very much." He added. Sabrina went down to the basement to set up the game table. André soon came down. He grabbed two glasses from the bar. "You're trying to get us drunk?" Sabrina asked. We'll be too drunk to make love tonight." "Nobody is going to get drunk." André replied. "We can sip on a little something. While we play this game."

"I'll have some Cognac and coke." He said. "What do you want?" "Let me get a little rum and sprite." Sabrina responded. After André poured the drinks, he handed a glass to her. "Alright now." André said. "Let's get this ass whipping on the road. I'm a gentleman. So I'll let you go first. Regardless of what letter I pull." They drew their letters. Sabrina started the game with a five-letter word. "12 to 0." Sabrina said. "I haven't even had my first turn yet." André replied. "You're acting like you did something big. He then laid out his word. "16 to 12." He said. "Get used to having the smaller number. For the rest of the game."

Sabrina then laid down a 27-point word. Taking advantage of a double word score. André then placed his letters on the board. "NEFU." He said. "That is not a damn word." Sabrina protested. "What do you mean?" André asked stunningly. "My brother's son is my Nefu." "I see now you're trying to cheat." Sabrina said. "Go ahead and put your sorry little letters down." André is then forced to put down a two-letter word, worth only seven points. "Umm Hmm. That's what I thought." Sabrina said. She then placed her letters. Using one of André's letters for 33 points. André swapped his letters and passed.

Sabrina took her turn for 15 more points. André laid his letters down. He spelled out "HEDON." "Oh My God!" Sabrina said. "What the hell is that?" André acted surprised that she was questioning him. "That is a word!" He said. "You know Pookie from around the way, right?" André asked. "Hedon" play that talking about his mama. Sabrina laughed mildly. "You are such a cheater." She said. "Get that off my board." André then played the word "Chess." He scored 31 points. "Now I've got some good letter finally." André said. "That makes one of us." Sabrina replied. They battled back and forth. Challenging each other's minds. At the end, the game was won by Sabrina. With a seventeen point margin.

"Like I said before." Sabrina taunted. "I don't talk trash. I bring the pain like Method Man." "You got lucky and won a game." André said. "Do you want a medal now?" "No. I just want you to bow down." Sabrina replied. "Acknowledge who is Queen around these parts." "Yeah, yeah, yeah, I hear you." André said. "Do you want to play another game? Give me a chance at payback?" "No Sir." Sabrina said. "We're about to role play. You go get in the shower upstairs. I'll shower down here. I'll leave your script on the bed. We'll see if your acting skills, are any better than your Scrabble skills." "Role play?" André asked. "You're going to fuck around. They're going to take your black card from you. You're going to be traded to the white folks."

"André I live in my own world." Sabrina said. "I'm not worried about anybody accepting me. I know I'm different than your average woman. I'm good with that. Now go get in that shower. So we can get this party started." André showered and dried himself off. He shaved his face. So his stubble wouldn't scratch her inner thighs. When he was done. He meticulously checked himself in the mirror. He walked out to his bedroom. Sabrina had laid out some clothes for him to wear. She had also left a folder on the bed. André picked up the folder. He found a few typed pages inside. He read them and thought to himself, 'This woman is off her rocker. I guess it takes some weird shit to get her off.'

He knew he didn't have to follow the script verbatim. He did however. Have to portray the character created for him in the manuscript. While reading the folder. He noticed that Sabrina had left her purse. Along with her phone in the bedroom. She was still downstairs taking her shower. He quickly tried to look at her phone. It was locked. He then went through her purse. He found some cash and her I.D. He also found some other papers. The papers appeared interesting to him. He put them back inside her purse. Then tried to place the purse back like he found it. After he got dressed, he looked over the folder again.

Sabrina walked into the room shortly after. He appeared to be still reading and thinking. "Are we ready, big daddy?" She asked. "Yes, I'm ready." André replied. "Let's go start in the living room, on the sofa." She said. André turned on the television as part of the script. He turned on one of the movie channels. They began cuddling like they were on a date. The movie they selected. Was almost over when they began watching. Sabrina lifted the bottom of Andrés' sweater and shirts. She began to caress the bare skin of his stomach and chest. The credits to the movie began to rise on the screen. "This is nice." Sabrina said.

"It's not bad." André replied. "I'm tired and about to turn in." "Can a sister get some love?" Sabrina asked. "You know how I like lying next to you. What it does to me?" "No." André responded. "Did you just tell me no?" Sabrina asked. "Yes, I did woman." He repeated. "I said no. I control your pussy and I will decide. When you may have an orgasm. How you will have an orgasm. So the answer is no." "What kind of bullshit is this?" Sabrina said. "This is not bullshit." He replied. If you want to cum. Then you have to play with your pussy and let me watch." Sabrina tried in vain to get him to touch her, but to no avail.

She wasn't going to let him stop her from getting hers. So she strutted to the bed room. In a very seductive way. Partly to try to change André's mind. Partly to show him she had changed hers. She was going to have all this sexiness to herself. He was no longer invited to join her. He followed her as she entered the bedroom. She got herself into position. She reached into the nightstand drawer and found a few items. Some lubricant and a small vibrator. "This is my trusted friend." She said. André watched with difficult restraint. While Sabrina pleased herself. He really found himself struggling when she'd open her eyes. She looked right at him. As if to ask. Are you sure you don't want to join me? Then she closed her eyes. Going back to work on her gorgeous pussy.

She toyed with herself until she reached climatic peak. André applauded her. He walked over and kissed her quivering inner thighs. Before lightly kissing her labia and then her mouth. Sabrina tried to push his head back between her legs. He firmly resisted. "Why are you being so mean to me?" Sabrina asked.

Chapter 6

The Submission Forms

"I'm not being mean at all woman." He said. "I just said you have to wait." "What the hell am I waiting for?" Sabrina demanded. "Until I am ready to give you some dick dammit!" André smartly retorted. "Man, you are being so cruel to me." Sabrina said. "Man?" André replied. "No baby, I'm Master today. Now get your sexy ass over here and give me a kiss." Sabrina got out the bed. Rolled her eyes and gave him a peck on the lips. "Didn't I just tell you woman to give me a kiss?" He asked. "Get on your knees!" He commanded. Sabrina lowered herself before him. He pulled out his swollen staff and stuck it on her lips. She opened her mouth. He hit her lightly with his manhood on her forehead. "Kiss it, don't suck it." He said. She did as instructed. He told her she could now touch herself. After only allowing her seconds to play. He stopped her.

"Now lower my pants." He ordered. She lowered his pants and he told her to lick his balls. She obeyed his command. She took his dick into her mouth but he stopped her. "I didn't tell you to do that woman." He said. "I said lick my balls, that's all." Sabrina felt he was having fun playing games. She didn't care. She knew she was playing and playing to win. She spent several minutes licking his balls. While letting his dick rub all over her face. "You can go get in bed now." André said. "I will get you some grapes shortly." He helped her stand and pulled her close to him. He looked into her eyes, his nose pressed against hers. "You are a beautiful black woman." He said. "You just have to learn to please me, understood?" He then kissed her passionately. Letting his hands run all over her nakedness. He squeezed her ass. Then brought his right hand around to rub her pussy.

"If you really thought I was beautiful." Sabrina said. "You wouldn't be just rubbing me there." "I do think you're gorgeous black woman." He said. "We're just not going to make love right now." "Well, I licked your balls tonight." She said. "The least you could do is lick me back." Sabrina protested. "Nope, not going to happen." André said. "Let me go find you some grapes and some toys to play with." Once in the kitchen, André began looking in the refrigerator. For grapes, whipped cream and other items he could use. He then called Sabrina from the bedroom. She walked to the kitchen. "Yes, what do you need?" She asked. "It's 'yes Master' to you." He replied. "Don't make me punish you for being a bad girl. I'll tell you what beautiful. Since you look so damn good right now. Sit up on the counter."

He helped lifting her there. She spread her legs. He sprayed her pussy with whipped cream. He began to lick her slit. He licked her pussy for about two minutes. He then told her to get down. "Is that it?" She asked. "I want more." "I know." André said. He took her hand and walked her back to the bedroom. Bringing the items with them. He sat the bowl of grapes and whipped cream on a tray. Over on his side of the bed was a wooden chest. It was mentioned in the folder Sabrina left for him. André opened it to find a collection of exotic toys. "I see I have a few options here." He said. He removed a padded neck collar. He placed it around her neck. Then attached a three-foot chain to it.

He then took out a blindfold and covered her eyes. "Now, get down on all fours and follow me." Sabrina obeyed. André walked her around the room. Being careful not to let her run into anything. He then returned to the chest to find a paddle. He had Sabrina turn away from him. He began to spank her ass cheeks with the paddle. To his surprise, her pussy got wetter. With each smack on her naked ass. He then walked in front of her and commanded her to kiss his thighs. Using the sound of his voice and her hands to locate him. She steadied herself and begin to kiss his body.

Still blindfolded, she felt him caress her scalp. Using the chain. He pulled her to stand. Then bent her body gently over to the bed. She then sensed him behind her. Without warning, he rammed his dick. Into her waiting and wet pussy. He wrapped the chain around his hand several times. To tighten his pull on her neck. The collar was only tight enough so she could feel slight pressure. André rammed his dick in and out of her for about two minutes. He pulled her around to face him. He made her kneel. Placing his dick over her closed lips. She opened her mouth to receive him. He forced her to suck her own juices off of him.

He then walked her around to the foot of the bed. Making her stand up. He returned to the wooden chest. Removing some Velcro restraints. Tying her arms to the top of the canopy bed. He then spread her legs. Tying each of them loosely to the foot posts. With her arms and legs stretched. She was now in the position of an X. He returned to the wooden chest. Removing a vibrating wand and turning it on. He started by rubbing it across the back of her neck. Then across her breast. He gave special attention to her nipples. Looking to make sure she couldn't see through the blindfold. He leaned closer to her. Softly speaking in her left ear. "What is it that you want chocolate doll?" He asked. "I want to cum for you, Master." She replied. With his knee, he nudged her legs. As far apart as they could go.

He then let the wand glide down her body. Until it found her pussy. Instant vibrating sensations jolted her clitoris. Driving her into a frenzy. André pressed it firmly against her. Her legs and arms were restrained. She could only grind her pussy against the wand. When he saw that she was about to cum. He took the wand away. Sabrina was breathing profusely. He leaned close and spoke in her right ear. "What is it that you want, chocolate doll?" He asked. "I want to cum Master." She begged. "I want you to fuck me." "I didn't tell you it was time to fuck now, did I?" He asked. "No you didn't Master." She answered. "Now you must be punished." He replied.

He grabbed the paddle and climbed on the bed. He began to spank her ass cheeks as he talked to her. "When will you get fucked chocolate doll?" He asked. "Not until you're ready to fuck me Master." She replied. He spanked each ass cheek a few more times. He then walked back around in front of her. Retrieving the vibrating wand. He placed it back on her clitoris. He took his free hand. Pressing his fingers inside of her pussy. Soaking up her juices. He then took those fingers and placed them in her mouth. While the wand sent pulsating shockwaves through her body. He began to tease her further. By removing the wand from her. Then placing it back on her clit.

He left the wand pressed on her pussy for about three seconds. Quickly removing it. He does that over and over again. Until the wand created and earthquake within Sabrina. Her body convulsed, pulsated, shook and rattled. With her limbs tied. A million volts of electricity riveted through her body. Culminating and exploding at her pussy. "Did I tell you to cum, chocolate doll?" André asked. Gasping for air, Sabrina struggled to speak. "No, no, no, you did not, Master. She breathlessly said. "I couldn't help it." "Oh, you couldn't help it." André taunted. "I'm very disappointed. You've earned a position across my knee." He then untied her arms and legs. Leaving her blindfolded. Taking a seat on the accent bench, he laid her over his lap. He began to spank her with his hand on her bare ass.

His fingers touch her pussy. With each swipe of his hand as he disciplined her. "Next time, you will not cum." He said. "Until I tell you to. Do you understand chocolate doll?" He asked. Sabrina was whirling between the pleasure and pain. Of not being able to see when his heavy hand, would come down on her ass. "Yes, I understand Master." She replied. He struck her ass twice more. He then pushed her onto her knees. "Now suck this dick for your Master." He commanded. Sabrina reached for his meat. He held her hands. He then placed his dick in front of her mouth. She began to suck him. André grabbed the back of her head. Forcing himself deeper into her mouth.

Sabrina gagged briefly. Adjusting to give him a masterful blowjob. André caressed her breast as she sucked him intently. "What is it that you want, chocolate doll?" He asked again. "I want your dick inside of me." She responded. "Now that you're being a good girl." André said. "I think we can give you what you want." He stood and got some pillows off the bed. He placed them on the floor. He then placed her knees on a pillow. He placed another for her head as he pushed her to the floor. The last pillow, he placed under his knees. He began to kiss the reddened areas of her cheeks. Where he had just spanked her. His kisses were gentle and soothing. As if to heal the pain. His hand and paddle had caused her moments earlier. She still couldn't see what André was doing. She could definitely feel him. When his tongue began to lick her pussy from behind.

Soon, she could feel his tongue inside of her. Followed by his fingers. He kissed the area of the small of her back. Loving the base of her spine. Before returning to her juicy pussy. "Do you like when your Master licks and kisses your pussy?" He asked. "Oh yes, I love it Master." Sabrina replied. "I love it so much." "Do you want to cum in your Master's mouth?" He asked. "Yes! Yes! Yes!" She screamed. "I want to cum in your mouth Master." She immediately felt his hand smack her right ass cheek. "You need to say 'please." He taunted. "Please Master, let me cum in your mouth." She begged. "I want to cum in your mouth so bad." André grabbed the wand off the bed. He re-applied it to her clitoris.

Her body was charged with high voltage and she quickly built to an epic orgasm. She came so hard. She squirted her juices onto the pillow and floor beneath her. André quickly inserted his dick inside of her. He fucked her at a frantic pace. Her pussy quickly synced with his rhythm. Sabrina began to cum once more. Her pussy was so sloppily wet. Soon, he announced to her that his own orgasm was pending. "Oh, fuck!" He yelled. "God damn, chocolate doll. You're going to make me cum all inside of this luscious chocolate pussy."

"Do you want me to cum inside of you?" He asked. "Yes! I want you to cum inside of me." She urged. "Cum for mama. Cum for this chocolate pussy." André firmly grabbed her hips. Ramming into her with passionate fury. His dick detonated. Gushing like a fire hydrant inside of her. Andrés body locked in place. Sabrina pushed back to milk every drop. Her hungry pussy wanted all of his cream inside of her. She pumped him until his sensitive dick couldn't take anymore. He pulled out of her. He then turned her using the chain and collar to face him. His dick was covered with the creamy mixture of both their juices. He placed his still erect dick inside of her mouth. Beginning a slow, deliberate movement.

His dick was still sensitive. He didn't want her to give him a full oral work out. Sabrina worked her mouth gently to suck him. She was making love to his penis with her mouth. After his dick was nice and clean. André removed her blindfold. "Ummm, that was good Master." She said. "What else do you have in store for your chocolate doll?" "Why don't we get in the shower and wash each other up." André replied. They got in the shower still kissing. Like teenage lovers. Letting the warm water run over their naked bodies. Sabrina turned to get the body wash to clean him. He turned her mouth back to him. He couldn't get enough of kissing her. Finally, he yielded and let her get the body wash.

She began to lather him up. He enjoyed the touch of her hands on his body. Sabrina turned her back to him. He soaped her down too. Giving special attention between her ass cheeks and pussy lips. Washing her back and neck. Sabrina got her face wash and began to wash her face. As soon as she was done, he kissed her again. "I just can't get enough of your lips, woman." He said. He ran his hands all over her body. They finished showering and dried off. They then got out of the shower. They went into the bedroom where they grabbed their robes. Keeping the chill off of them. Sabrina headed to get some water from the kitchen. André grabbed her arm and tossed her onto the bed.

"What are you doing?" She asked. "I'm kissing your pussy black woman." He replied. "I'm not doing anything to you. So you can go on to the kitchen. This is between your beautiful pussy and me. "Did you have fun tonight?" He asked her vagina. He gave her pussy another kiss. Finally letting Sabrina go to the kitchen. When she returned, he was lying naked on his back. "Okay, it's time for you to sit on my face!" He said. "You are a stone-cold freak." Sabrina said. "Aren't you, Mr. Nichols?" "Is that rain I hear starting to come down?" André inquired. "Yes, it is supposed to rain tonight." Sabrina replied. "Were you supposed to go out?" "No, I wasn't supposed to go out." André said. "We're about to go out." "Where are we going in the rain?" Sabrina asked. "At this time of night?"

"Why do you ask so many questions?" André said. "Can we just go have some fun?" He walked over to his walk-in closet to her things. "Just put this dress on and let's roll." Sabrina did what was asked of her. André also got dressed. "Hey Breen." He said. "Which one of these guns do you think goes best with my outfit? The black Beretta .40 cal Glock? The chrome .44? This Smith & Wesson 5906 9 mili? Or this Ruger P97 .45? I have more guns to choose from. If you don't like any of these." "I'd go with an external hammer with that outfit." Sabrina replied. "So that rules out the Glock. The .44 is a bit too shiny and bulky. The P97 is a Ruger so it's not one of my favorites. Unless it's a throw away gun. So, I guess that leaves the 9-millimeter.

Plus, it holds 15 in the clip and one in the chamber. More than enough to keep us out of danger." "Listen at you." André said. "You sound like you know a little something about guns." "Uh….I may have shot a gun or two." Sabrina said. "When I was growing up in Georgia." "You know a little something about wearing dresses too." André added. "Woman you look delicious." "Well, thank you Sir." She replied. "You don't look so bad yourself. Now are you going to tell me where we're going?" She asked. "I've just been hit with inspiration." André said.

"I want to go donate some money to charity." He continued. "In Atlantic City. I thought we could take a scenic route up Route 40. Enjoy some time together outside the house." "Alright, Mr. Spontaneous." Sabrina said. "Let me grab my purse and phone." "No baby, I'm taking you to Atlantic City." André said. "You don't need a purse or money. I will buy you whatever you want. "Oh, that's so sweet of you André." Sabrina replied. "However my mama always told me. To have my own. Just in case a man decides to put you out. I would have to find my way back home." "First of all." André said. "There is no way I'm going to put you out. Secondly, here's a thousand dollars cash."

"More than enough for you to get a plane." He continued. A train or an automobile. Plus a hotel if you needed it. Put that money in your pocket. Grab your phone and let's go. Your stuff is safe here. I'll set the alarm and we can be on our way. Just grab some sweats or casual change of clothes. In case we end up staying over." Sabrina was reluctant but eventually relented. "Hey, let me send a text." She said. "To my nephew in Michigan real quick. Then I'll be ready to go." "I didn't know you had a nephew in Michigan Brine." André said. "That's cool. I need to check on something as well. I'm going to run down to the basement. Sabrina waited for André to leave the room. She began to text. Down in the basement. André went over to his bar. He opened one of the cabinet doors.

He began moving drink mixes and other items. Well behind all the items he soon found an old flip phone. It was connected to a charger. "I wonder if this thing still works." He pondered out loud. "I have to scroll through the entire alphabet to send a text." He began pushing the number buttons. Sabrina was upstairs frantically texting someone. André called out to her as he was coming back up the stairs. "Are you ready?" He asked. She looked at her phone. A text from 248-555-5555 returned that read "OK". "Yes, I'm ready André. I'm grabbing a pair of sweats now." André grabbed a small duffle bag. Sabrina looked at her purse one last time.

She followed André out the door. After a short drive down Route 24. André was quickly onto to I-95 north. Moments later they were in Delaware. "Oooh, I hate driving over this bridge." Sabrina said. "Why are you hating on the Delaware Memorial Bridge?" André asked. "I don't hate the bridge silly." Sabrina said. "It's just that it seems so high up." "It always seems to be windy whenever I come across it." Just as she spoke, a strong cross wind rocked the car. André had to grab the steering wheel with both hands. "See?" Sabrina said. "That's what I'm talking about." "It's raining out here. It's foggy and I don't even know how you can see."

"I can't see more than twenty feet in front of us." She continued. "You don't need to see more than twenty feet to drive." André replied. "People like you panic in conditions like this. That causes accidents. As long as you can see the center lane markers. Or the shoulder lane markers. You can drive. Both lines glow in the dark. So most of the time, you can see them. If I can only see the center lane marker. Then I know where my car should be. In relationship to that marker. If I can only see the shoulder marker. Same thing. As long as any vehicle in front of me, has brake or tail lights. I won't hit them. So, I don't focus on what I can't see down the road. I focus on what I can see."

"That allows me to drive." He continued. "Like anything. If you don't have confidence in your skills. Then don't try this shit at home. I'm sure you've driven. While reading or sending a text before, right?" "Yes, I have." Sabrina answered. "Did you crash and die?" André asked. "No, of course not, silly." Sabrina replied. "That's because." André said. Even though your mind was fully focused on your phone. Your brain had already processed information about the road. To keep you from crashing. You knew approximately where the curb was. How far the next vehicle and other critical info. It's no different if you're driving on highway and some kid throws a brick into your windshield.

"People die because they panic." André said. "Reality is, at the moment that brick would hit. You should know if cars are behind you. Trust once you hit the break, they will react too. Eliminate them out of your thought process. Now just focus your mind. On where you estimate the shoulder is. If there is a rail or wall? You want to slow the vehicle down. So that you don't hit something at high speed. You're going to crash from such an event. Hitting a wall or tree at 30 mph. Is a lot better than hitting it at 80 mph." "Oh, so you're like the Terminator?" Sabrina asked. "You can drive in complete darkness?"

"That is, correct." André answered. "I see everything. I see you looking sexy." "Oh, you think I'm sexy, do you?" Sabrina asked. "What are you going to do with a sexy woman?" "I was sent back from the future to pound on your pussy." André said. "Who in the hell would have sent you?" Sabrina asked. Back from the future for that?" "You did." André replied. They laughed. Soon they crossed into rural New Jersey. "Now, I do love traveling Route 40." Sabrina said. "It's so nostalgic and peaceful, day or night." "Yes, it is that." André said. "There are so many farms and open fields. You seem to have the road to yourself on this Route." They passed a sign which read 'Cape May 42 Miles'. Suddenly a down pour of rain started.

There was an open field off to their right. It stretched as far as their eyes could see. There was a very limited amount of light available. No Street lights, no lights from buildings. Only the light of the moon peeking through the clouds. André pulled the truck over onto a muddy road. He turned off his headlights. They rode far from sight of the main road. He stopped and removed the keys. Asking Sabrina to get out of the truck. Sabrina didn't know what was going on. She was too nervous to obey. The rain was pouring. André spoke to her as a Police Officer would. Ordering her out of a car as he opened her door. Sabrina was afraid. She thought of screaming for help. Then she realized they were so far from any homes or buildings. No one would hear her.

Especially over the sound of the pouring rain. She decided to step out barefoot. She knew she would not run far. Especially in the high-heeled shoes she wore. André led her to the front of the vehicle. Between the headlights. She stood facing him. Suddenly he commanded her to turn around. To face the windshield. Standing in a puddle of water and mud. Sabrina could feel the rain beat on top of her feet. She turned to the vehicle. Thoughts began to rush into her head. "Why would he bring me here? Where did I slip up? How did he figure out my intentions? If I run now out of the headlights, can I hide in the darkness?" André stood still behind her in complete silence.

Sabrina wanted to cry. If this is what she thought, it wouldn't help her. He couldn't see her tears with the pouring rain anyway. Suddenly, the song, "In the rain" popped into her head. She could hear herself singing. "I want to go outside, in the rain." She was startled. By the feeling of André's hands on her shoulders. André bent her over the hood. Like a suspect. It felt like he was searching her. Then he lifted her dress up and pulled her panties down. "Damn, you look so good out here." He said. After he removed her panties, he used his feet to spread her legs. He held her hands behind her back. He knelt and began to eat her pussy from behind. Sabrina enjoyed every delicious lick. He jammed a finger in her pussy. Like a bear trying to draw honey out of a honeycomb. He licked his fingers the same. He released her hands and spread her ass cheeks apart. So he could have unabated access to her treasure.

"What do you want me to do Sabrina?" He asked. "I want you to fuck me André." She answered. "How do you want me to fuck you baby?" He asked. "Fuck me from behind, just like this!" She urged. André unzipped his pants and removed his throbbing dick. Rubbing it on her ass. He told Sabrina she had to suck him in the rain. Before he would fuck her. She turned and stooped down. So that she could follow the officer's order. He thrusted his dick in her velvety mouth. Just hard enough to tap her head lightly on the vehicle.

She soon had his dick nice and hard. He turned her back to face the truck. Spreading her legs once again for search. He slid his dick up and down her slit. He lifted her hips slightly. So that he could access her pussy. He began to fuck her furiously in the pouring rain. "Take this dick woman and tell me you like it." He ordered. Sabrina was in delirious ecstasy. "YES! YES! YES!" She screamed. I want to be fucked by you André. Just like this." "No you don't." He rebutted. "You wish you had my vibrating wand on your pussy, don't you?" When she didn't answer. He slapped her wet ass slightly hard. "You wish you had two dicks in you again, don't you?" He asked.

"Yes! I want both of your dicks at the same time again." She cried. "Do you want to eat that bitch's pussy again? André asked. "Do you want her eating your pussy again?" "Yes, I loved it when she ate my pussy." Sabrina grunted. "Oh, My God! André, FUCK! Me harder!!!" "Did you love all that hot sticky cum?" He questioned. "All over your pretty brown face Sabrina?" "Oh, Fuck I'm Cummmming!" She yelled. "Yes, I loved all that cummmmm. All over my face, baby!" She exclaimed. Her body rocked back and forth wildly. Meeting his every thrust into her. "Fuck! Oh yes!" She moaned. "I want you to cum on my face again. I want your cum and the rain to wash over my face. Cover me with your cum." Sabrina was ramming her hips back to André. Her first climax built, erupted and subsided. Suddenly, she pulled away. "Oh baby, I need you in my ass." She said.

André quickly pulled out of her pussy. He pushed his dick in her ass. Using only the rain for moisture. "Sabrina, you just can't get enough of my dick in your ass can you?" He asked. He began to fuck her intently. Drilling his dick deeper and deeper inside of her. "Tell me how much you like this dick." He said. "Oooh fuck, I like, and I love this dick." She replied. "You can't get enough of it, can you?" André asked. "No, I can't get enough!" She moaned. "I love that dick in my ass!" "Good, then get your dripping ass in the back seat." André led her to the back seat and reached into the cargo area.

There, he had a bin with some fresh clean towels. He laid the towels across the leather seats. Escorting Sabrina inside the vehicle. She laid across the back seat of the truck on her stomach. André climbed on top of her. Aiming his dick straight into her ass. He began pounding her hard. Hard enough to turn the truck on its side. "I'm fucking you in your ass Bree" He said. "You're going to take this dick like a good little whore." "Yes!" She screamed. "Ram that big black dick in my ass André." She said. "I love it soooooo much." "Oh yeah take this big chocolate dick is in your ass." André uttered. "Beg for this dick, baby." "Please give me that dick." She cried. "Give me that dick in my ass."

From this position he touched her G-spot perfectly. Her orgasm was beginning to intensify insanely. André told her he wanted her to cum for him. He started rubbing her clit with his fingers. While he drove his dick deeper in her tight, dark asshole. "I'm cumming in your ass, Sabrina." He moaned. "I'm going to fucking cum in your ass Bree! "Whose ass is this? Whose pussy is it?" "It's your pussy André!" Sabrina yelled. "It's your ass too baby. Fuck me any way you want to." "I'm going to spray this creamy cum in your ass." He said. "I'm going to stamp my dick print in your ass. You beautiful black woman." "Ooooh FUUUUCCCCKKKK, André! Sabrina yelled. "I'm cuuuuuummmmming again. Damn what are you doing to me baby?"

Sabrina's ass began to spasm as she climaxed. This caused a chain reaction with André. He began to pound her from the roof of the vehicle. As if dumping all of his cum into her. Sabrina tried to spread her legs a little wider. Holding on for the ride. They collapsed on the seat as André's dick trembled inside of her. It sputtered out more droplets of cum into her. After resting, they climbed out of the truck. Standing naked in the rain. Letting the natural water rinse them off. André handed her some clean towels to dry off with. They got back in the truck and drove to the road. "Sabrina." André called. "Yes baby." She replied. "I could get use to you being in my life woman." He said.

"Ummm, that would be nice if that could happen." Sabrina said. They made their way down the highway. Eventually they saw a rest stop. They pulled in to get fuel. One of the station attendants came to pump their gas. "Yes Sir, what can I get for you?" The attendant asked. "Fill up please." André responded. "I could move to Jersey." Sabrina said. "Just on the fact that I don't have to pump my own gas." "I don't know if I could deal with the smell." André replied. "Too many chemicals floating around in the air here. After he's done pumping our gas, I'm going to go inside. To use the bathroom." André continued. "Yes, I have pee too and I could use some snacks." Sabrina said.

André tipped the attendant for pumping the gas. He then parked the vehicle. "Don't try to spend any of your money woman." André said. "Whatever you want or need, I got you." After they used the restrooms, they decided to get some fried chicken. "We need to have something on our stomach." André said. "I'm going to get my drink on at the casino." "That's how they get you. Sabrina responded. "To keep dropping money on those tables." "Well, that doesn't work on me." André said. "All I do is play the slots." "Slots, tables whatever." Sabrina replied. "Those free drinks. Give the illusion that you're about to win. So you keep playing. Next thing you know. You're homeless in the soup kitchen line."

"God damn." André said. "You sent me all the way to the bottom. I go to A/C with a five hundred dollar limit. If that shit lasts 6 hours, then I'm here 6 hours. If it's gone in 30 minutes, then I'm gone in 30 minutes. I don't go to the cashiers. Trying to get a lien on my house for no damn slots." "I hear you talking." Sabrina said. "Don't make me have to drag you out of there. When they're about to take your ride." They ate and got back on the road. They decided to scan the radio for songs as they drove. They picked up WDAS in Philly. The song playing was 'Is It Still Good to You' by Ashford & Simpson. They sang it to each other. With the passion of long time lovers. They came across another station playing, 'I Can't Tell You Why' by The Eagles.

"What do you know about The Eagles?" André asked. "Are you kidding me?" Sabrina replied. "This guitar solo at the end is everything." Sabrina bought trail mix from the store. She poured some into her hand. She then fed some to André while he drove. He gently bit her hand. After he had all the raisins in his mouth. "You old, greedy dog." Sabrina said. "Greedy?" André repeated. "Keep talking about me. I'm going to pull this truck over again and fuck you……up." "Oh you want to fuck me….up?" Sabrina asked. "Yeah, that's what happens to people who talk a lot of trash." André replied. "Well, I might just have to keep talking trash to you." Sabrina said. "You greedy punk!"

They laughed and then paused. The song; 'Sailing' by Christopher Cross came on the radio. "OH, I USED TO LOVE THIS SONG!" They both yelled at the same time. "My Older brother used to play this song to death." André said. "Mine too!" Sabrina replied. They began to sing it. As they sailed on up the road towards Atlantic City. The drove through Cape May still scanning. An oldie station played; 'How Much I Feel' by Ambrosia. "OH, MY GOD!" Sabrina said. I haven't heard this song in forever." "I heard it a few years ago." André replied. Playing in a pharmacy store on Howard and Lexington Street in B-more."

"I had to pull out my phone to get the name of it. Then I downloaded it. There were a lot of great white bands and artist, back in the day. They made some good Ballard music." "Yes, they did indeed." Sabrina added. "Now be quiet, this was my jam!" She turned up the radio. The song; 'Summertime Anthem' by Eric Roberson came on. They both sang to the music. Karaoke style. Laughing in their own world. Soon, they arrived in Atlantic City. André tried to find a place for them to park. He checked Atlantic Avenue. Near the Boardwalk. They found a hotel parking garage. Then drove their way up to a parking space. "Give me a kiss for good luck." André pleaded. Sabrina leaned over and kissed him passionately. Giving him a long, tender kiss from her full, soft lips.

"Damn, I think I just had the best luck." He said. "In the whole world. André got out of the vehicle. He walked around to open the door for Sabrina. They took the elevator down to the Casino. They began to look around. "I think the machines over there are calling my name." André said. "Okay." Sabrina replied. "The ones on the row behind them is where I will be. André walked over to his chosen machine. He slid in a twenty-dollar bill. "Oooh Mr. big spender." Sabrina teased. "I'm not in a hurry." André said. "To donate all of my money to this charity." "I try to make this five hundred last. "As long as it can. Once it's gone, I'm done." "That's why I'll be on the .25 cent machine." Sabrina said.

"Now, let me go win this $100,000." She continued. "So I can buy me a new dress. "I'll buy you a sammich André." "Oh, you want to be funny now?" André asked. "Don't think that you can't get fucked……..up right here. In this Casino. I will pull down your panties right now. You beautiful black woman." "Go ahead." Sabrina teased. "I dare you." "You're lucky the spirits just told me to pull this lever." André said. "Instead of your panties. Besides, I don't need you dripping my DNA. All over these people's carpet. You do remember you being nasty? On the way up here, don't you?" "I wasn't being anything but a lady." Sabrina replied. "I was kidnapped and taken into an open field. I was made to do things against my will. Now I'm reporting that to you. Mr. Officer."

"I need you to catch the guy that did it." She continued. "Let me have some time alone with him to pay him back." "I'll look into it." André said. "If there's a place that sells Krispy Kreme nearby. Otherwise, I can't help you." They both laughed. She pinched him on his arm. "I'm going over to play my machine." She said. "I should have known better. Than to come to the Police for help without a doughnut." "Just for that." André said. "I'm going to find the guy. Then tell him to kidnap you again." They were interrupted by a waitress, coming to take their drink orders.

"Can I get you two anything to drink?" The waitress asked. "Yeah, she'll have a Malibu and pineapple." André said. "I'll have a Crown and Coke." The waitress wrote down their order and left. "Hey, give me ten dollars for her tip please." André asked. "All of my money has been designated for various charities." "No Sir." Sabrina replied. "You made me leave my purse. You told me to use my money only for emergency. You trying to get us drunk is not an emergency."

Back near André's house. A Commercial Plumbing truck was coming down his street. The occupants in the commercial truck spotted André's house. They then saw an SUV leaving from in front of Andrés' house. "Isn't that the house we're going to boss?" The driver of the plumbing truck asked. "Yeah, that's the house." The passenger said. Nobody was supposed to be here." "Maybe they were just pulled over to text someone." The Driver said. "They saw us coming and figured we lived here. So they left." "Well, that could be it." The passenger said. "People are bold. To park in front of someone's house this time of night." Their truck backed into André's driveway. Parking outside his garage.

The driver sat and appeared to fill out a form on a clipboard. He and the passenger walked around to the back of the house. "Oh, how nice." The passenger said. "The customer left his ladder back here. Laying on the ground. "We don't even need to use ours." The Driver said. "This will get us to that window." "Yeah, we're good on that." The passenger responded. "Let's go get the tool bag, my cell phone and charger. Then you can take the truck. Park it back at the port." "Sounds like a plan." the driver said. They walked back up to the truck and took their respective seats. The driver handed over the requested items.

"Hey, are you sure you're going to be alright boss? The driver asked. "Yes, I'll be good for the time this job may take." Michael replied. "Okay cool." James said. "I have to get back down to the job. We have a ship coming in tonight. With some new luxury vehicles. One of those cars may get lost and end up at my house." "Oh, is that what you guys do down at the port?" Michael asked. "I have to pay for my shit. You guys just take them off the docks." "Membership has its privileges." James replied. "It also has some risk too." "What do you mean?" Michael asked. "Well, sometime around 1:00pm tomorrow. We're expecting a Russian cargo ship."

"It's coming into the Dundalk Marine Terminal." James continued. "Reportedly, people in our Government. Are very interested in that shipment." "Is that unusual or something?" Michael asked. "Not necessarily unusual." James replied. "I mean. We have had plenty of instances. When Government agencies, have been interested in ships coming to port. Like the FBI may want to meet a ship. Suspected of carrying drugs or other contraband." Or the State Department flags a ship. That may have sanctioned individuals on it. What's weird about this is. Nobody will say which Government agency. Is pegging this ship. All we know is. They absolutely don't want us to open any of the containers. There is supposed to be some sort of Military convoy arriving."

"They're taking possession of whatever is on that ship. Which is really weird." "Do you know the name of the ship?" Michael asked. "It's called the Kidslovus or something like that." James replied. "Could it be the Kislovodsk?" Michael asked. "Give me that clipboard and pen you're holding." Michael said. He took the pen and wrote the word; 'Kislovodsk.' "Is this the name of the ship you guys are waiting on?" "Yes, that's the name on the manifest list." James replied.

"Except we don't know what's being carried." James continued. "Or offloaded onto our piers. That's making most of the guys really nervous." "Do you know where the Military convoy is taking the containers?" Michael asked. "When they load them onto the trucks?" "Man, they won't tell us shit about this cargo." James said. "Normally, we open one or two containers on a ship. Just at random. To make sure. It is what the sender said it was supposed to be. They are not letting any of our guys. Near that Russian ship when it arrives.

Chapter 7
What kind of ship?

"In fact, we all had to sign a waiver." James continued. "Saying we will not even discuss the ships arrival. It's cargo or departure with anyone. For telling you, I could be fired. I just heard you speaking Russian a few times. Which is weird for a black man. No offense." "None taken." Michael replied. "Anyways, being that you're a black guy." James said. "I figured you couldn't be a Russian spy. Just maybe. You might be able to make sense out of this." "Let me reach out to someone." Michael said. "See what I can find out." He then unlocked his phone and opened his secure email. He began to type.

To: Apsk13@gmail.ru.

Hey Atpyt,

How are you, my friend? I hope this email finds you well. I need a favor from you. I hope you can help me out with. I have Intel that the Kislovodsk is headed to Baltimore Md. With cargo that nobody here can discuss. I know it is a great risk to you. If you can find out what is on that ship? What's the purpose of it coming here? I would be very grateful. I look forward to returning to Saratov. Sitting in your study to play another game of Chess. I do understand if the risk is too great for you. So don't trouble yourself unnecessarily. However, any information you may find. May help me figure out what these two countries are up to.

Sincerely;

Michael Baryshev Kungawo

Хорошо мой друг

P.S. There is an unopened bottle of premium Vodka. In the kitchen cabinet of my apartment. You have the key. Go on over and have a drink for me. Make yourself at home.

"Who were you texting?" James asked. "I wasn't texting." Michael said. "I was sending an email to an old friend of mine. Actually, he was a friend of my mother's." "Does he work for one of the Government agencies here in Maryland?" James asked. "No, he works in Russia." Michael responded. "Russia!" James replied astonishingly. "Yes, my mother was Russian." Michael said. "My father is Nigerian. They met at the University of Baltimore Law School. They fell in love and poof. I was born. Both of them insisted on two things for me."

"That I visit both of their homelands." Michael continued. To know my origins. Then I had to learn to speak multiple languages. When I visited Russia. It was like, surprise. Racism is there too. Despite that, I made some friends. Because my mother had taught me the language. She also introduced me to some of her friends. Some of them had strong ties. To Russian Intelligence and the old GRU. Through those contacts. I can often find out what is going on in the Kremlin. The guy I just emailed, is a good friend of my mother. He really helped protect me from bullies. When I visited as a child."

"When I visited Nigeria. It was amazing. I felt more at home than compared to America. Over there, you motherfuckers are the outsiders. We're just brothers and sisters." "Yeah, but in Nigeria, they have a lot of warfare correct?" James asked. "Not as much as they have in Russia." Michael replied. "Nigeria hasn't invaded neighboring countries. Such as Cameroon the way Russia did Crimea. Killing people and stealing resources. Like your ancestors did. You white motherfuckers kill me. Always trying to put down non-white nations. When you fight among yourselves ten times more viciously and violently. Russia, truth be told, is a violent country.

Most of those motherfuckers don't have billions. Like their ruthless so-called leader." "Well, I have to get this truck back." James said. "To the port and start my shift. Besides, it's going to be daylight soon. So you should get inside before traffic picks up. We wouldn't want someone to see. The plumbing guy climbing up through a window." "Yeah, you're right." Michael said. "Let me get inside with my empty pickle jars. My food water and toilet paper. Most importantly, my only connection to the outside world. My cellphone. Thank God you can watch television shows on these things. Or I might go crazy. Next time I see you James. I'll let you know about that Russian ship."

"Sure Mr. Kungawo. Next time you see me." James replied. Michael exits the truck and walked to the back of the house. He then put his duffle bag strap over his shoulders. Climbing up to the guest room. James places the ladder back and leaves. Inside Michael found a small refrigerator. Sabrina had stocked it with sandwich meats. Along with fresh fruits and vegetables. There was also a case of water in the closet. "Damn, this is going to be even better than expected." Michael thought. "Now all I have to do is lay low. Wait for the opportunity to kill this motherfucker. Meanwhile, let me log onto my television app. Put on my earbuds to pass the time. The shit I do for love. Oh and half a billion dollars too. He smiled to himself. He scrolled through his App in search of something to watch.

Later that day off the coast of San Francisco. A tour boat arrived at Alcatraz Island. Several anxious tourists clamored to the side of the boat. It was within a few hundred yards away from docking. Tourists have been told that there was a special guest on the Island. The Chairman of the House Intelligence Committee. He was taking the tour with his family. The tourists have been told that Security was tighter than normal. They were aware they may have to wait. To go into some areas instead of having the freedom to walk around.

As the tour boat docked, the tourists could see the Chairman. He was giving an interview to various media groups. Tourist saw their opportunity to move freely on the island. They were directed to put on their headphones. So they could listen to the voices of some of the actual inmates. Recorded when prisoners were there. In the middle of their tour, the guests were asked to clear out. The Chairman had made his way into the cellblock area. With his family and the media in tow. The Chairman took some photos. In front of the waxed uniformed guards. He then remarked. Saying how courageous men and women like these were. To live on this island to keep us safe.

He paused again under an old photo. It was of inmates being admitted. The picture had a caption. Which read; *"Break the rules and you go to prison, break the prison rules and you go to Alcatraz."* The Chairman stopped again to speak. "We need to bring a place like this back." He said. "To finally get tough on crime. Too many criminals in our society. Know they can get away with murder. Because the courts won't punish them. Thank God our President is putting Judges in place. That will finally address that issue." "Congressman, are you advocating for Alcatraz to be reopened?" A reporter asked. "Well, we have to do something." The Chairman said. "Alcatraz closed because it was too expensive. For the Government to operate."

"However, if we could have private businesses find a way." He continued. "To make it cost-effective. I'd certainly look at their proposals." The Chairman then headed to D-Block. To the cell that used to house the one and only. Alphonse Capone. "In this very cell." The Chairman said. "Was one of the most ruthless and violent criminals. That ever preyed on our society. "Congressman, can we get a photo?" Another reporter asked. "Of you inside the cell." The Chairman smiled and happily obliged. He stepped inside the cell. Making sure his Security detail was nearby. The cameras flashed. They took his photo numerous times. One particular flash was very bright. It caused the Chairman to squint. Putting his hand in front of his face.

"Speaking of criminals, Mr. Chairman." A voice yelled. "We've been watching you in the shadows." The Congressman instantly recognized the phrase. "Security, it's time to leave." The chairman said. He tried to step out of the cell hurriedly. A large man wearing a hoodie, blocked his path. The hooded man stepped inside the cell with him. The Congressman again called for Security. They, along with everyone else. Was being pushed out of the area. The only one left outside the cell was Mr. C. "My family is right upstairs." The Congressman pleaded. "I'll give them your regards." Mr. C. replied. Mr. C. then nodded to the man in the hoodie.

The hooded man started viciously stabbing the Chairman. On the side of his head and neck. The Congressman's head was almost severed. He fell lifeless to the floor. "Shall we do lunch after you get cleaned up?" Mr. C. asked. He put on his dark shades and baseball hat. The hat looked extremely out of place with his suit and coat. However, it did provide an adequate cover for his face. He walked up to the dock. Where tourists were boarding the boat to return to San Francisco. He walked up to the boat and was handed a megaphone. "Ladies and gentlemen." Mr. C. said. "I do sincerely apologize for the abrupt end to your tour."

"However, because you have all been so wonderfully cooperative. The tour will reopen in about two hours. You can come back then. If you don't wish to come back, we can understand that. Since you all paid with credit cards. We have your information on file. You can just request a refund. When you get back ashore. Oh, I almost forgot. None of your cellphones are working right now. We had to pull data from them. They all pinged off the cell tower here. From your cell phone and credit card information. We can find anyone of you. That is should you want to talk. About what you think you may have seen here today. Don't panic good people. Nobody is going to harm any of you. What kind of people do you think we are?

"We will however." Mr. C. continued. Upload to your phones hidden files of child porn. Perhaps Anti-Government sentiment. Maybe requests on making bomb material. By the time you get out of prison. You would have long forgotten. Whatever it was you thought you saw here. That's if you're lucky. I mean. I've seen people get stabbed in prison before. They didn't make it. I can remember it like it just happened. Now should you doubt who I am. I'm going to turn your cellphones back on. I'll call each one of you right now." Mr. C. nodded his head. Suddenly, everyone's cell phone began to ring. The tourists were all shocked. They showed each other their cell phones. Showing an unknown number calling. They each also received a text message on their phone.

"If you should ever discuss this day with anyone. Jesus will not be able to save you from me." After about 25 seconds, the text disappeared. When they finally looked up, Mr. C. was gone. "Where did he go?" One of the reporters asked. A voice over the P.A. system called out. "Don't worry, I can still see you. When you're home tonight with your families. I'll still be able to see you. Enjoy your trip back and thank you for visiting Alcatraz." "This is unbelievable." A white woman in her 40s said. "What's unbelievable?" A black woman in her 30s answered. "I have no fucking idea what you're talking about. Your stupid ass needs to not know, what you're talking about either. I don't know who that was. But THAT motherfucker is not to be played with." Everyone around the two ladies nodded their heads in agreement.

The boat arrived back onto the mainland of San Francisco. The tourists debarked and some were obviously shaken up. They walked past various shops in Pier 39. They saw televisions in some of the stores and shops. The televisions were all playing breaking news. The Chairman of the House Intelligence Committee. Had announced his abrupt resignation from Congress. A spokesperson for the Congressman told Joy Reid. That the Congressman's wife had a severe medical crisis.

The family was flying immediately to Europe. Where she would be able to undergo a stem cell procedure. Other members of Congress reportedly were shocked. They had no idea the Chairman was considering this. A Statement from the Speaker of the House read in part; *"The Chairman is a dear friend of mine. I wished he had shared with me his family's crisis. So that we could have been more supportive to them. In this time of crisis. However, nothing is more important than family. So I completely understand."*

When asked who may be up for taking the Chairman's place? The Speaker stated that it had not been decided yet. "Wow, they have it on all the news stations that he resigned." The white woman in her 40s said. Another middle-aged white male who was on the boat spoke. "That's because, that's what the fuck happened. You dumb bitch! Your ass will be the next motherfucker. They'll be talking about on the news. If you think that guy was a joke."

Back in Atlantic City. André and Sabrina were having lunch on the boardwalk. "Thanks for getting us a room here." Sabrina said. "I didn't know if I could have made it. All the way back to Maryland this morning. Besides your being naughty on the way up here. Then keeping us in the Casino until almost 4:00am this morning. I needed sleep. "That was a lot of money to spend." André said. "For just about seven hours in a damn hotel room. Plus, I didn't get my dick sucked because you were tired."

"Negro, you took your shower." Sabrina replied. "Left me in there, and was sleep before I dried off." "I don't need to be awake to get my dick sucked." André replied. "My dick has Auto-suck pilot." "You are a damn nut job." Sabrina laughed. "Hurry up and finish your food. So you can buy me a funnel cake." "Oh yeah." André agreed. "We cannot come up here to the boardwalk and not get a funnel cake."

"Funnel cake, lemonade, the boardwalk with a nice warm breeze." Sabrina said. "Not too many things are better than that." "Nothing." André said. "Except funnel cake, lemonade, the boardwalk. With a warm breeze and you sucking my dick. While I'm eating funnel cake and spilling powdered sugar in your hair." "Is that all you think about all the time?" Sabrina asked. "No, not at all woman." André said. "What kind of pervert do you think I am?" "I think about ice cream and you sucking my dick too." Sabrina pinched him on his arm again. "What am I going to do with you?" She asked.

"Can I make some suggestions?" André asked. "No, I already know what you're going to say." Sabrina replied. "Now, let's go get that funnel cake and lemonade. I want powdered sugar and strawberries too." "Damn, you know that's going to cost about $20 right?" André asked. "Getting you all of that stuff. What am I getting for spending all of that kind of money?" "I'll give you a kiss and let you hold my hand." Sabrina replied. "In that case." André replied. "Money is no object. I may even spring to get you some napkins." "Oh, you're going all out for a sister, aren't you?" Sabrina joked.

Back at Andrés' house. Michael was laying in the guest bed when his phone vibrated. It was a notification of an email. It was sent from Apsk13@gmail.ru.

Michael, I looked into that information you asked me about. It is quite alarming. You need to call me immediately!

Your friend;

Atpyt

Michael carefully got up to check. Making sure he heard no voices in André's house. He then dialed the number. Atpyt answered on the first ring. "Michael, Holy shit!" Atpyt said. "I don't even know where to begin."

"It appears Russia and members of your Government. Have come up with a truly horrifying plot. Russia has been trying. To become a major player in the pharmaceutical industry. Except the Government won't spend the money. Necessary to fund such grand aspirations. What Russia will fund fully without any hesitation. Is chemical warfare. It appears your President had a side meeting with ours. At a summit the two of them attended. During that side meeting, our Presidents solidified a deal. First brokered by your National Security Advisor. That deal was to supply your Government, with a cheaper flu shot."

"Intelligence agents from the Kremlin first pitched the idea. When your National Security advisor Mr. Davenport. Attended a function here. Other operatives have compromised members of your U.S. Congress and Senate. We launched campaigns to help them gerrymander and win elections. By providing them with sizable contributions. The pitch for our flu shots. Was that it would save your country money. Also, it would help Russia establish itself. As a viable alternate to U.S.-made medicines. In exchange for your President signing this deal. Russia is going to send $150 billion dollars into his personal account. Russia will make that money three-fold. By getting your health insurance companies to pay for this vaccine."

"This deal also includes significant cash windfalls. For several key members of your Congress and Senate. Money for their personal accounts as well. The issue is. The flu vaccine Russia shipped to your country. Contains Novichok-5 broken down in molecular composition. They took science intended to save life. Then found another way to destroy it. A Ugandan Scientist named Adroa Kiyonga. Found a way to kill the AIDS virus. By resurrecting the dead T-cells. That die in battle fighting the disease. He found the cells could be isolated. Just as they attack the AIDS virus. Once isolated, they could be made dormant. By an injection of a derivative from the Button spider. The Button spider as you know. Is found commonly in Southern Africa. It's venom causes paralysis.

"These injections to the T-Cells. Prior to them being killed by the AIDS virus. Tricks the virus into thinking the T-Cells are dead. The T-Cells remain dormant for approximately 90 days. In their dormant state. The T-Cells are no longer attacked by the AIDS virus. The T-Cells then recover stronger. Becoming immune to the AIDS virus. These T-cells now full of life, violently attack the AIDS virus. The AIDS virus doesn't fight back. Due to its sensory perception telling it. That these T-Cells are already dead. When the AIDS virus realizes it's being attacked by the T-Cells. It mounts a gallant attempt to fight back. By then the AIDS virus is wounded so immensely. That any resistance to the T-Cells are futile."

"They kill the virus and wipe it completely out of the human body. Russian scientist took the published research. Done by Doctor Kiyonga and duplicated it. However, they found a way. To separate the non-toxic components of the drug Novichok-5. Which digest and absorb slowly over time. They put separate components of the drug. In the dead flu virus which is standard in a flu shot. The other components in the dormant T-cells. This flu shot your government will fail to disclose. Came from Russia. Once injected into the human body. The T-Cells will begin their 90-day recovery period. Once all the components meet in the human digestive tract. They will become super reactive causing death within hours."

"Now that these shipments are being delivered to your country. They will be transported to every Military base. Along with as many hospitals as possible. Your President will sign an Executive Order. Directing all members of the Military. They must get the new flu shots. As you know, most members of the Military. Will not be able to refuse such a directive. Ninety-percent of your men and women serving in the Military. Both there and abroad, will be dead by the time the season changes. As well with a significant portion. Of your civilian population. Death will be far away in time. From when the flu shots were administered.

"Doctors will struggle to find a cause. We're talking about 45% or 135 million people in America. Infected with this deadly toxin. Within six months of your President signing this Executive Order. Another 60 million will become infected. From the contagion of the virus being passed on. By those that come in contact with infected persons. Immediately after signing this Executive Order. Your President will travel to Moscow. He will claim his Secretary of Health won't let him return. Until they find out what's going on. However, he will really be there to watch his country die. Your streets will be littered with dead bodies. From Vermont to San Diego. Michael, if the Kremlin and your President carry out this plan. Two-thirds of the entire population of America will die."

"They will be dead before the end of this year. With the $150-billion-dollar windfall. Your President will jump to the number one spot of wealthiest Americans. He is surpassing Mr. Bezos in a single bound. By murdering most of your country. Almost certainly, there will be no one to challenge him. For authoritarian rule. Every person who doesn't die will be filled with grief and fear. From losing so many loved ones. They will be in no mood or condition. To stand up to your President. Russian Military and tanks will roll down Pennsylvania Ave. Backing and establishing your President as a dictator. However, he will reign to only do the beckoning of the Kremlin."

"He will turn over nuclear codes. Security codes and any information the Kremlin demands. Moscow will be granted rights to American-made movies. Music, and television shows. They will become the owners of Technology companies in Silicon Valley. They will then imprison without charges. All Asians, Jews, poor Whites and of course, African-Americans. Those prisons will become concentration camps. After Russia has the vast majority of Americans in these camps. They will make Nazi-Germany look like a nice place to vacation. The Kremlin, at some point. Will direct its troops to seize your President. Along with the members of Congress who helped them."

"They will be brought to the concentration camp in Lorton, Virginia. Where they will be tortured for any intelligence information. About operatives and facilities abroad. Then they will be murdered on a live streaming broadcast. By decapitation with a guillotine. Russia began making and shipping these devices to Isis and Al-Queda. Back in the late 90s. After Osama Bin Laden turned his anger towards the U.S. These two former enemies began a backroom partnership. That partnership remained relatively obscured from the world view. The two continued to act like enemies in public. Yet, both had the goal of destroying America."

"My enemy's, enemy is my friend." Michael said. "This cannot be right. I knew the President wasn't shit, but I could never have imagined he would do this." "Michael, the vaccines are in similar bottles." Atpyt continued. "To the standard flu shot bottles typically used in the U.S. However, you can tell which are toxic. They are marked with the word Novck-5 on the label. However, you can only see it using ultraviolet light. They will most likely be stored with flu bottles. Left over from last season. The vaccines are headed first down to a storage facility. On the Snowden River Parkway in Columbia Maryland. Not far from the NSA. There, they will be divided. Then designated for delivery to locations. They will be loaded onto military convoy trucks."

"Those trucks will be headed down to Andrews Air Force Base. In Capitol Heights, Maryland. Michael, I don't have to tell you. Once those trucks reach Andrews. It will be nearly mission impossible to get on base and stop this plot." "Fuck!" Michael said. "What the fuck is this stupid ass, motherfucking excuse for a President thinking?" "I don't know what he is thinking either." Atpyt said. "However, I also found out there are a few containers on that ship. That are actually carrying, Russian Special Forces personnel. They are being smuggled into your country. With full knowledge of the White House. Their containers have air holes and food. Even an opening to relieve themselves off the side of the ship.

"Once they are let out of the containers. They will spread out and cut off the water supply. At water treatment facilities by blowing up the infrastructure. In Baltimore, Washington, Philadelphia, Newark, New York City and Boston. Your President will tell you everything is under control. That they are working to fix it. These cities will be left devastated like Puerto Rico. Store shelves will go empty. People will panic. The one place your citizens can get free bottled water. Will be at the same locations they can get the flu shot. A case of water for each member of the family. If they get a flu shot."

"Every mother will bring her children down. To their imminent death in search of water. I'm going to send you the identifiers for the containers. The ones housing Russian Special Forces. If you can stop them before they are let out. You will save millions of lives. Let me attach the file with all the information on it. I'll email it to you right now Michael. Hold on. Atpyt paused. "I just heard a noise in the other room." "GET THE FUCK OUT OF THERE, ATPYT! Michael yelled. "It's okay Michael." Atpyt replied. "If I can help stop something this horrific. Then I am prepared to meet my fate. It was a pleasure watching you grow up. Into such a fine example of a man."

"Be well, my friend." Michael heard the sound of a door burst open. He heard Russian voices yelling in the background. He heard his friend Atpyt, speak also in Russian. "Fuck вы демонов!" Atpyt said. Multiple automatic rifle shots. Rang out on the other end of the phone. Michael heard his longtime friend murdered. The roar of automatic weapons goes on for seemingly forever. Until a voice said, "достаточное" (Enough). He heard footsteps walking towards the phone. Then the phone being picked up off the floor. He then heard someone breathing. Michael quickly hung up the phone, as he grieved his friend. The tears began to flow down his face. Suddenly his phone rang. The caller I.D. read Atpyt. Michael knew that it was not his friend calling.

Michael was about to smash the phone. Then he suddenly remembered. He looked at his phone and saw an email notification. He tried to open the email but his phone rang again. Once again, the caller I.D. read Atpyt. He allowed it to ring until voicemail picked up. He knew rejecting the call would confirm to the caller. That someone saw the call coming in, chosing not to answer. When the phone stopped ringing, he attempted to open the email. His phone began to flash. He knew someone was sending a virus to his phone. So he quickly switched it off. He knew if that virus was allowed to upload. He would not have access to any data on his phone.

He removed the sim card and went to his duffle bag. There, he had a backup phone. He removed the back cover from it. He inserted the sim card into a small Ziploc bag. Placing it inside the duffle bag. Using his pre-paid phone. He now logged into all his accounts individually. He quickly went to his secure email, where Atpyt had just sent the file. He forwarded that email to his personal unsecured email. He sent a copy to Jasmine and two separate accounts of his. Accounts from different internet service providers. Now, who in the fuck, can I get this information to?" Michael pondered. "That might stop this shit? This is truly some unbelievable shit. Jasmine, I hope you check your email woman, I could really use some advice."

At Union Station in Washington DC. A small Congressional delegation was assembled. They were boarding a Maryland Commuter Rail train to West Virginia. Capitol Police were also traveling with them. They were there protecting the congress members. Once onboard, they saw three officers from the Maryland Transit Police Department. Officer Wiggins of the Capitol Police walked over to the MTA Police. "Wow, we don't usually see you guys travel this far down from Baltimore." Officer Wiggins said. "Not unless it's one of your motorcycle officers."

"Yeah, we know." Officer Gaines replied. "Our Chief, Colonel Delaney wanted us to be here. "You know how that goes. It's not like we had a choice." The train started moving. The standing officers grabbed the rails to hold on. Officer Stewart grabbed the mic of her Police radio. "9Mary23 to KMT. We are in motion southbound. En-route to the end of the line at this time." "10-4 9Mary23." Dispatch replied. "Your time is 1343 hours." "He told our Captain Nichols." Officer Gaines continued. "To pick three people." "For some reasons, he picked me. Officer Stewart and Officer Bellamy.

I'm a motorcycle patrol officer. Officer Bellamy is a pistol range instructor. Officer Stewart does Cyber Investigations." "Oh, she hacks into people's computers? For your department?" Officer Wiggins said. "Mostly cell phones but I can hack into computers too." Officer Stewart said. "A few of us wanted to get that training." Officer Bellamy said. "Our Captain picked her. Probably because she wears knee pads, when she goes in his office." "Excuse you." Officer Stewart said. "I don't use knee pads. I use a towel." They all laughed. "She's probably not lying." Officer Gaines said. "He does call you to his office a few times. Then you're in there after work sometimes."

"That's because his computer is the one with the hacking software on it." Officer Stewart replied. "They don't want just any officer or cleaning personnel. To be able to log into that stuff. I have people's personal information I need to print out for court. He has a private printer in his office. They want the least number of eyes. On people's personal information as possible." "Well, at least, you don't have to babysit." Officer Wiggins said. "A bunch of Congress people who think they're elected by God. Talk about multiple pains in the ass. Getting fucked by King Kong in my ass wouldn't hurt as much. Compared to dealing with these pricks. "Boy, I could only imagine how quickly." Officer Stewart said. "I would have been fired if I had to deal with them."

"Yeah, Stewart has no filter on her mouth." Officer Bellamy said. "She would have cursed the Speaker out." "He'd be like, 'Officer, can you get my coat?' Officer Stewart said. "I'd be like, 'Get Deez tits out your mouth motherfucker'" "I'd either get promoted or fired." They all laughed. "So where in West Virginia are they going?" Officer Bellamy asked. "Oh, they're going to The Greenbrier." Officer Wiggins said. To look at the old Congressional Bunker. The one that they designated for Congress. To survive nuclear war. They have a ride waiting at the train station. It is going to take them to Sulphur Springs."

"That place was deactivated in the 90s, wasn't it?" Officer Bellamy asked. "Yes, once the public found out." Officer Wiggins said. "About the amount of money it cost. And that they weren't included in the survival plan." "Excuse me but is anybody wondering?" Officer Stewart asked. "Why they are going there now? I mean, do they know of some pending shit? That we might need to know?" "I've asked myself that same question." Officer Wiggins said. "If I see these motherfuckers, start to bring their families down here. I'm calling in sick. Then I'm getting a one-way plane ticket. For me and my family out of the country." "You don't think they would tell the Capitol Police?" Officer Stewart asked. "You have protected them all these years. They should tell you what's going on?"

"Man, these folks only love us." Officer Wiggins said. "When the cameras are on. Next week, they are making all of us, get the flu shot at work. They say they don't want us to get sick and pass it on to Congress." "What?" Officer Bellamy asked. "They can make all of you get a flu shot? Even if you don't want to get one?" "Yes, this order didn't even come from our Police Department." Officer Wiggins said. "It came from Congress. All of us who work on Capitol Hill has to get a shot. Or we can't work on Capitol Hill. If we can't work on the Hill. Then we cannot possibly do this job. It involves working in and around the Hill mostly. So, we have a choice. Get a shot or put in our papers to retire or resign."

"That's fucked up." Officer Gaines said. "I don't get flu shots because they give you the flu virus. To supposedly protect you from it. What kind of shit is that? Half the people who get the flu shot. End up getting sick. From that motherfucking shot anyway." "I don't know if it's half the people." Officer Wiggins replied. "But yes, people do get sick from the flu shot." "It would be interesting if we could pull the data." Officer Stewart said. "To see if all the people who died from the flu. In the last year. Had a flu shot in the last few years? I wouldn't put nothing past those motherfuckers sitting up there. They'd kill our ass in a heartbeat. For a check from the pharmaceutical industry. That's why they should put term limits on these motherfuckers." Officer Bellamy said.

"Make drug companies work to cultivate relationships. That would be better. Than having one in their pocket for twenty or thirty years. Making policies that hurt the public." "These bastards don't give a damn about the public." Officer Gaines said. "They get elected and will have a pension and health insurance. For the rest of their lives. Healthcare we pay for. Then they do everything they could. To take away our healthcare." Suddenly, the train slowed down. Everyone looked out the window. They were not pulling into a train station. Officer Wiggins was summoned back. To where the Congress personnel were seated. "What the hell is going on out here?" Officer Bellamy asked. "I don't like being stopped in a wooded area. With a bunch of white men on the train."

"If those motherfuckers try something funny." Officer Stewart said. "It'll be a shootout on this bitch. Hell, I got PMS. I have ADD, N.W.A and any other alphabets I need. I'd rather be judged by 12, than carried by six any day." The train came to a complete stop. The detail of Capitol Police were standing in guard. Of the Congressional delegation. Suddenly, the conductor came back. He opened the door to the train car. Then placed a stepping stool on the ground. Stepping onboard the train was Mr. Vailati. Along with Chief Delaney.

Chief Delaney was not wearing his Police Uniform. He was wearing a double-breasted suit. Boarding behind him were Director Tolbert and Baker. Wearing black suits and dark glasses. Both carried Bushmaster AR-15 rifles with extended clips. "Good afternoon." Mr. Vailati said. Ladies and gentlemen of Congress. My name is Mr. Vailati. "This is Colonel Doug Delaney of the Maryland Transit Police Department. There is a security threat. We need you to exit the train and come with us." "I'm sorry." Congressman Grimes said. "You said he was Chief of the Transit Police, correct?"

"What department did you say you were with?" "I'm with the department." Mr. Vailati replied. "That is telling you to get your old ass off this motherfucking train. Notice I didn't say I was asking. That's who I am. Now ask me another stupid question. The last vote you cast in Congress. Is going to be the last vote you casted in Congress. Mr. Vailati then turned to the officers. "All of you Capitol Police are relieved of your duties. Go to the rear car and read the Post or something. Right now, your radios and cell phones do not work. So don't think about pushing that Signal-13 button. No sending a text or making a phone call either. In approximately 27 minutes. A northbound train will arrive at this location. Taking you back to Union Station."

"You'll be met by Lieutenant Rustin who will brief you. On what you can and cannot talk about. I strongly suggest you take heed to his words. As if your life depended on it. Oh, one last thing." Mr. Vailati continued. "You guys are valiant officers with excellent records. One of you may feel a little heroic and want to hatch a plan. To save these Congress people. Let me assure you of two things. These bastards would let you die for a few rubles if given the opportunity." As Mr. Vailati said those words, Congressman Henson bowed his head. "Secondly, let me assure you that your service weapons and vest. Will not stop these armor-piercing bullets. Bullets that penetrate the metal of this train and will seek you out.

"That will really mess up." Mr. Vailati continued. "Your family dinner tonight. When that plate is just sitting there waiting. Go home and eat dinner with your families." The Capitol Police walked towards the back of the train. "MTA Police." Mr. Vailati said. "Help us escort these Congress men and women. Off this train. If any one of them tries to run. I need you to make sure you duck to not get shot. The Police assisted all the Congress persons off the train. They walked them over to a non-descript black van. The van had District of Columbia tags. The tags read "BShadO." Congressman Henson took mental note of the tag. He and the other nine members. Were loaded into the van by the MTA Police. Mr. Vailati and Chief Delaney looked on.

Officer Bellamy then closed the side panel door. Ensuring everyone was inside. The van began to drive off. As it does, the tags changed to Virginia tags. They now read; "End-5385". The van drove up the dirt road and made a right into the wooded area. "Thank you, Chief Delaney." Mr. Vailati said. For assisting us with this critical matter. I knew you would come around to wanting to help us. You can send your people back. On the train to Washington. You can come with me and the Directors. I'm going to show you proof. That you're playing for the right team." "Officer Stewart." Chief Delaney yelled. "Get everybody back on the train. Wait for that northbound!" "Yes Sir." She replied. "Do you need me to stay with you Sir?"

"No, I'm good Stewart." Chief Delaney said. "Advise KMT to have a unit pick you up at Penn Station. "You guys can go 10-7 once you get to the office. Head home to your families." "You don't have to tell me twice Sir." She said. "Just call me if you, oh. That's right our phones and radios don't work." "Service will return." Mr. Vailati said. "To both devices once you're briefed at Union Station. Then you'll have a non-stop train to Baltimore's Penn Station." "Hey, that sounds like a plan." Officer Stewart said. "You gentlemen have a good evening." "Oh, Officer Stewart." Mr. Vailati said. "One more thing. "Yes Sir." Officer Stewart replied.

"You seem to be a sharp officer." Mr. C. continued. "A very observant officer. If you ever find yourself in some scenario. Where you may need resources above the norm. Dial this number." He handed her a black business card. "No one will answer." He said. "The number will go immediately to dial tone. However, someone will call you back expeditiously." Back on board the train. Officer Bellamy and Gaines approached Officer Stewart. "What the fuck was that all about?" Officer Bellamy asked. "Probably some nut case threatening the Congress." Officer Stewart said. "It probably came in as a credible threat. You know they will do anything to protect Congress."

"If that's true?" Officer Gaines asked. "Why was that man talking all nasty to the Congressman?" "You know how it is." Officer Stewart said. "They probably don't have time to be explaining everything to them. They knew that Congressman. Was about to ask a whole bunch of dumb ass question. That man was like. Look motherfucker, I'm trying to save your life. "Well, maybe they will tell us more at this briefing in DC." Officer Bellamy said. "Once we get to Union Station. Speaking of the devil. Here comes the train we need to switch to right now."

André and Sabrina were on the New Jersey Turnpike. Returning from Atlantic City. "Thanks for taking me to have such a good time André. She said. "This was a really nice trip." "Don't try to be nice to me now." André replied. "You're just scared that I may take you off the road again. That you might get fucked……………………up." "I wish you would call yourself trying to fuck me……………..up." Sabrina teased. "I would really have to show my ass. If you put your hands on me." "Oh you're trying to get fucked…………up." André said. "Talking all of that trash." "I want to see." Sabrina responded. If you're big and bad enough to fuck me………..up." "You're lucky it's broad daylight out here." André said. "Wait until we get home. I'm going to fuck you……………..up good."

"Oh, you're afraid of the sunlight too?" Sabrina teased. "What are you? A Vampire and a punk?" "Oh, you're running your mouth." André said. "Over there in that seat. I'm going to see what your mouth can do. When we get in the house." André said. "Whatever you say, Chicken George." Sabrina joked. "Oh okay, keep talking over there." André said. "We'll see how much you have to say. When I ram this big chocolate dick in your pussy." They arrived at the toll booth coming back into Delaware. André looked over at Sabrina. "Let me get a few dollars." He asked. "To pay for this toll. Since you spent all my cash on funnel cakes and lemonade." "You told me this cash was for me." She replied. "Since you've been a gentleman. I guess I can let you have a few dollars."

She handed him the money for the toll. André paid and drove on. "Hey, do we need to stop anywhere." He asked. "Before we get back home?" "I guess we could get some solid food." She replied. "Before we go in. Lord knows I don't feel like cooking tonight. I know you don't either. You have to go in for that ceremony tomorrow, right?" "Yeah." André replied. That stupid idiot they call President. Will be here in Baltimore." "That motherfucker is not my fucking President." Sabrina huffed. "My President was the black guy that left office. Without him or any of his people. Being investigated or indicted." "Oh, you mean back in the day." André asked. "When they had real Presidents?"

"What do you want to get to eat woman." He asked. "I don't know." Sabrina replied. We can stop at that nice Caribbean spot. The one off of Route 24 in Edgewood." "That salmon is the God's honest, gospel, Holy Ghost, sanctified truth." "Yes Lawd." André added. "We can eat there and then go home." "Sounds like a plan to me." Sabrina said. They arrived at the restaurant. André went around to open her door. Sabrina turned her phone on, as they entered the restaurant. Her phone started to ding and ring. From all the emails, texts and social media notifications.

She began looking at her phone. She could see she received an email from Michael. It was marked "urgent". André was speaking to the waitress. About where they would sit. He turned to see Sabrina wasn't paying attention. So he gently pulled her arm to follow the waitress. Sabrina typed a quick text to Michael. Letting him know they were not far from the house. She advised him that they were eating at the restaurant. So he had time to shit, shower and shave. If he had not done so. She reminded him to make sure he cleaned the restroom. To dry out the shower. On the rare chance André comes up there. She got a response text.

Michael: Have you read the email I sent?

Sabrina: No, I haven't had time yet, but I will soon. I have to go, ttyl.

"Now what are we having, Mr. Nichols?" She asked. "The way you look." André said. "I'd like to come across this table. Have you right in this restaurant." "Is that right, Officer?" She said coyly. "How bad do you want it? Sabrina asked. "Drop those panties and I'll show you." He said. They were suddenly interrupted by the waitress. With a heavy Jamaican accent. "Hi, my name is Nicole." The waitress said. "I'll be your server today. What can I get you to drink?" "I'll have some Sorrel drink." Sabrina said. "I'll have some cream soda." André added. "Okay, I'll be right back to take your orders." Nicole said.

She walked away and André continued. "Take off those panties. I will eat you right here in this restaurant." "Now who's talking trash?" Sabrina said. "You live right down the street from this place. You do not want these people calling your department. Telling how freaky you are." "I'm not scared of these moarfuggers in here." André said. "You're just a punk, Sabrina." André said. "Anyway, I think I'll have the Salmon." She said. "What are you going to have André?" "I think I'm going with the Jerk chicken." He said. Just then, Nicole returned with their drinks. "Now what can I get you two?" She asked.

André placed their orders. He asked Sabrina if she needed to go to the restroom. Before he did. She excused herself. Going to wash her hands and freshen up. As soon as she left, André went out to his vehicle. He opened the rear door of his SUV. He grabbed his pre-paid phone. Sending a text and anxiously awaited a reply. After an entire minute, he got a response. He smiled at the message. He then put the phone back in the case. Closing the vehicle door. He walked back into the restaurant. Sabrina was already back at the table. "What's going on André? She asked. "Were you texting your sidepiece already? Dag man, let me fall asleep first. Before you start creeping. You don't even know how to play the game right." "No, I was using my work phone." He said. "To check on things at work."

"My sidepiece is going to meet us here." He continued. In five minutes so scoot over." "Oh, and order you something else to eat. She loves salmon." Sabrina kicked him lightly and laughed. "If I wasn't afraid of spilling our drinks." She said. "I might come across this table and strangle you right now." "Why do women always want to resort to violence?" André asked. "Why can't you all be loving, sensitive souls like us men?" "What men are you talking about?" Sabrina asked. "ALL men." André said. "You know, honest, truth-telling, faithful men. Loving, caring, compassionate men. All that is built into our DNA. That's why you never hear of stories about men lying to women. We're incapable of doing such a thing. Due to our religious values."

"Man, I'm going to move from this table." Sabrina said. Before God sends down a parade of lightning bolts." "What, are you calling me a liar?" André asked. "No, I'm not." Sabrina said. "I'm calling you a damn liar." They laughed. André could no longer carry his far-fetched exaggeration, with a straight face. "Okay, you got me." André said. "Maybe one man may have told a lie once upon a time. It's such a rare occurrence that nobody keeps records." "Ask Anita, Janet, Michelle or Tia." Sabrina said. "We all have detailed records of men lying."

"Hogwash." André retorted. "Bullshit." Sabrina countered. "Oh, such language you're using." André said. Around my virgin ears." "There is nothing virgin about you." Sabrina replied. "Mr. Kidnapping women on the side of the road. Then having your way with them." "Do I look like the type of man?" André asked. That would do something like that" "You look exactly like the kind of man." Sabrina replied. "That did that to me." "I loved it though." She continued. "Yeah, that was really nice." André said. We should go behind this building and do it right now." "Ah, it was warm the other night." Sabrina said. It's a little chilly out there tonight." "Ah man, you're always whining about something." André said. "I bet if I wanted to make love in a lion's cage at a zoo. You would find something wrong with that too."

"What the hell?" Sabrina asked. "Why would we do it in a lion's cage?" "Man, you are stupid." She laughed. Nicole returned with their food. Then made sure that everything was to their satisfaction. Sabrina asked for some additional napkins. She grabbed Andrés' hands to say grace. "Are you going to say grace? Or do you want me to say it?" Sabrina asked. "I will say it." André replied. They bowed their heads. André began. "Grace." He said. He then lifted his head and Sabrina lifted hers. "Man, you are retarded." She laughed. "What?" André asked astonishingly. "You asked me to say Grace and I did. "You women are never satisfied. I do exactly what you asked and you're still complaining."

"Whatever man." She said. "Just say the grace correctly please. So I can eat." André prayed over their food and they started to eat. On the television in the background. The All News Network was on. Panelist were discussing the pending trip to Las Vegas. By several members of Congress for a controversial fundraiser. "Isn't that guy they are meeting a felon?" Sabrina asked. He did time for armed robbery in London right?" "Yeah, he did." André replied. Supposedly, he's connected to the Russian Mafia."

"Kind of makes you wonder." André said. "Why those demons in Congress would be meeting with him?" "I can answer that." Sabrina said. "They only have moral values when it's to shame someone else. When it comes to them doing dirt. They pretend like they don't know what you're talking about. They're just like those devil ass Evangelical Pastors. They suddenly forgot what God wanted. When they got a Klansman in the white house. "They are just like the Pastors of 1619." André said. Preaching the Bible and Slavery at the same damn time. They couldn't have held Slavery together. Without the Bible." André said.

"Why do you say that?" Sabrina asked. "Think about it." André said. "What if I grab anybody in this restaurant? Drag them to the car, take them home. Then chain them in my basement. Every chance they get, they would try to escape. Call 911 or kill me to get out of that situation. However, if I can convince them, that God wants them to stay in my basement. They will stop trying to be free. That's exactly what happened in Slavery." "Then if you make them study this holy book." Sabrina said. "That's in a language foreign to them. That they couldn't possibly understand or verify for accuracy."

"So now, they are relying on my interpretation." André said. "Of this book to know what it says and means. I then become their god. I'm the one teaching them what I consider good and evil. They will love what I love and hate what I hate." "You're probably right on that." Sabrina said. "I just think it's far deeper than just that book. The beatings, torture and trauma. Definitely had to play a significant role." "No doubt about that." André said. "Let me get a piece of your salmon. It looks and smells delicious." "Why didn't you order salmon, greedy man?" Sabrina asked. "Because I wanted Jerk Chicken." André replied. "Now I want some salmon and don't back talk me woman." "Yassa, Massa." Sabrina joked. "I's mapoligize for me manners. Is you goan flog me? If you are. I have a whip at the house you can use."

"Well, just remember." André said. "You asked for this spanking. I'm going to give it to you. Then I'm going to give it to you." "Oooh promises, promises." Sabrina said. "Tonight, I may want to be the dominant one." Having my way with you." "What kind of domination are we talking?" André asked. "I told you, I'm not into no urine or other crazy stuff." "No silly, I just want to tie you up." Sabrina replied. "Kiss you all over. When I'm sucking that dick. You won't be able to stop me." "Hmmmm, I don't know about that." André responded. "I am intrigued though. My gut is telling me don't do it. My dick is saying hell yes!"

"Well, like every man." Sabrina said. "Aren't you going to listen to your dick?" "Probably." André said. "Now that's the kind of man I can work with." Sabrina replied. "One who doesn't think his dick will lead him to danger. You men are hopeless as a species. You could see a beautiful naked woman. On the other side of the Grand Canyon. Then watch a million men try to jump to that side. Falling to their death. Despite all those dead bodies. Your dick will say. You can make it bro! Then you'll jump." "Hey, that's enough of that dick bashing stuff." André said. "The only dick bashing I want. Is you bashing your body on it."

"Well, let's pay for this delicious food." Sabrina said. So we can go home and get it on. "Hold up." André said. "We're back from Atlantic City now. You can pay for food now and leave a tip. No less than $20.00 for the tip. We have to keep great black businesses in business." "Damn, you're trying to break a sister." Sabrina joked. "If I pay for food and tip. That's over $60. I will only have. About twelve hundred dollars left on me." "Listen to you." André said. "You have twelve hundred dollars. Yet complaining about paying this little bill. I should pull out my gun. Then rob you my damn self." "You're lucky I like you." Sabrina said. "So I'm going to pay for your food this time." Sabrina said. "Just don't make this a habit."

On the 27th floor. Of a building that sits on the corner of St. Paul and Baltimore Street. Chief Delaney and Commissioner Riggs meet. In an office facing the inner Harbor. They were joined by Acting NSA Director Baker. Along with FBI Acting Director Tolbert. They were soon joined by Maryland State Police Superintendent Scales. "Do you know why we're here, Chief Delaney?" Superintendent Scales asked. "I figured since your bosses work out of this building. That you would know." "All I know." Chief Delaney said. "Is we were told to be here at 1900 hours. It's 6:55pm now so this should get started within 5 minutes" "I can tell you all why we're here." Director Tolbert said. "We're here because Mr. C. wanted us to be here."

"That's right, gentlemen." Mr. C. said. "I called you all here." He walked into the room with Mr. Vailati. "Tomorrow is our big day. I wanted to make sure we are all on the same page." "How is one of us?" Superintendent Scales asked. "Supposed to get close to the President?" "That's the brilliant part." Mr. C. replied. "You're Law Enforcement in uniform. The President trusts you. Probably more than he does his own Secret Service. I just need you all to show up. Look enthusiastic about meeting your Commander and Chief. You three being the leaders of your respective departments. Is the perfect cloak. Nobody is going to think twice about why you are there. You three provide the cloak. I'll provide the dagger."

"That's why it's imperative. That you have Major Carver there, Commissioner. For you Chief Delaney. It's imperative that you have Captain Nichols there. Standing next to you. Superintendent Scales. You can have any ranking personnel you choose. Standing there with you. They are just a part of the cloak. The reason we're meeting here. Is because we can see the harbor from this location. Without actually being at the harbor." "Yes, it wouldn't look too good for us." Director Tolbert said. "To be pointing at locations in the area. The day before the President is shot."

"Yeah, all we'd need is some tourist." Director Baker added. "To capture us on pic or video." "Their nice trip would end in a terrible tragedy." Mr. Vailati said. "Let's not talk down that road." Mr. C. said. "That's why we're here. So gentlemen, here is the plan. The President is going to fly into Baltimore. On board Marine One. He is scheduled to land at 1315 hours. On top of Shock Trauma. They picked this location. So that he would have the shortest ride possible." "Wait." Commissioner Riggs said. "This asshole is going to land on top of Shock Trauma?"

"This is where our critical patients are sent. Hell, who cares if a patient has just been shot? Or having a heart attack? They can wait. So the President doesn't have too long of a drive." "May I continue, Commissioner?" Mr. C. asked. "From Shock Trauma. He is going to travel south on Greene street. Greene Street will be closed to all traffic. With the exception of ambulances, three hours prior to his arrival." "Duh, can't somebody put a bomb on an ambulance?" Superintendent Scales asked. "Yes, they could." Mr. C. replied. "Which is why Secret Service will be there. With bomb sniffing dogs. Before the patients are off loaded and brought into the hospital. They will be sniffed."

"Oh, I'm sorry." Chief Delaney sarcastically said. "You're having a stroke Mr. Williams?" "Our dog is taking a shit right now. As soon as he's finished shitting. He'll sniff you. Then we'll get you in for your operation." The room broke into quiet laughter and even Mr. C. smiled. "Are you over there talking shit, Chief Delaney?" Mr. Vailati joked. "He's talking dog shit." Commissioner Riggs added. "Anyway, back to the schedule." Mr. C. continued. "The motorcade will travel south on Greene street. Until Greene becomes Russell street. They will make a left on Lee Street. Bringing them into Camden Yards. All North and South Bound traffic. Onto I-395 will be shut down. No Light Rail Service will stop. From Lexington Market to the Stadiums.

"Passengers will catch a bus at Westport and Centre Street stops. Which will route them around North and South. Via Mulberry and Franklin streets. Down Fulton and Monroe to Annapolis Rd." "Man, if I was catching the Light Rail." Director Tolbert said. "And had to go all the way around Robin's barn. I'd pitch a bitch!" "Continuing." Mr. C. said. "The motorcade will exit Camden Yards at Conway and Howard. Heading North up Howard to Pratt Street. It will then go East on Pratt up to the Harbor. Where the President should arrive at about 1330hrs. Needless to say. The Governor and other dignitaries will be there. The President will spend about ten minutes. Shaking hands and greeting folks."

"There will be local, National and International news media. As well as supporters and protesters. Commissioner Riggs. Your department along with Baltimore School Police. Will secure the harbor from errant school kids. Foot patrol units will route them. To Lombard or Baltimore Street. That's if they need to go East or West. To or from the harbor. Secret Service and FBI will secure. The actual perimeter of the Harbor itself. The President should take the podium at around 1345 hours. He should speak for about 30 minutes. Until about 2:15pm. As he speaks. Secret Service will stand in front of him. Just below the stage. They will also be positioned behind him on each wing."

"However, when his speech is over. He is going to come down to the audience. Shaking hands with the non-dignitaries. Most notably. The men and women in uniform. From the National Guard and various Police Departments. At this time Commissioner. I'll need you and Major Carver to step in front of Captain Nichols. Major Carver is significantly taller and bigger than Captain Nichols. The Captain will not be able to see. You will inadvertently step on his foot. When he makes any movement, that's when the shot rings out. Captain Nichols will be the only one in movement at that time. Ironically where the shot appears to have come from.

"At that time, he'll be injected. With a high dosage of GHB. This should cause him to collapse. In the commotion of the President being shot. Fewer eyes will be on Captain Nichols. When he does get attention. He'll be found with a gun in his hand. A gun matching the bullet that shot the President. The Captain will be arrested and taken to 300 E. Madison. For his initial arraignment and processing. Then he'll be turned over to Federal custody. Then recharged under Federal law. Once Law Enforcement studies the video. It will appear that Major Carver was an accomplice. He will also be arrested. You gentlemen will have your wish. Of removing two people. You don't like out of your departments."

"Well, this sounds like a flawed plan." Chief Delaney said. "Captain Nichols won't raise his arm. Not high enough to shoot someone above the waist. Plus we are near Shock Trauma. Where they have saved many gunshot victims. I know they will have their top Doctors on standby. Just because the President is visiting." "Ah, now you're thinking Chief Delaney." Mr. Vailati said. "However. We thought of this weeks ago. The President will be rushed into his motorcade. In the commotion, no one will notice. That one of the men who appears to be Secret Service. Is not. He is actually a member of The Black House. As the President is being carried to his Limo. He will be injected with a lethal dose of pure Heroin."

"Come on, Sir." Commissioner Riggs said. "Do you really think the public is going to believe? The President is a Heroin user?" "The better question Commissioner is." Mr. C. replied. "Do you think the White House? Would ever go public with that information? It's far more heroic to say he died from a gunshot wound. Than to smear his legacy. As being a drug addict. Like I said earlier. I just need you people to be the cloak. I am the dagger. Prior to this administration. We would never even have thought of. Involving local Law Enforcement. Alas, the Federal level is in such disarray. All because this idiot has allowed the Russians. To infiltrate almost every agency and branch.

"Nobody knows who to trust." Mr. C. said. "So the fate of this country. Is in the hands of you gentlemen. Please don't fail me. If you and your people don't show tomorrow. I will have to come looking for you. However, once things go according to plan. All of your Departments. Can look forward to a significant boost in Federal subsidies. You'll also get unprecedented training offers. Recognition in the national spotlight. We will monitor every officer in your respective departments. For a three-year period. As well as your Police radio transmissions for that time. Any rogue or corrupt Officers you may have. Will be dealt with. Long before their deeds become public. Embarrassing your departments."

That means you will not have any scandals. During that period. Director Baker will head up the team listening in. To not only your Department's radio transmission. But the phone calls of your officers. Director Tolbert will head up the team. That will visit your officers with questionable character. Most cops who know they are being watched will walk a straight line. If there are a few who test our resolve, that would be tragic. They may end up dying in in the line of duty. Or meeting a fuel tanker on the way home from working a double shift."

"Basically gentlemen, you help your country tomorrow. Your country will be indebted to your departments." "This shit is just weird." Chief Delaney said. "Being asked to be involved in taking out the President." "Here's the choice you have, Chief." Mr. C. replied. "Do unto others or they will do unto you." "Was the President talking about doing something to Baltimore?" Chief Delaney asked. "You're thinking too small again Chief." Mr. C. replied. "Whatever they're planning will have ramifications well beyond Baltimore." "Wait, was he dropping a bomb on us or something?" Superintendent Scales asked. "No," Mr. C. said. "We don't know yet fully what they are up to. We just know it's probably not good. Let's adjourn this meeting. So everyone can get home. To their families at a decent hour. Are there any more concerns about tomorrow before we depart?"

"Yes, I have one Sir." Commissioner Riggs said. "You told us where we are going to be. Where will you be?" "You won't see me Commissioner." Mr. C. said. "Rest assured, I will see you. You will see Director Tolbert and Baker. As well as other members of The Black House. Don't forget to eat lunch. You both will face intense questioning and request. For personnel files on your men. I apologize in advance. For the yelling that you will both get from your bosses. Rest assured, neither of you will lose your jobs. I'll make the State and City offers they can't refuse. In order to keep you on." "Damn, is there anybody you can't blackmail or reach?" Superintendent Scales asked. "There have been a few people." Mr. C. responded. That we haven't been able to blackmail or persuade."

"God rest their souls in peace. In the world of shadow government. It's dangerous in the shadows. Folks that refuse to cooperate. Have to go out into the shadows at some point." "So, you kill people in the shadow of the night?" Chief Delaney asked. "When most people are not likely to see?" "No Sir, that's just a figure of speech." Mr. C. replied. "If we want to kill you in broad daylight, we will. There are so many ways to kill someone. The possibilities are endless. Accidents, stray bullets, overdose. Or we can just plain snatch you off the street. The public will not think twice. About who they think is Law Enforcement putting you in a van. They will think you really did something big. No search for you, no posters, flyers. You're just gone.

We can drive you to wherever and do with you what we will. That's actually how we were going to kill you Chief. If you hadn't agreed to help. With that situation on the train out of DC." The Chief raised his eyebrow in surprise. "It's not personal Chief. It's just to protect the country. If you're not involved. You're more likely to go talk to someone. Then we'd have to kill all those people. It's so much easier just to kill you. Commissioner Riggs. Would you like to know how we were going to kill you?" "No thank you Sir." Commissioner Riggs answered. "I'd like my day and way of death to be a surprise."

"Very well then." Mr. C. replied. "You'll all be glad to know. Rarely does lightning strike twice in the same location." "What does that mean?" Commissioner Riggs asked. "It means you were selected." Mr. C. said. "To do a favor for The Black House. Chances are you will never be asked again. We try to not use the same citizens more than once." So we can go on living our lives?" Chief Delaney asked. After this event I mean?" "Yes." Mr. C. replied. "We try not to focus our attention. On anyone or anyplace too long. That's how you get people to start asking question."

"Then we'd have to kill those people." Mr. Vailati said. "Damn, you all are some cold motherfuckers." Superintendent Scales said. "I'm in the Black House, because The Devil is in the White House." Mr. C. responded. "Cold would be killing for personal gain. The Black House never kills. For personal or selfish reasons. We only kill to maintain the foundation. Of this republic. We kill to stop those who would try to destroy. The principles of the nation for their own personal gain. Sometimes, it's necessary to enlist assistance. Of people outside of The Black House. When that is needed. We employ various means to acquire compliance. Including murder. That's just a necessary tool of compliance."

André and Sabrina were driving home. They noticed a marked patrol car parked in front of his house. "That's a car from your department isn't it? Sabrina asked. "Yes, it is." André replied. "They probably need me to sign off on some papers. Some administrative bullshit probably. When they pulled closer to the house. Captain Nichols could see the officer in the patrol car. It was Officer Stewart. André pulled into his garage and parked. "Hey I'll be inside shortly Sabrina." André said. "Go ahead and get yourself comfortable. What do you have in that envelope Officer Stewart?" "Some very important papers." Officer Stewart replied. They require your signature, Sir."

"I don't have a pen." Captain Nichols said. "I should write you up." Officer Stewart replied. "For not being prepared Sir. I'll let you go with a warning this time. You can use one of my pens." "What am I signing again?" André asked. "Sir, can you just sign the papers?" Officer Stewart jokingly insisted. "Before I have to charge you with obstructing and hindering?" "How am I obstructing and hindering?" André asked. "You're keeping me from my lunch Sir. Officer Stewart remarked. "That's a felony."

Chapter 8

Sign and a date

They both laughed at the joke. Captain Nichols got into the passenger seat of the patrol car. He began to sign the documents. "Make sure you have the right date." Officer Stewart coached. "On all these documents Sir. We don't need any problems. With you having to come in and do this over." "No, we wouldn't want that at all." Captain Nichols said. "Will you look over everything? Make sure it's correct for me please Officer Stewart?" "I'm watching you sign and date as you go Sir." Officer Stewart said. "So far, you haven't messed up anything." "I think this is the last one." Captain Nichols said. "Yeah, good thing I filled out most of this for you." Officer Stewart said. "All you have to do is sign and date." "Yes, you're a very good officer." Captain Nichols said.

Inside the house, Sabrina called out to Michael. "Hey, are you in here, babe?" She asked. "Don't talk. He could be walking through the door at any moment." Two light taps came from upstairs. Confirming that Michael was in position. "When he and I make love in the morning. Come into the Master bedroom. Do what you have to do." Again, she heard two taps. "Try not to pay attention." She said. "To what you may hear tonight babe. It's just acting." She then heard a single tap from upstairs. Followed by a long pause. Finally, the second tap came.

Back outside in the patrol car. Captain Nichols and Officer Stewart were still talking. "Now, can you do a favor for me? Captain Nichols asked. "Make sure my backup and transport arrive on time? I'll be on a tight schedule. I don't need any mishaps." "Well, I guarantee the transport." Officer Stewart said. "Will be where and when it's supposed to be. Now your backup is not my call. I could fill in if you need me to." "No, that won't be necessary Officer Stewart." Captain Nichols said.

"My backup is solid." Captain Nichols said. "I just need you to turn in those forms. First thing in the morning when the office opens. Get a receipt for both of them. Then take care of my transport for me please." "Man, I got you." Officer Stewart said. "Stop sweating me Yo." "Excuse you, Officer?" Captain Nichols said. "I meant. Officer Stewart corrected. "Stop sweating me Yo, Sir." "I'll deal with you later." Captain Nichols said. "I have to get in the house." "Yeah, I'll bet you do." Officer Stewart said. "I'll deal with you later as well, Sir." "Just don't lose those papers Officer." Captain Nichols said. "Oh, I have those papers." Officer Stewart replied. I'm safeguarding them." "Have a good evening, Officer Stewart." Captain Nichols said.

He then walked back into the house. "Hey Breen, where are you hiding?" He called. "I'm in the bathroom. Sabrina replied. "Just getting out the shower. Hey, what was the officer doing here? Is everything okay on your job?" "Yeah, everything is fine." André said. "They just needed me to sign some papers. About an upcoming event." "Is that for the Presidential thing tomorrow?" Sabrina asked. "No, this is not related to that." André said. "I don't want to talk about work tonight. I don't want to think about, that stupid ass ceremony tomorrow." "Yes, you're right baby." Sabrina said. "Why don't you go get in the shower? Get cleaned up, so I can suck your dick." "Damn, now that's an offer." André replied. "I don't think I can refuse."

At Drexler's house. He and Deer Dog were counting cash deposits. Brought in by lower level crew. "Hey Drexler." Deer Dog called. "This Russian heroin is some pretty good shit." "It's selling better than the shit we were getting from the Italians." "It ought to be." Drexler said. "They get their heroin straight from Afghanistan. Then ship it here. The Italians were getting theirs through a Mexican cartel. They got it from a South America. So that shit was cut three times before we got it." "The dope fiends are laying out in the streets." Deer Dog said.

"From North and Greenmount to North and Milton streets. These junkies are passed the fuck out. Hell, we're making most of our money charging the white boy price." "Yeah I know." Drexler said. "Word is out that our stuff is so good. Those white motherfuckers from Towson U and Loyola are loyal. Of course, we have to charge them the premium white boy price. They don't face the same risk. If they get caught with drugs. So we have to seek justice somehow." Drexler and Deer Dog both laughed. "Hey, if one of those motherfuckers O.Ds." Drexler said. That's one less future Klansman in the world." "Speaking of paying the price." Deer Dog said. "We need to go meet Ms. Parsons about that flag on our field."

"Oh, that little young hopper?" Drexler asked. "Up in Edmondson Village? Which car are you rolling down there in?" "I'm rolling in the Yukon and yeah." Deer Dog said. "That lil motherfucker. Mama P. thought it would be a good idea. To have him know who you are. So he doesn't get any more penalties." "Hey, you go ahead and take that meet for me." Drexler said. "I have some personal business that came up. I need to attend to it tonight." "Where are we going?" Deer Dog asked. "You are going to that meet with Mama P." Drexler said. "I have to make a run." "When are we going to go and take care of that broad?" Deer Dog asked.

"You know? The one staying at your brother's house?" "The next time you see me." Drexler said. "You'll have the answer to that question and more." "Next time I see you?" Deer Dog repeated. "Nigga, are you going to get some pussy? Or rejoin the Army?" "Hold on, let me send this text real quick." Drexler said. "I'll let you know everything when you see me again." "That's not the burner phone for today, is it?" Deer Dog asked. "Did you use all the minutes? On the one I gave you this morning? Drexler was engaged in typing his text. He didn't respond to Deer Dog. "Oh, now we're keeping secrets from each other?" Deer Dog asked. "Negro, we're brothers. We don't keep secrets from each other.

"Now if you have beef with somebody." Deer Dog continued. "You need to let me know. You probably should let me kill them anyway. So we don't get your hands dirty." "No, there's no beef with anybody anymore." Drexler said. "I don't need you to kill anyone. "It's all good, I promise." "Alright nigga." Deer Dog said. "Don't have me coming down to Central Booking. Trying to get you out on bail." "Man turn on the television." Drexler said. "You're way off base." Deer Dog turned on the television. He began to flip through the channels. "Let me hold the keys to the black Camaro." Drexler said. Deer Dog threw him the keys. "Don't be out there racing my shit." Deer Dog said. On I-95, 195, 295 or 395." "Bro, nobody is going to be racing tonight." Drexler responded. Not on 1, 2 or 395."

"Don't take your ass down the way." Deer Dog continued. "Racing on 495 or out in the County to 695, 795 or 895." "Yes mama." Drexler replied. "I promise I won't be racing." "Do you want to fix my lunch too? Make sure I have my jacket?" "No, but you can make sure." Deer Dog said. "To put some gas in that motherfucker. Before you bring it back here." "Hey, you got that my brother." Drexler said. "Your car takes unleaded and granulated sugar combo, right?" "Man, you better not." Deer Dog said. "Put some damn sugar in my tank." "I'll be around here singing the blues. With a guitar like I was B.B. King." "Can you just be quiet?" Drexler asked. "Let me hear what they're saying in this movie."

"I've been trying to watch this movie." Drexler continued. "For about two months now. I always catch it after it has started. I finally caught it at the beginning the other night." "You know you can stream it back." Deer Dog asked. "To the beginning, don't you? "Since the system is connected to the internet. You can do that with much of this stuff on T.V." "Yeah nigga, I know I can do that." Drexler said. "I saw it from the beginning the other night." "Now if you'll shut the fuck up. I can watch the rest of it. Unless you want to have deep meaningful conversation." "Nigga fuck you." Deer Dog laughed.

"I'm about to roll out. Go take this meet with Mama P." Deer Dog said. "I bet she is going to be disappointed that you aren't there, bro." "Let her know that I will make it up to her soon." Drexler said. "I would love to be there. I just have to take care of this thing tonight." "Alright, I'll catch you later my brother." Deer Dog said. "You're missing a meeting with Mama P. This girl better be fine. Fine enough to follow into shark-infested waters. Carrying a bucket of tuna." "Who said I was going to meet a girl?" Drexler asked. "I hope it's a girl." Deer Dog replied. "I know you're not gay. So it's either money or pussy." "Okay, you caught me." Drexler said. "I'm going to see your aunt named Clara Mae. She is paying me to fuck her." "Fool go head." Deer Dog said. "My aunt is named Cora Jean." They both laughed. Deer Dog walked out the door.

At the Edmondson Village Shopping Center in West Baltimore. Dirty Red was coming out of a carry-out restaurant. With two chicken cheese steaks, fries and two drinks. He walked over to his brand-new BMW 535i. He opened the driver's side. In the passenger side of his vehicle was a young lady. He entered the vehicle and handed the young lady the food. He then drove up Edmondson Ave. and turned onto Old Fredrick Road. He turned up Scarlet Oak Ln. There he saw the road blocked by a blue Yukon truck. The Yukon was driving on the wrong side of the street.

He drove slowly towards the Yukon. The Yukon drove slowly towards him. Dirty Red put his car in park. He got out to find out what the driver's problem was. As he left his vehicle, another vehicle pulled up beside him. Ms. Parsons was sitting in the rear passenger seat. Her window rolled down and she called out to him. "Dirty Red, how are you, son?" She asked. Stunned, he turned to see who it is. "Hey, Ms. Kitty. How are you?" He replied. "I'm fine son, but it looks like you've committed a foul. I warned you about going out of bounds in this area of town.

You're trying to turn my MLB into the NFL." "No ma'am." Dirty Red replied. "I'm not trying to mess with your Major Large Bakeshop. It's not good if there's No Food Left." "So, you didn't drop that body?" Ms. Parsons asked. "On Pulaski and Smallwood? Right in the middle of my district." "I didn't think that was your district Ms. Parsons." Dirty Red replied. "I thought your district was Mondawmin to North Ave." "See." Ms. Parsons said. "This is why you young niggas, shouldn't even be allowed in the game." "You don't even take the time to learn the fucking rules." "Whatever, old lady." Dirty Red said. "That nigga disrespected me. He got dealt with where we found him."

"I don't have time to be pausing the game." He continued. "Calling your old ass. Or that retarded ass son of yours to get permission. Those older cats call you the referee. Or whatever but you ain't shit to me." Dirty Red raised his shirt to expose a 9mm black handgun. "We younger cats don't need no fucking referee. And you're about to get your old ass shot talking shit. You need to take your old ass home. Breast feed that retarded motherfucker you call a son. He probably home right now crying in his fucking diapers." Ms. Parsons removed her glasses. Dirty Red looked at the lady in his car. Ms. Parsons then spoke. "When I drove up here. It was to just tell you about the foul you committed. Assess you a 15-yard penalty. Now you've committed unsportsmanlike conduct. After the play was over.

I'm afraid that's going to get you ejected out the game son. At that moment a black Jeep drives up behind the BMW. Out stepped Crazy Ronnie James. Wearing a black and white striped poncho and a werewolf mask. Ms. Parsons threw a yellow flag from her vehicle. She hit Dirty Red and rolled up her bullet proof window. Dirty Red went for his weapon at his waistline. Ronnie James pointed a doubled barrel shot gun at his head. Deer Dog exited as the driver for Ms. Parson. He had a chrome .44 pistol pointing at Dirty Red. Ronnie James removed his mask. "It can be just you." Ronnie James said. "Or you and that bitch in the car."

Dirty Red turned around. He saw Ms. Parsons also with a .45 pistol pointed at his back. Clearly seeing he had no way of winning this gun battle. So he laid his gun on the ground. He stood, facing Crazy Ronnie James. "All this time you've just been pretending to be retarded?" Dirty Red asked. "Hey, those disability benefits come in handy." Ronnie James replied. He then pulled the trigger of the shotgun. Blowing Dirty Red's head to bits. The woman in Dirty Red's car screamed in fear. Ronnie James pointed the weapon at her head. She stopped screaming and Ronnie James lowered the gun.

"Don't make me come looking for you." Ronnie James said. "Because you don't know how to be quiet." The woman, obviously terrified, shook her head that she understood. "You heard me, right?" Ronnie James asked. "Yes." She whispered. "Hey, let me get his sandwich?" Ronnie James asked. "Since he won't be eating it. No sense in food going to waste." The woman took one of the sandwiches out of the bag. "Hey, wipe his brain matter off the foil for me please." He said. She took some napkins and wiped off the foil wrapper. "Thank you, sweetheart." Ronnie James said. "I appreciate that. Hey are you seeing anybody, because you're kind of cute? The woman didn't react. She sat there stoned-face.

"Boy, bring your ass on!" Ms. Parsons yelled. "Let's get out of here! Shift change is almost over. You know somebody has called 911 by now. There is your Liftee ride home young lady." Ms. Parsons continued. The fare has already been paid." The young lady got out of the BMW. She walked over to the waiting car. A red Ford Expedition also arrived. Driven by a woman in her 50s. Deer Dog and Crazy Ronnie James placed all the guns in her vehicle. "Make sure these guns get dumped." Deer Dog said. "In Anacostia Park down in DC." The woman nodded that she understood. She then drove off the lot towards Cooks lane. "You both need to go dump those ponchos." Ms. Parsons said. Dump the gloves too. Be careful putting them in that hydrochloric acid barrel.

Any gunshot residue the cops would be looking for. She continued. Is on those things." "Mama Parsons." Deer Dog called. "How do you get to keep a barrel of hydrochloric acid anyway?" "One of the Deacons at St. Mary is a Chemist. For the big Defense Contractor Company, out by BWI airport. He was able to get me a 50-gallon plastic barrel. He's one of our laundry men too. For the money the church washes for our street business. So, it wasn't hard to coach him into doing more favors. Once I had the plastic barrel. I had him bring me any acid he could. Sometimes, he could only bring one-gallon. Other times, he could bring four or five.

Eventually, I got close to 50 gallons. He showed Ronnie James and me how to handle it safely. Gave us protective suits. He even checks on it every Sunday after church. To make sure it's secure. My late husband built that underground fallout shelter. Because he was sure war was coming. It has a network of ventilation. To keep fumes from building up. It's also sound proof with the thick cement walls. Unless you leave the entry door open. Enough of talk about shelters and acid. Where is that damn Count Drexler?" "I don't know." Deer Dog replied. "He said he had to make a run right about this time." "A run to where?" Ms. Parsons asked. "I wish I knew but he wouldn't tell me." Deer Dog said. "He's been acting a little off lately. I can't figure out what's going on." "I'll say he's acting off." Ms. Parsons said.

"He seems to have forgotten." She continued. "Who made sure he had the best product? On this side of the Mississippi river. Who refereed the game? To make sure everyone could make some money. Without always going to war. I focused on straightening out disputes. So they all could just focus on distribution. I plugged him into this church network. So his money could be clean. Hell, I bailed him out of jail. When his own punk ass brother arrested him. Now we got some bitch I asked him to go get. He's got me waiting? Listen Deer Dog. We need to make that change in leadership now.

"There is over half a billion dollars on the line." Ms. Parsons continued. "Which is more than enough for us all to retire. I mean now is the time to retire. The Russians killed my Italian supply crew. But not before they found out how we ran business. They reached out to me to keep things running smoothly. So our business was pretty much unaffected. Still, I trust these motherfuckers, less than I trusted the Italians. I didn't trust those motherfuckers at all." "So, what are you thinking about doing mama Parsons?" Deer Dog asked. "I would like to promote you to run your crew tomorrow." Ms. Parsons replied. "In order to do that. The current leader has to fall. Once he goes down. You and Ronnie James can go get that evil bitch. Out at his brother's house.

"Hell, if we have to kill his whole family. Then so be it. We get that bitch and the code she has to those funds. We can walk away from this business, the Russians and this fucking country. Do you think you're ready? "Hey, Drexler is my man 100 grand." Deer Dog replied. Yet him I will kill for half a bill." "Well, get to the house." Ms. Parsons said. "Drop those ponchos in the barrel. Grab a matching one out the spare room. You never know who the fuck is filming. With a cell phone around here." "Alright, after we change clothes." Deer Dog said. "I'm going to get a hotel on Security Blvd. Then I'll wait up for Drexler tonight. In the garage until he brings my car back. I'll take care of him there. Then drive his body over the Bay Bridge.

I can get rid of that stolen Accord at the same time. I'll put him in this abandoned house. Down in Salisbury. I'll borrow a phone to call a Liftee ride back to Baltimore. I'll leave my personal phone at the hotel. So they can't back track it moving. To the same place where they will find the body. I'll have a burner phone. I will only turn on if it's an emergency. When the cops check my phone movements. They will think I was in the hotel all night. I'll say I was with some married woman. Which is why I didn't get much information about her. I have to have all my bases covered.

"We know the cops will come talking to me." Deer Dog continued. "Once Drexler is reported missing or found. The beautiful thing is. This bitch we're going to get is off the radar. Nobody will be looking for her. We'll make Drexler's cop brother, look like he just ran off with the broad and money. By the time they find her and Drexler's body. It will be long after we are out of their reach. We'll do what we have to do to her. In the basement of the church to get that code. Then we can baptize her in that barrel of hydrochloric acid. Toss the bones in the woods down in Dru Hill Park. Day after tomorrow. We'll all board a plane for Cape Town. Go mansion shopping when we arrive."

"I'm going to go mansion shopping." Ms. Parsons said. Then I'm going man shopping. With the kind of money I'll have. I'm sure I can find me some nice Scientist, Engineer or Doctor. All he will have to do is service me in my old age. Keep me happy. I'll keep him rolling in dough. I need to get me some new dick. Pastor Kingsley just ain't hitting it right. Now let's get back to the house. Take care of this evidence before we get pulled over."

André was getting out of the shower when Sabrina walked in. "Are you all nice and clean for me, baby?" She asked. "Yeah, I'm all clean." André answered. "Now let me put some lotion on. So you don't have to call me ashy Larry." "Oooh, you're going from ashy to classy on a sister, huh?" Sabrina asked. "I'm not mad at you." "Yeah, I'm all about class." André said. "I'll finish with some cologne and I'll be ready. The question is, are you ready?" She lifted her robe, reached her fingers down between her legs. She covered them in her moisture. "Look at my fingers." Sabrina said. "Doesn't it look like I'm ready?" André took her fingers into his mouth. He sucked the wetness from them. "Ummm, that tastes good." He said. "I can't wait to get some straight from the source."

"Looking at Mr. Friendly down there." Sabrina said. "It looks like you're ready too." They walked out into the bedroom. Sabrina had adult toys laying all over the bed. Bondage restraints, edible lotions, blindfolds, a paddle and whip. Vibrating wands, bullets and a host of other things. "What is all of that for?" André asked. "Well, right now, it's for me." Sabrina replied. "Maybe later on, I can use some of this on you." "I want you to tie me up and have your way with me André." She said. André smiled at her in a sinister way. "I told you up front I wasn't shy about my freakiness." Sabrina said. "Tonight, I want to submit to your every desire."

"Damn, this might be my lucky night." André said. He walked over to the bed and looked over the various items. "Hey, you have real handcuffs here." He said. "Where are the keys? That shit will not be funny if we can't find them?" "André you have cuff keys all over this house." Sabrina answered. "I'm sure we will be able to find one. If you lose all three that are on your dresser." "Okay woman." He said. "Let me put this blindfold on you. Now to make sure you can't see. He waved his hand in front of her face and she didn't flinch. He then placed his hands on her shoulders. Pressing her gently down to her knees. "You know what to do woman." He ordered. Sabrina opened her mouth and began to suck on his engorged shaft.

André grabbed her curly strong hair. He caressed her scalp as she worked her juicy full lips on him. "Oh my God." He moaned. "Baby you make me feel so damn good when you do what you do." He reached down and pinched her nipples as she sucked him. After several minutes, he stood her up. Then backed her towards the bed. "What are you doing?" She asked. "I wasn't finished yet." André picked up the pair of handcuffs. Cuffing her hands in front of her body. "Am I being arrested, Officer?" She asked. "No, you're being detained." He replied. "I'm going to have to search you."

"What on earth are you looking for Officer?" She said playfully. "I'll let you know when I find it." He replied. He then turned her so her back was to him. His hands began to caress up and down the sides of her body. Up and down over her back. Gently massaging her shoulders and neck. "Ummmm that feels good officer." She said. "Give me the confession paper. I'll sign it for whatever the crime was." André did not respond. Instead, his hands drifted down to her round ass. He firmly rubbed her luscious mounds in his hands. He then turned her to face him. Laying her on the bed. He began to kiss the top of her feet. Sucking her pedicured toes.

Sabrina tried to pull him up to her. He stood and placed her still cuffed hands, over her head. Then he went back to work. His nibbled on her inner legs. Alternating from right to left and working his way upward. When he reached her knees, he lifted her legs. So he could kiss behind her knees. Along with the meaty part of her calves. Sabrina moaned in approval. His kisses seemed to be all over her legs. He then lowered her legs and worked his way up to her thighs. He kissed the top of them. Again alternating from left to right. Eventually, his head fell between her thighs. He began to suck her inner right thigh. He sucked her firm enough to leave a passion mark. Then did the same to her inner left thigh.

His hands were busy caressing the top of her thighs. His tongue skillfully played. Just below the center of her joy. Sabrina was moving her hips. Trying to get his mouth to connect. With her wanting, wet and waiting pussy. André teased her by pretending to start. Then kissed her in her shaven pubic hair region. He did this several times before finally being ready to please her. His fingers found her labia and spread her open. His mouth then followed. He placed a gentle hello kiss on her clitoris. Sabrina moaned in approval. His tongue started at the bottom of her slit. Zig zagging upward to her clitoris. His lips caught her swollen bud. He began to suck her gently.

Sabrina's hands moved down to caress his head. He pushed them back away from him. "Don't try to stop me from eating this pussy." He mumbled. "You beat me in playing Scrabble the other night. So now I'm going to spell some words. With my tongue on your pussy." He called out an "S" and started writing with his tongue. From her clitoris down to her entry way. He then called out an "A" and started at the bottom of her pussy. His tongue moved upward to her clit. From the left side and back down on the right. He then added the cross bar. He then called out a "B." Proceeding to draw that letter with his tongue. Sabrina was then aware of what he was spelling. Her mind anticipated each letter in her name.

After he was done writing her name. He came up for air briefly. "Only 90 more letters left in the game and I think I have a 'Z'." He said. Sabrina smiled in delight for the man she could only hear. She still couldn't see past the blindfold. André inserted two fingers inside of her pussy. Beginning to rub her G-spot. He continued his oral assault on her delicious pussy. "I want you to cum for me woman." He commanded. "Can you cum for daddy?" "Oooh, yes I want to cum for you baby." She moaned. "I want to cum and glaze that handsome face of yours." "Prove it to me." André urged. "Let me see if you really want to cum." His fingers rubbed intently on her G-spot. Her vagina poured like a raging river. His tongue was the damn trying to contain the flow.

"Oh, fuck!" Sabrina cried. "André right there, right there, baby!" "Oh yes, that's it! You're going to make me cum." He worked his fingers faster on her G-spot. Sucking her clitoris with determination. Soon, her hands came down on the back of his head. Clamping him like a vice grip. André pulled his fingers out of her. Letting his tongue do all the speaking. Sabrina's breathing became heavy. Suddenly, her scream rattled the room. She came so hard it squirted from her vagina. She sprayed Andrés' face and the bed. Her body convulsed wildly.

André was still licking, sucking and fucking her with his tongue. Her body was on edge. "Oh my God!" She panted. "Oh my God! Oh my God!" She tried to push his face away from her." André grabbed and held her cuffed hands. So they couldn't push him anymore. He continued to eat her pussy. In a matter of a few short minutes, she was cumming again. Grinding her pussy all over his face. Her legs clamped tightly around his head. Her sounds were rabid as she came three times in succession. Finally, André relented. Taking his mouth off of her pussy. He then kissed her stomach and worked his way up to her breast.

"I think I like playing Scrabble this way better." He said. "It just seems more fun when you hit a triple this way." Sabrina, still fighting to catch her breath, looked at him and smiled. "You are a nasty man." She said. "Oh, you didn't like that?" He asked. "Liked it? I love it!" She replied. "Well, this night isn't about you." André said. "You're my sub tonight so get up." He gently helped her to her feet. Then turned her to face the bed. He bent her over the bed and grabbed the spreader bar. He secured the leather straps around her ankles. Spreading her legs the length of the bar. He then grabbed the vibrating wand. Rubbing it up and down her inner thighs.

Soon, he found her dripping wet pussy. He pressed the wand on her clitoris and labia. Sabrina struggled trying to close her legs. Trying to escape the intensity of the vibrations. With the spreader bar, she had no such luck. She was quickly cumming all over the wand and floor. "I don't think I told you to cum just yet." André said. "You must want to be punished." He picked up some of the strawberry edible lotion. He bent her down further and spread her ass cheeks. He then poured some of the lotion directly on her ass. He picked up some anal beads and pressed them into her ass. Each bead was bigger than the last. Sabrina eagerly held still as he pushed each one inside. "Now turn around and suck this chocolate dick for me woman!" He commanded.

Sabrina did as she was told. As she turned, André removed her blindfold. The dimly lit room slightly required adjustment for her eyes. As the beads slightly moved inside of her ass, she began to suck his dick. "No, no, no." André said. "I need you to swallow this dick." He then pushed it deeper into her mouth. Until she began to gag. She quickly took it out of her mouth. "I didn't say stop now did I? André asked. He rubbed his wet dick all over her pretty face. Making sure his balls rubbed across her succulent lips. "Ummm, do you like the taste of my balls in your mouth?" André asked. "Ummm, I love it." Sabrina replied.

He held her head steady. Slowly and gently he pushed his dick deeper into her mouth. All the way back into her throat until he heard her gag. He then began to fuck her mouth wildly. Causing her to gulp and gag. Tears begin to flow from her eyes. Yet Sabrina urged him not to stop. Her saliva was also flowing heavily from her mouth. Her soft tender lips gripped his meat as it went in and out. Her hands ached to hold him. They were still restrained in handcuffs. So, she resorted to touching herself. Rubbing her clitoris as the beads continued to move inside her ass. His dick continued to stroke in her mouth. Sabrina looked up at him with those warm watery brown eyes.

Her beautiful chocolate face was too much for him to take. He grabbed the back of her head. Forcing his dick deep down her throat. He released his hot and creamy cum in waves onto her tonsils. He grunted with each pulse. Sabrina held her head steady. She received all his deposits and greedily swallowed them. When his orgasm began to subside, Sabrina started to work her mouth. Up and down his now sensitive shaft. Forcing him to tap out. "Damn woman, your mouth is amazing." André said. "Is my master pleased?" She asked. "Did his sub do a good job?" "Yes, you did an excellent job woman." André replied. "I think you deserve a treat." He helped her to stand and turned her to face the bed once more.

Her hands were still cuffed in front of her. She placed them on the bed for balance. The spreader bar kept her legs spread. Like she was being searched. André grabbed the vibrating wand. He turned the speed up high and stuck it close to her ear. Allowing her to hear the hum. Rubbing it on her ass cheeks before sliding it between her legs. He soon found her wet pussy and clitoris. He pressed the wand firmly there. Sabrina's body began to react immediately. The stimulation on her clit was beyond intense. Powerful waves of orgasm washed over her. Again and again. André held the wand steady with his left hand. Then tugged gently on the beads with his right.

Her ass was convulsing with each orgasm. When the beads were removed. Her body exploded, imploded and disintegrated. Her legs held open by the spreader bar went weak. She began to crumble towards the floor. André follows her collapse with the wand. Keeping it trained on her pussy. At the same time, he pulled the remaining beads out of her ass. He was drove her to the brink of insanity and ecstasy. Until it felt her body couldn't take any more pleasure. As he removed the last bead, Sabrina fell onto the floor. Simply unable to stand any longer. Her breathing was intense. Her body was super charged with what felt like high voltage electricity. "Damn I, I, thought I." She huffed. "I was, I was going to, to over-dose from, from, k,k, cum-ming."

André tried to kiss her. She pulled quickly away. "Fuck!" She exclaimed breathlessly. "It should be illegal for a man. To be able to do that to a pussy." He gave her a few minutes to float back down to earth. Once it appeared she was only 20,000 feet up, he touched her. As she lay on the bed, he began to rub her back. He kissed her spine in soft sporadic kisses. His hands worked on her shoulders. He gently massaged her neck and kneaded her muscles. "Ummmm, that feels so good." She said. He caressed her skin and mixed it with kisses. On her shoulder blades, collar bones and all over her back. Just as she was falling into the relaxation of the massage. He lifted her up.

Now up on her hands and knees. He slid his dick into her pussy from behind. Sabrina gasped as his throbbing hard flesh, met her soft yearning flesh. He began to fuck her wildly. Holding her hips firmly. Sabrina screamed as she could feel his passion in each thrust. He rammed his dick into her with incredible force. Making her juicy ass bounce with each pounding. Sabrina was only too happy. Bouncing her well-rounded ass back to him when he pulled out. He stroked her intently for several minutes. Then suddenly he stopped. He found the edible lotion. Pouring more of it between her cheeks.

Once she was moistened there. He grabbed one of the vibrating bullets Sabrina left out. He turned it on and slid it gently into her ass. He then returned his dick into her pussy. Fucking her nice and slow. Her body began to adjust to the rhythm. Of both the two-inch bullet and his rock hard staff. Sabrina was soon ascending back into the clouds. She felt heavenly pleasure as they made love. The vibrating bullet was sending shockwaves. Of delightful sensations through her body. His dick did the same as it invaded her pussy. He rammed his dick into her like an angry black man. A black man just turned down on his third job interview. Sabrina screamed in delight. She loved the feel of him taking out his frustration on her pussy. His dick worked in sync with the shockwaves of the bullet.

"God Damn!" She moaned. "That dick feels so fucking good." "God Damn Sabrina!" He moaned back to her. "This pussy is incredible. You're going to make me cum all inside of you." Sabrina bent her head further onto the pillow. She began to bite it. André seemed to be driving his dick deeper and deeper. Each stroke intensified the feeling of the vibrations in her ass. "Your chocolate skin glistening is so fucking sexy." André said. I just want to fuck you all night." "Oooh!" Sabrina moaned. "Fuck me however you want to." He pulled out of her and turned her over onto her back. He quickly climbed on top of her. Kissing her all over her gorgeous face. Soon, his dick was pushing inside of her. He lifted her legs up over his arms.

He locked his lips onto hers. Their tongues wrestled as he began to thrust his dick deeply. His hands found their way under her soft round ass. He lifted her cheeks off the mattress. Her legs were pinned and pussy suspended in air. He began a furious pace of pounding inside of her. Sabrina wrapped her arms around the back of his neck. Pulling him to keep his face close to hers. He met her at eye level. Looking deep into her eyes. He drilled his dick into her soft and wet pussy. No words were spoken but they communicated through their eyes. He told her he controls her pussy now. Her eyes spoke back to him in submission and compliance.

His dick seemed to be coming down. From atop the Empire State building as he crashed into her body. With each stroke. He looked into her open eyes. So she could see who was ravishing her body in such a manner. Both of them felt the sweetest pleasure. While they indulged in beautiful lovemaking. André drove her long and deep. Making sure to grind his pubic bone, on her clitoris with each stroke. The intimacy of looking into each other's eyes, caused passion's fire to build. The fire roared. To an unbelievable amount of equitable heat between them. They both could feel that pending climax. André was determined. To make sure that they both climax at the same time. His hands gripped and re-gripped her ass. Keeping it suspended, above the mattress as he pounded into her. Sabrina's vaginal walls clamped onto his shaft. Each time he pulled upward.

They quickly sucked him back inside of her magical tunnel. Swallowing him whole. Each time they envelope him. It sent tidal waves of pleasure through his body. Sabrina moaned with each thrust. The feeling was just too damn good and all she wanted to do was cum. André had found her spot. He was beating on it like a skilled drummer. Sabrina knew exactly when to clinch onto his shaft. She played his organ in beautiful song. Together, they made the sweetest symphony of music. Their raging climaxes began to meet each other on the moon.

Sabrina wrapped her legs around his waist. Her heels tapped his ass cheeks. Urging him to fuck her harder. The intensity of her kinetic energy. From her heels, through his hips and back into her body was godly. Both of their bodies seemed to be shattering. Sabrina began to moan in between breaths. "Oh F, Fa, Fuuuuuck! She said. "DON'T STOP! Ooooh, YESSSSSSSSSS! André you're making me…. OH MY GOD! OH MY GAAAWWWWD!" André sensed her orgasm. He found the right angle inside of her. The angle that would stimulate him. To release all of his pent up energy. Sabrina felt as if her cum was being held by a damn. Suddenly the damn just broke.

Her juices rushed out of her like a waterfall unleashed. Only to be met by André's hot molten lava. Realizing that they both were cumming at the same time. Sabrina wrapped her arms and legs around him even tighter. She strained to hold on. They both were covered in glistening perspiration. She thrust her hips upward as the only direction she could. André held her ass lifted still in suspension. He pounded her. Emptying every single drop of semen into her soft and wet pussy. Moaning and grunting with each powerful thrust. His body shook as he poured everything he had into her. She felt his remaining spasms of joy mix with her own climax. Gently, his hands lowered her body back onto the bed. Then slowly into reality.

Sabrina relaxed her legs from around his waist. They kissed tenderly over and over. "Damn woman." He said. "You feel like the world's finest chocolate. Your body is so sweet. So chocolate, so delicious and so addictive." "Thank you." Sabrina replied. "I love your chocolate bar with nuts too. "You know that melts in your mouth?" André asked. "As well as your hands." "So I've heard." Sabrina replied. "You'll have to show me." "Well, you're going to have to give me a minute woman." André said. "You took almost everything I had." "Almost?" Sabrina quizzed. "You mean you have something left? I'm going to need you to hand that over right now."

"Damn, I'm about to call the Police on you woman." André said. "I think you're trying to kill me." "Why would you say that?" Sabrina asked. "I'm just saying." André replied. "You're trying to work a brother to death." "Well, this was your turn to be in control." Sabrina said. "In the morning, before you go to that ceremony. It'll be my turn to be in control." "What?" André replied. "In the morning? I may not have recovered by then. Why can't we wait until I get back from the ceremony?" "No, Mr. Lover man." Sabrina replied. "Rules are rules. You had your way with me when you wanted. I want you in the morning. Don't worry. You'll be done long before the ceremony begins."

"Now, I'm going to go take a shower." She continued. Would you care to join me?" "I'm scared to get in the shower with you." André said. "You may try to get me excited again. I won't be able to do anything with you in the morning." "Oh, you'll be able to do everything I need you to." Sabrina assured. "I'm sure of that. After I get out of the shower. I'm going to make a grilled chicken salad. Would you like one as well?" "Yeah, that sounds good." André said. "Something light and healthy. So I can get to sleep. Then wake up and see what the hell you have planned. Before going to this stupid ass ceremony." Sabrina got out the bed and headed to the shower. "I'm going to go ahead and change these sheets." André said. "While you're in there." "Good idea." Sabrina said.

"Since you got sweat and stuff all over them." She said. "Ah, my back wasn't on these sheets." André replied. "That was you, ma'am." "I'm too cool to sweat." Sabrina said. "So that had to be you." "Your ass wasn't too cool." André said. "To be making all that damn noise in my ear." "Why Sir, I have not a clue as to what you are referring." Sabrina said. "I'm a lady and I don't partake in any such things." "Yes, you're a lady in public." André retorted. "In this bedroom though? Anyway, get in that shower woman. Let me change these sheets and get my shower. So we can get some rest."

Down in the fallout shelter in West Baltimore. Ronnie James and Deer Dog were putting on their protective suits. To open the 50-gallon drum of hydrochloric acid. They deposited the poncho and clothes they wore. Where most of the gunshot residue was deposited. "Man, this is brilliant." Deer Dog said. "That your mom has this shelter down here. In the middle of the hood. How do you all get rid of this acid? When it's time to change it?" "Behind that steel door is a tunnel." Ronnie James replied. "This house used to be a part of the church across the street. There is a conveyer belt that can transfer shit. From here to there and vice versa." "Man, that door is probably heavy as a motherfucker." Deer Dog said. "Yeah, we had to put hydraulics on it." Ronnie James said. "In order to get it open. Or else, we'd need like 6 people down here to open it."

Chapter 9

The Clean Up

"Those stairs going up to the back yard." Ronnie James continued. "Is the only other way to get down here. Even that takes time. The staircase is so narrow. Only one person can get down here at a time." "Does the sprinkler system work?" Deer Dog asked. "Yeah, that shit better work." Ronnie James replied. "It takes time to get down here, it would take time to get out too. The walls, floor and ceiling. Are made of seven and a half inches of solid concrete. Behind this plastic coating. The plastic is to contain the acid. Should this barrel leak out. That's why I left the door open up there. This shit will burn almost anything it touches. For some reason, it will not eat through this plastic."

They heard a loud crash come from upstairs. Deer Dog immediately looked at Ronnie James. "What was that?" Deer Dog asked. "Mom might have fallen again." Ronnie James replied. "She does that about once every year. Trying to walk around without turning on the lights." "Is she alright?" Deer Dog asked. "That was a loud crash." "Yeah, let's find out if she's alright." Ronnie James said. "HEY, MA! MA! ARE YOU ALRIGHT?" They then heard footsteps coming down the stairs. "I think she's coming down here." Deer Dog said. "No, those footsteps are too fast to be hers." Ronnie James said. "Grab that shotgun out of that cabinet." "No, don't touch that shotgun, Dog."

Drexler appeared as he descended down the stairway. He held a .357 in hand. He was wearing a pair of gloves. "What the fuck are you doing here, nigga?" Ronnie James asked. "I just stopped by to say goodbye." Drexler replied. "Goodbye?" Deer Dog asked. "Are you going somewhere else?" "I would be gone if it were up to you." Drexler replied. "My dear brother." Drexler removed a digital recorder from his pocket. He then pressed play and held it up. Allowing Ronnie James and Deer Dog to hear it.

"Once I secure the funds, he and Drexler will shake hands. You'll be standing behind Drexler and I want you to blow his brains out. This serves two purposes. It will get Drexler out of the way, so you can run things. Two, it will send a clear message to Dirty Red. That I'm not to be fucked with." "Okay, if that's the plan then that's what I'm rolling with." Deer Dog said. "What the fuck man?" "What's wrong?" Ms. Parsons asked. "This damn Transit cop has been following us.

"Drexler, you have to know." Deer Dog said. "That was just bullshit talk. I was just feeding shit to Mama Parsons." "I just told her at the meet I wouldn't do it. You can go ask her." "How am I going to ask her?" Drexler replied. "Did you forget? A dead bitch can't tell a nigga shit!" Ronnie James charged at Drexler upon hearing the news. Drexler fired two rounds at his chest. Ronnie James fell to the floor and Drexler fired another round at his head. "Drexler, come on man." Deer Dog begged. "You know I would never sell out my brother. I was just telling that bitch what she wanted to hear. I was going to bring her scheme to you. See how you wanted to handle it."

"When were you going to do that?" Drexler asked. "When you lured me to that meeting with Dirty Red? Then blew my brains out? Or were you going to tell me about it at my funeral?" "Look Count man." Deer Dog said. "I know how it looks man. You have to believe me that it wasn't like that. We have that bitch who took our money. She is up there right now in Harford County. We can go up there together. Grab her ass. Walk away with more money than we ever dreamed about. I'll help you give your brother the punishment, you've always wanted to give him." "Motherfucker! Drexler replied. "I don't need your help working out my family issues. Turn around, nigga. I'm going to shoot you right where you planned to shoot me." "I'm not turning around man." Deer Dog said. "If you're going to shoot me. You would have to look me in the eye and do it."

"Have it your motherfucking way nigga." Drexler replied. He fired one shot to Deer Dog's forehead. He then stood over him. Firing two more rounds into his chest. He calmly walked over and switched to protective gloves. He carefully opened the barrel of acid. He gently dropped the gun inside. He took a look around at the two bodies on the floor. He then changed his gloves again. He walked upstairs through the back door of Ms. Parson's house. He looked at her body lying still on the kitchen floor. "I told you." Drexler said. "I'd make sure you were taken care of Ms. Kitty. At least, for your funeral. You don't have to go far."

"They can just roll your old ass across the street. Oh, I meant to tell you. I've been thinking about making a change in leadership. I was thinking I would do better. Not needing a damn thing from your ass." He walked to her refrigerator. He took a bottle of water before walking out. He closed and locked the door. He then removed his gloves. Then walked to his car while drinking his water. He took a look around the dimly lit street. Taking a mental picture of how everything looked. He then entered his car and drove away.

The morning light began to peer. Into the closed blinds at André's house. He appeared sound asleep. Sabrina nudged him gently. She began to kiss his neck. Trying to slowly wake him to reality. "Ummm, what are you doing?" He mumbled. "I'm trying to wake you." Sabrina replied. So I can have my way with you." "It's too early for this, isn't it?" André asked. "Oh, it's never too early to cum." Sabrina responded. "Especially after what you did to me last night." André stretched his arms and yawned. He got up to make his way to the bathroom. Sabrina followed him. Kissing him on his shoulder. "Let me rinse with some mouthwash first woman." He said. "Take a quick shower. Obviously, you've been up and done all of that." "I'll be out here waiting on you, Officer." She said. André went to the sink and began to rinse his mouth.

He washed his face with cleanser. Gently drying his face with a cloth. He walked over to the shower and turned the water on. He waited for his shower head to change from blue to green. Signifying that the water was warm so he could enter. After his shower, he dried off. He tossed the towel into the dirty clothes bin. He lifted a few layers of clothes. Verifying that a 9mm pistol he put in there, was still there. As he put on his robe, he called to Sabrina. "Hey Breen." He said. "Are you going to feed a brother first?" "Or are you just going to catch a rape and a negligent charge? First thing in the morning?" "From the looks of what's hanging down there." Sabrina replied. It doesn't look like you feel rape is happening."

"Excuse you." André replied. "It's scientifically proven that men can have an erection out of fear. Or other emotions. That doesn't mean they are looking for sex. Just as women can become moist out of fear. Or other emotions. I thought you knew something about science. Now I see I'm dealing with a kindergarten dropout." "Damn, you didn't even let me make it to first grade?" Sabrina asked. They walked to the kitchen where Sabrina had made coffee. She also made light breakfast sandwiches and grits. "Oh." André said. "I see you got up real early and got this day started. You must really have some big plans for me." "I just want to get you back in bed." Sabrina replied. "Work out all this pent-up energy in me." "Well, are we going to save anything for tonight?" André asked.

"Don't worry about tonight, sweetie." She replied. "Let's just enjoy this morning and see what happens." "Is something raunchy supposed to happen?" André joked. "Something like that, nasty man." She responded. "Nasty man?" André said. "You're the one talking about having your way with me." "I'm just trying out my fantasy of being a dominatrix." Sabrina said. "I want you to play along, that's all." "This better not be painful or no crazy stuff." André responded. "Or I won't be playing anymore. We might have some problems then." "I promise I won't hurt you my sex toy." Sabrina said.

"Now hurry up and finish your breakfast." She urged. "So you can come and do as you're told." "Yes, ma'am Sergeant. Right away, ma'am." He washed down his breakfast sandwich with some coffee. Sabrina took the dirty dishes to clean at the sink. Once she finished, she went to meet André in the bedroom. He was already in bed watching television. She slid under the covers next to him and laid her head on his chest. "So, what are the rules of this game?" André asked. "These rules are simple." She replied. "I'm going to tie you up and give you commands. All you have to do, is everything I say or….." "Or what?" André asked.

She turned to reach under the bed. Producing a plastic whip and spanking paddle. "Or I'm going to have to correct your behavior." She continued. "That whip doesn't hurt, does it?" He asked. "No, it's plastic for the most part." Sabrina replied. These tassels only sting a little bit." She hit him across the arm twice. "See?" She said. "It's all fun and nothing that you can't handle." "Is my uniform ready?" He asked. "For this stupid ceremony later today?" "Yes, I ironed your shirt and pants." Sabrina replied. "Everything is laid out. In the powder room. Are you excited about possibly meeting the President?" "Hell no!" André answered. "I don't want to meet that motherfucker. This bitch has committed treason. He is incompetent, a racist and everything I hate."

"Why don't you tell me how you really feel?" Sabrina joked. "I feel like that motherfucker belongs in prison." André replied. "Maybe he's not all bad." Sabrina said. "Do not tell me you support this bastard in any way?" André said. "All I'm saying is." She continued. "Maybe there's a reason he does some things." "Yes, there are very good reasons." André said. "That bitch is a criminal." "I don't know about criminal." Sabrina replied. "Sometimes, people do things because they have an opportunity. That will never come again. Sometimes, they do things for personal reasons. Or it could be. Because they want to make amends. For wrongs that happened in the past.

"Well, while our food settles." Sabrina said. "Let's not talk about him. Let's not talk government. Or anything that's going to get us angry. I'll pull up an old episode of "Sanford & Son." On demand and we can laugh together." "Now that sounds like a good idea." André said. "See if you can find that one. Where Lamont got a ticket in Beverly Hills and they went to court. I split my side open every time I see that episode." "Is that the one where Fred questions the cop?" Sabrina asked. Asking if he ever gave tickets to white people?" "Yeah, that's the one." André said. "The cop said, 'yes.' Then Fred said. 'Well, where are they? Look around this courtroom. They're enough niggers in here to make a Tarzan movie!'"

They both laughed out loud recalling the episode. Sabrina went through the episodes on TVOne on demand. She found the episode. They laid in bed together laughing. As if there was nothing else going on in their lives. She laid her head on his chest and they watched the show. The episode went off. Sabrina began gliding her nails across André's chest. "Let me go get my high heels and lingerie." She said. "I'll be back to tell you what to do momentarily." "Didn't I show you last night?" André asked. "That I know what to do?" "Yes, you did baby." Sabrina replied. Last night you were the Dom and I was Sub." "This morning, I'm the Dom and that makes you my Sub.

"Just like a good Sub sandwich." She continued. "Made at any carry out in Baltimore. I want everything on my Sub with hots." "I think I might need to tell my mama on you." André said. "Oh no!" Sabrina replied. "Your mama can't save you now boy. I'll be right back." Moments later Sabrina returned. Wearing black lace lingerie, exposing her breast. Her lingerie also had no crotch material. Exposing her vaginal area. She was also wearing high-heeled pumps. Her accessories included satin arms-length gloves. A mask that covered her eyes and nipple clamps. To top off her outfit. She wore his 8-point Policeman's hat. She also carried a duffle bag with unknown items inside. André, sitting on the bed stared at her in disbelief.

Partly because he couldn't believe she liked to role play this way. Partly because she looked so sexy. "Get down on your knees boy." She ordered. "Your Mistress wants to be pleased now." André was slow getting to his knees. Sabrina opened the duffle bag and removed the whip. She whacked him with it. Letting him know that she meant business. André hurriedly got on his knees. Sabrina slowly walked up to him. She walked close to him. So that her vagina was right before his face. Close enough where he could smell her sweet scent. "Say hello to your Master Sheba." Sabrina commanded. André tried to kiss her labia. Sabrina pulled back. She then lifted her right leg and stepped over him. Letting her crotch rub across the top of his head.

Once behind him she spoke. "You didn't ask permission to kiss Sheba." She said. "That is punishable by arrest." She went into the bag grabbing a pair of Velcro cuffs. Dropping the bag she tied his right arm. She secured that arm inside the restraint and then his left arm. She lifted her right leg. She stepped back over him as before. Letting her crotch rub across the top of his head. Before turning to face him again. "Now, let's try this again." She said. "Say hello to Sheba for me." André called out to her vagina. "Hello beautiful Sheba." He said. "That's a good boy." Sabrina said. "Now you may kiss her." André stuck out his tongue and tried to lick her. She grabbed him by his forehead and stopped him. "Didn't I just say you may kiss her?" Sabrina asked.

"I said nothing about licking!" She then hit him across his chest with the whip. "You're going to learn to follow my orders Sub. Or your punishment will be severe." She then stepped closer to him once more. She grabbed the back of his head. With her hand gently guiding him forward. He began to kiss her vulva area. After he kissed her several times, she broke the silence. "Enough of that." She said. "You may kiss me from behind." She then turned around and presented herself to him. She leaned slightly. André did as he was told again.

"Yes, I like that my Sub." She said. "You're learning very quickly to please your Mistress. "Enough!" She said. She turned around to face him. Removing her right shoe. "Now bow and kiss my foot." She ordered. André leaned forward to obey her. She lifted her left leg, placing her heel on his shoulder. She gently applied pressure to force his face down. Only relinquishing when his lips touched her. "Kiss my foot and shoe." She demanded. André alternated kisses. Between the top of her foot and top of her shoe. "Ummmm, I like that darling." She said. She then stopped him. Going into her duffle bag once more. She removed the padded collar with the short chain on it.

She sat her bag down and placed the collar around his neck. She then carefully walked him over to the accent bench. She sat on the bench. She removed her other shoe. Ordering him to suck her toes. "Which set do you want me to start with madam?" He asked. "DON'T SPEAK!" She commanded. "Just do what you're told." She slowly moved her left foot up to his mouth. André began to suck her toes. She leaned back, bracing herself on the bench. She soon offered him her right foot. André sucked her toes on that foot as well. Her legs were spread slightly. So André could see all of her treasure.

All he wanted to do was drive his dick balls deep inside of her. Sabrina could see the look in his eyes. She knew what he was thinking. "You'd better not rise up to touch her." Sabrina said. "Not without my permission." Stunned that she seemed to have read his mind, André continued. Sucking and kissing her feet. Sabrina presented the bottom of her feet to him. He kissed them as well. She then sat up and rested her feet on his thighs. His kneeling before her provided an excellent stool. Her crotch was only inches from his face. She made sure she kept her legs open for him to bask in her scent. The strawberry fragrance she applied there, along with her natural scent was intoxicating. André wanted to stop playing this submissive game. He wanted to fuck her silly.

That was also evident to Sabrina. She just knew she was in control of this show. She got up and helped him stand to his feet. She removed a cuff and placed his hands in front of him. She reapplied the restraints. She laid him on the bed. His naked body before her, she climbed on the bed as well. She moved her crotch over his face. She took a seated position and simply said one word. "Eat!" She ordered. André wanted to use his hands to help him access her jewels. However, he couldn't get them past her waist. Her weight was firm as she sat on him. She grinded her pussy into his face. Pouring her juices and scent all over him. Rubbing her clitoris on his nose. Then back down to his mouth. She covered his mouth completely with her labia.

Her right hand grabbed the whip. Her left hand grabbed his forehead. She guided his face where she wanted him to lick. She enjoyed the control she was exerting over him. "Are you trying to make me cum Sub?" She asked. André tried to speak. She pressed her vagina more firmly over his mouth. All he could do was mumble. "You do like to please your Mistress don't you?" She asked. "So, I think you deserve a little treat." She climbed off of his face and moved her face down his body. Leaving kisses as she went. His hands reached for her breast as they brushed his arms. Sabrina pushed his hands away. She slowly made her way down to his semi-erect penis. She took it in her hand. She put her face close to his shaft and began to talk. As if she was speaking to it. "Do you want me to put you in my mouth?" She asked.

"Yes ma'am, I do." André said. She gently squeezed his penis and pinched his thigh. "I wasn't talking to you, Sub!" She snarled. "Only speak to me when spoken to. Understood?" André did not respond and she got up. She went to her duffle bag. She produced the paddle and walked back to the bed. She smacked him hard across his right thigh. "Do you understand, Sub?" She asked. "Yes ma'am. I understand Mistress." He answered. She laid back next to him. Taking his rod back into her hand.

"Now do you want me to put you in my mouth?" She repeated. "That throbbing in my hand tells me you do." She kissed the tip of his penis. Then stared at its reaction. "I like what I see." She said. "Do you want me to do it again?" She asked. André tried to move his hand to reach out to her. Again, she refuted his gesture. "Why are you trying to come down here?" She asked. "All in our conversation?" "When I want you to do something, I will tell you." She grabbed her paddle again. Whacking him across his left thigh. André moaned in the slight pain. Which he forgot when she her placed her mouth on his shaft.

His erection had begun to fade. Until Sabrina started to rub it with her satin gloves. In seconds, he was erect once again. She then took his dick into her mouth and began to suck it. Like a food-starved person. André tried in vain to get his hands onto her head. To make her suck him deeper. She was able to keep his hands away. They were still restrained together. Once he stopped trying to reach out to her. She moved his dick out of the way. So that she could lick his balls. André was delirious with pleasure. She seemed to be spelling the entire alphabet. With the tip of her tongue over his balls. She then moved back to sucking him.

Her mouth moved as if she was making love to his cock. Sabrina sucked until he was nice and stiff. She sat up and reached for her duffle bag. She seemed to be searching for something. Shortly, she emerged with a vibrating cock ring. "What the hell is that?" André asked. "Did I tell you to speak Sub?" She asked. "It's a cock ring if you must know. It will squeeze the base of your shaft. Delaying your orgasm. It also has a little vibrator for my clit. When I glide down on you. Now silence and let me work here." She stroked and kissed his dick a few more seconds. Assuring his stiffness. She let her saliva moisten it. So the cock ring would slide on more easily. She gently worked it down to the base of his shaft. Next she turned the vibrator on.

She then climbed on top of him. She moved forward towards his face. Using her hand on his chest to balance herself. She assumed a seated position and gave out the command. "Eat it!" She said. She began to ride his face. André could only offer his tongue in service. His hands were still bound. Sabrina made sure he licked every place, she wanted to be licked. She soon stopped her clitoris right over his mouth. She had him lick it repeatedly. She was grinding her clit over his tongue and mouth. Her climax was beginning to build. She then quickly moved down to André's dick. Guiding it into her dripping wet pussy.

She rode furiously up and down his dick. Mashing her clitoris on the waiting cock ring. The vibrations touched her clitoris. Sending pulsating tsunami waves of pleasure through her body. Her entire body shook. Her orgasms came so fast and ferociously. They even caught her off guard. Her body was bucking wildly. The intensity of her climax was like a volcanic eruption. She tried desperately to hold onto the ride. She had to hold herself still to keep from falling apart. As her climax subsided, she began to release her grip. She slowly lowered her body frozen in air. As her vagina moved down his shaft. The vibrating cock ring touched her clitoris again.

Her orgasm was once again off to the races. She was fucking André. Like she was taking his dick against his will. She slammed her pussy down most of his rod. She slowed when she got the bottom. She did this to make sure her clitoris grinded on the vibrating ring. "OH MY GOD! OOOOH FUCK YEEEEEEEEEEEEEEEEEEEEEEEEESSSSSSSSSS! Whose dick is this?" She asked. "Say my fucking name." André called out her name as instructed. "It's yours Sabrina." He replied. "Fuck this dick. Use that dick to make that pussy cum." Sabrina relished the feeling of the dick inside of her. Along with the vibrations of the cock ring. Meeting her clitoris with each thrust. She came in one violent explosion after another and another. Finally, she had to throw herself off of André. To stop herself from cumming.

She collapsed next to him. Breathing heavily into his face. Gathering herself. She let him kiss her as her faculties began to return. "Let me take this ring off." She said. "We don't want to leave that on there too long. It will cut off all your circulation." She removed the cock ring. Before lying back next to him. "You pleased your Mistress very well." She said. "I guess you deserve to be pleased as well. Don't worry I'm going to make sure you get what's coming to you." She started to kiss his face and neck. Making her way down his body. Her hand found and caressed his semi-hard dick. She began to make it animated again.

She moved her head down and kissed it. Before taking it into her mouth once more. André tried to reach for her head. He desperately wanted to go deeper. "I have to do something about those hands." She said. She motioned for him to move closer to the headboard. She then went to her duffle bag. Removing some longer Velcro restraints. She tied one end to the right corner of the head board. She then removed the cuffs André was wearing. Placing his right arm into the longer restraint. She tied the second restraint to the headboard. Adding his left arm. "What are you doing?" André asked. "I'm making sure your hands don't try to stop me." She answered. "From sucking and kissing you. Relax and just let what's going to happen, happen."

She picked up her duffle bag once more. Removing two additional long restraints. "What the fuck?" André said. "Are we making a BDSM movie in here? "Shhhhhhh." She replied. She tied a restraint to the corner at the foot of the bed. Then she wrapped his left leg inside the other end. She then placed the remaining restraint on the bed, tying his right leg. "Now, that's a good boy." Sabrina said. "You want your Mistress to sit on your face again, don't you?" She seductively crawled onto the bed. Then up to his face. This time, she turned her back to his face. She steadied herself with her hands on his thighs. He stuck his tongue out for her service. She made him lick her up and down repeatedly. She began to work towards her next orgasm.

"Yes, that's it baby." She said. "Make your Mistress happy and I'll let you cum." She leaned down into the 69 position. Taking his dick into her mouth. He tried to pull his arms from over his head. From out of the restraints but to no avail. He was helpless to control her motions. Or what part of her he could lick. Sabrina took full advantage of him. She rubbed her clitoris madly into his face. The fact that he was struggling to reach her. Only turned her on even more. She worked her mouth up and down on him. Her tongue flickered like a snake. Especially when she reached the tip of his dick. She then gulped it back into her mouth. Deep-throating it onto her tonsils. "OH GOD. DAMN!" André moaned. "That feels so good. Suck it deep like that again."

This time, Sabrina took an order from him. Her mouth engulfed his dick. She took it deep again. She got it all the way in her mouth. Then took her tongue and licked his balls resting on her lips. André was desperately trying to free himself. So that he could keep her mouth right where it was. Her mouth felt delicious to him. He wanted to make sure she didn't stop. She used the side of her legs to nudge his head. She wanted to remind him to focus on her pleasure. André got the message and returned to licking her wildly. His lips grabbed her clitoris and labia. Whenever Sabrina slowed down enough for him to do so. She took her hands off of his dick. Keeping it in her mouth while reaching back.

She spread her cheeks to give André the access he had been searching for. He could now lick inside of her pussy and everywhere. The feeling of control was overwhelming to Sabrina. She began to feel atomic-like intensity building inside of her. She grinded her pussy savagely over Andrés' face. With only one concern in mind. She wanted to cum. "OOOOOOOHHHH FFFFFUUUUUUUCKKKKKKKK!" She screamed as she exploded! Squirting her eruption all over him. She thrashed her pelvis. As if shaking out each wave of cum onto his face. He was unable to push her away. He could only endure her waterfall.

Sabrina paused as she tried to regain her composure. She also had to regain his dick inside her mouth. Somehow, she released it. When she was in the apex of her orgasm. She took it back into her mouth and began to suck it. André tried to push his hips upward. Trying to go deeper and she let him. She then turned to face him and sat on his dick. She began to ride him and encouraged him to pump into her. André did his best. He was limited in how strong his thrusts were. In his current position. "That's right, officer." Sabrina said. "I'm in control now. Your orgasm is in my hands." André pulled at his leg and arm restraints. His efforts were futile. Sabrina rode his dick and began to talk to him.

"Do you like when other people have control over you?" She asked. "How does it feel?" "Oooh yeah, keep riding that dick." André replied. "OH, I'm about to cum in your pussy. Oooh FUCK! I'm going to cum in that fucking pussy. That's it woman. Make it cum in that pussy. Here it comes Sabreeeeee…." As he called her name, Sabrina got up swiftly. She took his dick into her mouth. André pumped madly. His impending body-shattering explosion took over him. He pumped her mouth. Blasting it with his creamy white cum. Sabrina worked her mouth to his rhythm. She took every drop of his love. André's eyes were closed. He had an out-of-body experience.

Sabrina sat on the edge of the bed. She watched and waited for him return to normal. "See, you didn't cum in my pussy." She said. "You came in my mouth." "So, you don't always get to call the shots. Let's call that your first lesson André." "Damn!" André replied. "That was good Sabrina." "Now take these things off of me. So I can shower and get ready to go." "I just told you." Sabrina replied. "That you don't always get to call the shots. Apparently, you don't pay attention in class very well. Maybe you'll learn better with your second lesson. She walked over to the duffle bag and looked for some items. "What is my second lesson?" André asked. "Oh, it's a lesson you'll never forget." Sabrina answered.

"It's called, 'Hell has no fury like a woman scorned!'" She then walked over to the headboard to his right arm. She placed real handcuffs on him. "What the fuck are you doing?" André demanded. She walked over to the left side. After a brief struggle, she handcuffed that arm to the bed as well. "I just saw to it that you came." Sabrina replied. "Now I'm going to see to it that you're gone." "What the fuck are you talking about crazy bitch?" André yelled. "Crazy bitch?" Sabrina repeated. "Oooooh are you mad at me? Or super mad?" She asked.

Chapter 10

We Had No Idea

"He's all yours Michael." She said. "Kill him and let's go catch our ride." "WHO THE FUCK IS MICHAEL?" André demanded. Michael then walked into the room. Carrying a Sig Sauer .40 caliber handgun. He pointed it at André. "Put a towel over this fool Jasmine?" Michael said. "I don't want to look at this motherfucker's dick. Especially after it was just in my woman." "Jasmine?" André repeated. Sabrina tossed Michael a towel. He got closer to André to toss the towel onto him. André noticed the tattoo on his neck. "Kings Get Better?" André read out loud. "You're the motherfucker from the swinger's club!" "Bravo!" Sabrina said. "You solved a mystery."

"You should become a cop or something." "Sabrina!" André called. "Jasmine or whatever? What the fuck is going on? "What's going on is." Jasmine said. "You're about to pay for ruining my family." "BITCH I DIDN'T KNOW YOU WERE MARRIED TO THIS MOTHERFUCKER!" André yelled. "Not him you fool." Jasmine said. "My brother." "Your brother?" André repeated. "I don't even know your fucking brother." "Oh, is that how you do?" Jasmine asked. "You ruin lives. Then just forget about them? "How did I?" André asked. "What are you talking about bitch?"

"Let's take a short trip down memory lane." Jasmine said. "Back to when you arrested two men. At the Mondawmin Mall station." "Bitch, I've arrested lots of men at Mondawmin." André replied. "Well, these two particular men." Jasmine continued. "Were involved in a prescription pill selling scheme." "A scheme that led to some prominent Doctors. Doctors you arrested. One of those Doctors was my brother. You had a good case with just the men and the woman. The woman was actually writing the prescriptions.

"Yet, you had to go after the Doctors. Arresting them. Ruining their career and lives. My brother and I were the first in our family to go to college. Not only did we graduate. He became a doctor. I am a former FBI Agent. As of five minutes ago because I quit." "Woman, I was a patrol officer back then." André said. "I arrested the two guys, that's true. However, they started singing to keep from going to jail. They told on the woman and your brother. They laid out the operation to our Detectives. Of course, the State's Attorney's Office and my department jumped. They pushed to set up the sting operation. At the next scheduled meet between the men and the woman.

She had dozens of prescriptions on her. Many from your brother's office. It wasn't personal. I was just doing my job." "Oh, you looked like it was personal." Jasmine said. "When you were all on T.V. during the press conference. Oh, I watched you. I was assigned out of the Detroit office. I had just come to visit my brother here in Baltimore. Just as you were ruining his life. He lost his license to practice. His family and all his savings. Trying to stay out of prison. Whatever things he owned like the house. His greedy ass wife took in the divorce. Now he's been reduced to drawing blood. At a few clinics around town.

I've been watching you since that press conference. I pulled your file and studied you. I found out you have some interesting family ties as well. I tried mightily to arrest your brother. Or set up a situation to kill him. That is until I found out. You two didn't really care for each other. When the bureau offered the opportunity to come to Baltimore. I jumped. When they added it was to infiltrate your brother's organization. I almost had an orgasm. They sent three of us here. At first, we were all about the mission. Then some strange things started happening in Washington. When your current President came to power. Policy became incoherent. One day, we're doing this. The next day somebody else is in charge. This is obsolete and now we're doing that.

"So, the other two agents and I." Sabrina continued. Came up with a plan. There was all this unmarked money floating around. A large amount was supposed to end up in your brother's hands. We figured out a way to rob your brother. But then he caught Cynthia. It's almost like someone set her up. Left her drugged in a parking lot or something. I don't know. Somehow your brother found out she was there. I heard what he did to her. He is really an animal. My only regret is that I don't get to kill him." "You said there were three of you." André asked. "Who was the other person?" "Excellent question André." Jasmine responded. "That was Agent Thompson. The man who was sent to protect little old Cynthia and I.

Of course he wasn't sure about taking the money. Then your brother asked us to move the money. When he found out about a raid that was coming. I convinced your brother to keep Ricky T. I'm sorry Agent Thompson with him. I said it would look less suspicious if Cynthia and I moved the money. Once we moved it. Poor Cynthia fell asleep in a car. Your brother didn't believe her story. Ricky knew I was the only one. Who knew where the cash money was. Cynthia had the encrypted code which he figured I had now. So Ricky started following me." "So, did you rat Agent Thompson out to my brother?" André asked. "Or did you kill him? "Neither." Jasmine said. "Actually you killed him André." "What the hell are you talking about?" André asked. "I didn't kill anybody."

"Remember the first time we made love?" Jasmine asked. "You slept really late afterwards? There may have been a little extra something in your tea. While you were sleeping. I took your department issued gun. I went to see Ricky T. By surprise of course. At this Light Rail station that's pretty secluded at night. I shot him with your gun. I shot his locally hired helper with a throw away gun. I left his helper there for the Police to find. Then Michael and I moved Agent Thompson's body. I cleaned your gun so you wouldn't know it was fired. I brought it back here where I got it from.

However, once we're safely out of the country. I'll make a phone call. When an FBI Agent's body is found. With bullets from your gun in him. You'll be disgraced in the death. There will not be any honorary services for you. No bagpipes. No flag. Just dump your simple ass in the ground and forget about you. Meanwhile, my brother and I. Oh and Michael too, will be living the rich life around the world." "You see, we've gathered all the cash money. That was to be distributed. In Charlotte, New Orleans, Detroit and here in Baltimore. "Yes, I painstakingly traveled to those cities." Michael said. "I relieved the holders of the money from their duties."

"Two of them were guys who worked for your brother. He sent them out to Detroit. They were on their way back to Baltimore. They got a flat tire somehow, on the highway and I killed them. Then I had a truck driver help me transport that money here too. We now have 100 million dollars cash money. It should be getting taken to the docks right now. I hired a little local crook down at the ports. He has a crew to put that cash on a ship for us. That ship will take us in Morocco. Then we will just disappear. Look at the bright side here André. You're going to die from a gunshot which is nice and quick. Not the agonizing flu shot." "What are you talking about?" Jasmine asked.

"The flu shot his President...." Michael said. "Didn't you read my email?" "What email?" Jasmine asked. "I was a little busy lately and couldn't read it." "Well, you may want to read it." Michael said. Then warn any of your family and friends. They may want to stockpile some food. Stay away from the flu shot. Also stay away from anybody who gets the flu. In the next 90 days. Your President is planning on killing two-thirds of the country. Becoming King or some shit." Jasmine grabbed her phone and read the email. "Oh my God! We have to warn somebody." She said. "Who are we going to warn?" Michael asked. "There are so many in Congress, the Senate. Every level of Government that are in on this.

"We tell the wrong person." Michael continued. They'll just move up the timetable. Unfortunately, we don't know who the right or wrong person is to tell." "Fuck! Fuck! Fuck! Fuck!" Jasmine yelled! "This is insane! We can't let all these people die. This is my mother. My cousins, uncles, aunts, nieces and nephews. My friends, colleagues and just innocent people." "Take these cuffs off of me Jasmine." André asked. "Let me help." "No motherfucker!" Jasmine replied. "You are the one person I will let die." "If you hadn't destroyed my brother's life. I wouldn't be here. Bringing shame on everything I've worked for. Consumed with vengeance."

"I'm going to let Michael kill you." She continued. "I'll feel nothing but joy when you take your last breath. We'll figure out something to try and save these people. After you're gone. Either way, you won't have to worry about it. When we transfer that half a billion into our account. You'll be a distant memory. Let me look at the code Michael. Those numbers get me all excited." "I don't have the code Jasmine." Michael said. "I thought you had it." "What do you mean you don't have it?" Jasmine asked. I texted you to come get it. When lover boy here took me to Atlantic City. He insisted I leave my purse here. The code was in a booklet in my purse when I left."

"When I got back, it was not in there. You were in the house." "Yes, I got your text." Michael said. "I came here like you asked. There was no booklet in your purse. I looked there and around the room. I assumed you changed your mind and took it with you." "Michael, no one else lives here." Jasmine said. "Nobody else was here so you have to have it! I am not in the mood to be playing these types of games." "Woman, I am not playing any games." Michael said. "We need to find out where the fuck that code is. Could this motherfucker have taken it?" "No." Jasmine replied. "I was the last one out the door when we left for Atlantic City. It was definitely in my purse then because I checked it. Then I was the first one in the house when we got back."

"He stayed outside." Jasmine continued. Talking to his little Officer friend. Signing papers." "Well, if you don't have it?" Michael asked. "And I don't have it? Where the fuck is it?" They heard footsteps approaching the room. Count Drexler appeared. Carrying a pistol grip pump, Mossberg .590 shotgun in his right hand. In his left hand was Smith & Wesson M&P9mm pistol. He pointed the shotgun at Michael. He pointed his pistol at Jasmine. "I have the damn access code." Drexler said. "Hey, fancy meeting you thieving bitches here. Did you all think you were going to steal my money? Without me seeking retribution? Is that my little brother over there? Tied up in his own damn house?"

"You always was into some weird shit. Even when you were a kid. Drop that gun motherfucker. Drexler said to Michael. Before I blow a 12-inch hole in your Nigeri-ussian ass." Michael carefully did as he was told. "Now kick it over here." Drexler ordered. Michael kicked the gun over to Drexler. Holding his hands in the air. "Now I thought I was going to be good." Drexler said. "With just the 25 million sent here to Baltimore. Then I find out Michael. "That you've been a busy little beaver. You've been to New Orleans and Charlotte. Even brought me my money from Detroit. Then you found you a little "criminal" as you said. Down at the port. To help you get that money out of the country. I'm going to forgive you Michael. Since you're from Detroit. How could you know?

Most of the "criminals," in Baltimore report to me. My boy James, is no different. That money his crew is getting out of the storage units. To load on the ship is actually my crew. That money is going to make a slight detour. On the way to Morocco." "Okay Drexler." Jasmine said. "You have all the money. You don't need to kill us." "You're right." Drexler replied. "I don't have to kill you." "I'm going to let my little brother. Deal with your trifling ass." "Yes, leave us to your brother." Jasmine agreed. "He's a good and honest cop." "He'll arrest us and take us in."

"Wrong bitch!" André responded. "Those papers I signed last night. Were my retirement papers. I have no obligation to turn your asses in anymore. Now if my big brother would be a gentleman. Take these fucking cuffs off of me please. Why of course, my dear little brother." Drexler replied. "When I got the text from your little flip phone to mine. After twenty-one years. I got excited. When I read to come over here and get the notepad, out of Jasmine's purse. I was excited and elated. When I looked in the notepad and read the amount of money. I was excited, elated, erect and damn near ejaculated." "Wait, you two actually get along." Jasmine asked. "This wouldn't be the first time you FBI folks got a profile wrong." Drexler said.

"We all remember the white man you were looking for? As the DC sniper. "Sometimes, shit is just not what it seems." André added. "My brother Drexler and I. Made a pact 21 years ago. We would work the system. From both inside and outside the law. We knew that there is a thin line. Between those that uphold the law and those that break it. So thin that somebody crosses it on a regular basis. For one reason or another. Somewhere with all that zig zagging across that thin line. A lot of money gets lost or misplaced. We didn't know who would cross the line or when. We knew if we were patient, it would happen. We had no idea that it would take over twenty years."

"Or that the motherfucker crossing that line." Drexler said. "Would be the President doing it in plain sight." Drexler told Michael to remove the cuffs off of André. He then told Jasmine to give André his underwear and pants. They both did as they were told. André quickly got up to get dressed. "Hey, little brother." Drexler said. "I believe they even brought you a gun that you can use." André picked up the gun off the floor. "Why, that was very generous of them." André said. "I'm almost inclined not to kill you. Then again, almost only counts in horseshoes and hand grenades." He stepped up to Michael. Pointing the gun at his forehead and pulled the trigger.

Michael crashed to the floor. André leaned down to fire two more shots to his head. "Please André." Jasmine begged. "You don't have to do this." "You can just take the money and run. Or I could go with you. We can make love in a different place around the world every day. I'll do all the things that you would like me to do. All the things, any time, any place." "No, that's alright." André said. "I know you will always be thinking about your brother." He then pointed the gun at her temple and pulled the trigger. "Let me take those thoughts off your mind." "Damn, you're a cold motherfucker little brother." Drexler said.

"We could have probably got her to suck our dicks one more time. Before you killed her. Damn trigger happy ass Police. That's why nobody likes you gangs in uniform. André turned to look at his brother. They stared at each other intently. The stare lasted for about 20 seconds. Until they flashed the biggest smiles. They sat their guns down and embraced. They looked at each other. They then embraced again. "Man, it's good to see you." Drexler said. Without having to pretend to be hating you." "Well, it looked like those days are about over." André said. "Almost little brother." Drexler replied. "We need to get out of here though. I made some rounds last night. It won't be long before people are looking for you and me."

"I took care of that." André said. "Let me take a quick shower and we're out. I'm supposed to be at the ceremony this afternoon." "Oh shit!" Drexler said. "What's going on?" André asked. "Jasmine's phone was still unlocked on this email." Drexler said. "Is this shit real? Let me see it." André demanded. He read the email and his mouth dropped open. "What the fuck is this nigga thinking?" André asked. "Print a copy of this to the printer in my office please. We can figure out what to do later. I'm going to take that shower."

Later that day. Hundreds were gathered for the ceremony at the Baltimore Inner Harbor. Lots of media presence and a few tourists. Along with folks whose jobs required them to be there. Chief Delaney's driver was making his way. Through a barricade at Howard and Pratt Street. They headed east towards the Harbor and all subsequent barricades. When he arrived he exited his vehicle. He was greeted by Commissioner Riggs and Major Carver of the BCPD. Standing close by was NSA Deputy Director Baker. Also FBI Deputy Director Tolbert. Along with Maryland State Police Superintendent Scales. A group of Troopers were with him. Governor Hicks was off to the side having a conversation.

The stage was surrounded by Secret Service personnel. There were Police from various agencies. In addition to some unknown men in black suits. Notably absent from the gathering was Captain André Nichols. "Where is your man Chief?" Deputy Director Tolbert asked. "He should be here by now." Chief Delaney responded. "He texted me saying he's running about 15 minutes late. That was about 30 minutes ago." "Well, we've had eyes parked out in front of his house." Director Baker said. Since about 1100 hours." "They don't believe anybody is home. He could be coming from some getaway with his girlfriend.

The President should be arriving here. In about an hour 15 from now. So, we need to have Captain Nichols here. On this platform within 30 minutes. They will close off access to the stage at that time. We'll have to go to plan B." "What's plan B?" Commissioner Riggs asked. "Let's just say I hope all of us here hugged our loved ones today." Director Tolbert responded. "That would include us and you too. Let's give Captain Nichols a few more minutes." Chief Delaney said. "I'm sure he will be here." "For all our sake." Director Tolbert said. "We better hope, wish and pray he shows up. Here in the next few minutes."

At Dulles Airport in Washington DC. Three Senators and Congressmen were exiting a limousine to catch a flight. There was a small press corps gathering. They began to shout questions at the men. "Gentlemen, what does it say that you're taking this trip?" One reporter asked. "While the President is just up the road?" "Do you support the President's initiative in Baltimore?" "Will you make the fund-raising numbers available from this trip?" Another reporter asked. "Are these funds for any specific candidate?" "Are you flying this commercial airline, because of the embarrassment? Of some in this administration's use of Military planes at taxpayer expense?" Senator Simpson stopped and then approached the microphones.

"With regards to the potential ethics violations." Senator Simpson said. "Of Military jets flown for personal use. The White House has assured this body, that they are conducting a full, internal investigation. They are also taking measures to ensure. If any violations have occurred, they will be rectified. We have no information on where they are in their review process." "Senator?" Jacqueline Hubbard with ABC9 News. "Will you demand if violations are found, that the tax payers will be reimbursed?" "This body is not conducting the investigation." Senator Simpson replied. "As such, we are in no position to dictate the remedies. For any ailments in judgement." Chuck Bass from WARC. "Senator, with all due respect. You are a member of the oversight committee.

If ever there seemed like a logical issue. For your committee to investigate. This would appear to be it." Senator Simpson replied. "At this time, we have no reason to believe. That the Administration's internal review. Won't yield a fair and unbiased report. If we deem the report to be hurried and not meticulous. We may step in." Janice Harper with ABC7 News. "So, you're leaving it up to the Foxes? To tell you that they didn't try to eat the chickens? Are you buying the bridge in Brooklyn from them as well?" "As I stated earlier." Senator Simpson said. "We will step in should we deem it necessary."

"No further questions." Senator Simpson said. "We do have a flight to catch. Commercial airlines don't wait. Even for sitting U.S. Congress persons." "Senator." Josh Campbell from WDC13 News. "Can you tell us…." "No further questions." Senator Simpson repeated. "We've got to get out to Vegas and attend this fund-raiser. To try and support our candidates." The group of Senators and Congress personnel walked into the airport. Their luggage was already scanned and checked in by their driver. Although they were well recognized, they presented identification. They were personally escorted onto the plane by U.S. Air Marshalls. The Marshalls would accompany them on this trip.

First class had been booked for just the six of them. Along with their entourage of Marshalls and staff. Once onboard the plane, they could talk more freely. "Did you hear that bitch?" Senator Simpson asked. "Asking me if I was buying the Brooklyn Bridge?" "That's why I didn't take any questions to begin with." Senator McCombs replied. "Especially not from that cunt who tries the "gotcha" questions. To boost her ratings." "That may be true." Congressman Hale said. "This idiot racking up over a million dollars-worth of military flights isn't pretty. People in my district will be asking questions I can't explain." "Just tell those idiots." Congressman Whims said. "That we're waiting on the White House findings. Which we all know is never coming."

"By the time you're home again. They would have forgotten all about this story." "I'll bet." Senator Simpson said. "That flu bug can be nasty. Deadly even. Most of them may not even be around. To ask about no damn Military jet expenses. We on the other hand, will be a lot richer." Senator McCombs said. "We just have to make sure. Our families and friends we care about are protected. They should have enough food and water stored. So that they don't have to come outside for three months. We'll pass an emergency bill. That no utilities can be cut off for non-payment. Since people will be discouraged from going out to work."

"For the ones who have enough food and water. There should be some great real estate deals." Congressman Whims said. "That is once we clean up all the dead bodies. The stench in the air will be unbearable, I imagine." Senator Simpson said. "We can get the Russian Army to come in. Help recover the dead. What will we do with all those dead bodies?" "Load them up on ships and carry them out to sea." Congressman Hale responded. "Then just dump them as shark food. Sharks don't get sick. That's cheaper than the cost to bury all those bodies. It'll be like Christmas for the Sharks. Call us Santa Jaws." They all had a hearty laugh at the joke.

A Stewardess entered and everyone went silent. The Captain announced that the plane was now ready for departure. Everyone should fasten their seatbelts. The Stewardess gave the customary safety rules and instructions. "This trip may be one of the last times." Senator McCombs said. "That we have to fly on a plane with the general public." "That's good because I won't have to sit next to you Thad." Congressman Hale replied. "Smelling you passing gas anymore. We should make your ass go back there and sit in coach. With the rest of those saps." "Don't worry about me and my passing gas. Congressman Whims replies. "Soon I'll have my own private jet."

"Yeah and your own private jet fuel it smells like." Senator McCombs says. They laughed again. The plane took off down the runway. Soon, they were airborne. The Stewardess came by to take their drink orders. She soon returned with the drinks. "I have one scotch on the rocks, two bourbons and coke, a vodka with O.J and two Gins and tonics." "Thank you, darling," Congressman Hale said. "Here's $200. Go on keep the change." "Thank you, Sir." The Stewardess said. "I appreciate it." "Anytime darling." Congressman Hale said. "Now give us some privacy, will you?" The Stewardess returned to the Stewardess station. "I'm going to feel a little bad." Congressman Whims said. "Seeing someone as fine as her laying out on the street dying,"

"Fuck her, there will be plenty like her left over." Senator McCombs said. "Ones who will be willing to do anything for a nice meal. I'll provide that meal. As long as she is willing to do something for me." "I'll drink to that." Senator Simpson said. "That reminds me. I need to tell my wife to get a flu shot this year." They all had a rowdy laugh. "Hell, we should all tell our wives to get a flu shot this year." Congressman Whims said. They laugh even louder. "If I wasn't afraid the dingbat would take my kids with her. I'd do it." Senator Simpson said. "Yeah, I wouldn't be able to do that to my children." Senator McCombs said.

At the Peace Bridge of Niagara Falls. A black SUV arrived from the American side to Canadian border. "Good afternoon, ma'am." The Patrol Officer said. "May I see your passport for everyone in the vehicle?" "Oh, it's just me and my girlfriend coming over for a visit." The driver responded. "How long are you planning to stay?" The agent asked. "We'll be here for about nine days." The driver said. "Do you have anything in the vehicle that you should declare?" The Agent asked. "Such as weapons or drugs?" "Yes, I have my off-duty weapon in the vehicle." The driver said. "Off-duty?" The agent repeated. "Yes Sir. I'm a cop in Baltimore." The driver replied. The agent took her passport, license and Police I.D. "Officer Pamela Stewart." The agent read. "Welcome to Canada Ma'am." He said.

I'm going to need you to pull over to that parking space. Do not take the gun out of the vehicle. I will need you and your girlfriend to get out." The agent then called for another agent to come and assist him. "Hey when you get off work officer." Officer Stewart said. "You should stop by the Sheraton over on Lundy's Lane. My friend and I could use some company. So bring one of your friends." "What, do you have man?" The second agent asked. "Just a female cop from Baltimore. Coming up to party with her girlfriend." The first agent replied.

"They have a weapon in the car." The first Agent said. "We need to get it out. They're talking like they want to get fucked tonight too. We may have to go by the Sheraton over on Lundy's." "Are we going to search the whole vehicle?" The second agent asked. "Nah, it's a cop." The first Agent replied. "Two lovely ladies in the car. We'll never be able to get what they packed back into that truck. I'm just going to have her fill out the Customs form. To declare her weapon. She can pick it up here on her way back to the States. Just run the drug-sniffing dog around the vehicle. To make it look like we're checking." The agents approached Officer Stewart's vehicle. Asking where her weapon was located. "It's under the driver's seat Sir." Officer Stewart replied. The agent went and recovered the weapon.

"Alright ma'am, if you'll follow me inside." The first Agent said. "Then you'll be on your way." Officer Stewart saw an agent coming with a drug-sniffing dog. She said rather loudly. "Oh, you're going to have the drug-sniffing dog check my car? There are no drugs of any kind in my car. Not even aspirin. I may have something in my panties. That may get you hooked tonight." We're supposed to check." The first Agent said. "I'm pretty sure you don't have anything illegal in your car. The first Agent motioned. Telling the other Agent to not run the dog around the car. Officer Stewart then followed the border patrol agent inside. She filled out the Customs form. "Alright ma'am." The Agent said.

"This is your copy. Just bring that here on your way back to the States. Your weapon will be returned to you." "Thank you very much Agent DeBreaux," Officer Stewart said. "We hope to see you and your friend at the Sheraton tonight." Officer Stewart and her friend got into the car and drove off. They drove around to Clifton Hill. They turned left onto River Rd. They drove down to a house and pulled into the garage. They closed the garage door. Officer Stewart opened the rear door of the vehicle. They removed suitcases and bags. Under the suitcases were two sleeping bags. They unzipped the bags.

Out stepped André and Drexler. "Damn, could you drive any slower, baby?" André asked. "Yeah, I thought you ladies were trying to suffocate us in back here." Drexler said. "What are you talking about?" Pamela asked. "You didn't get in the sleeping bags until we left Buffalo." Bridgette said. "Now see, that's my Candy." Drexler said. Ready to fight before she gives me a hug." "Negro, don't ever call me Candy again." Bridgette said. "I don't work at that funky ass strip club anymore. I'm not his or your informant. I'm just your wife Bridgette. A newly rich bitch."

She and Drexler hugged each other tightly. They then kissed like long-lost lovers. "Yes, and I'm just your wife André." Pamela said. "So, the last time I called you Sir. Or you called me Officer Stewart. You better had enjoyed that shit." "Girl, all I want to do." André said. "Is take you in this house and make love to you all night. "Yes Sir." Pamela said. They quickly stepped towards each other and kissed. "No more sneaking quickies in the office at work." André said. "No more sneaking anything." Pamela said. "We can be Mister and Misses out in public from now on. As we travel the world." "That reminds me. André said. We need to look at this email." "What email are you talking about?" Bridgette asked.

"Show them the printout." André said. Drexler removed the papers from his pocket and unfolded it. He then handed it to Pamela. "What the fuck?" She asked. "Where did you get this from?" "This was emailed to Sabrina. I mean Jasmine. From the half black, half Russian dude she was with. Apparently, he was connected. To some KGB guy over in Russia." "If this is right. That asshole of a President and those demons in Congress. Are going to murder most of the country." Bridgette took her key and opened the door to the house. They all walked inside and into the living room area. "This is the type of shit you'd report to the FBI." André said. "Under normal circumstances. We just don't know if whomever we report it to. May be in cahoots with those fools."

"We have family and friends still living there." Bridgette said. They will die." "I'm at a loss for what to do on this one." Drexler said. "I'm trying to think of who we can let know about this." André said. "I got it." Pamela said. "You've got what?" André asked. "I know what to do." She answered. "I know who to call. Hand me that black business card in my purse. I need your pre-paid flip phone too." "Whose card is that?" André asked. "Some guy that hopefully can save the day." Pamela replied. "Hopefully save a lot of lives." "Hey, we don't need to be making any phone calls." Drexler said. No calls or connecting to any internet until we're out of Canada."

"That's why I'm using this old flip phone." Pamela said. We bought this in Vancouver over 20 years ago. Right when we all made this pact to work the system. I later programmed it. So that it pings off of a cell tower first in South Korea. Then Ghana, and about 170 other places around the world. She looks at André and smiles. My Captain in my old Police Department, made sure I got top-notch Cyber Security training. We're both retired now but I still have those skills." She dialed the number on the card 202-000-9999. Immediately she got dial tone. "Oh great." Bridgette said. "The guy that can save the day can't even pay his phone bill."

"No, it's supposed to do that." Pamela said. "Now, we just need to wait." "Wait for what?" Drexler asked. "For somebody to call me back." Pamela said. "Hey, a lot of people are about to die." André said. "We don't have time to be playing phone tag." At that moment, the phone rang. Pamela answered quickly. A voice on the phone immediately spoke. "At the tone. Please leave a message." "This is Officer Stewart. You gave your card to me south of Union Station in DC. She read from the email printout. The Kislovodsk ship should now be docked in Baltimore. It transported highly toxic chemical, Novichok-5. Broken down in molecular composition. The President and other members of Government. Are going to unleash this chemical through mandatory flu shots.

"Hack into email from Apsk13@gmail.ru." She continued. It will tell you everything." Pamela hung up the phone. Only to find everyone staring at her. "I sure hope that shit works." Drexler said. "Maybe we should call the U.N." André said. See if they can do anything." "I think we just made the only phone call." Pamela said. "That we needed to make." "I sure hope you are right." Bridgette said. "How will we know?" Drexler asked. "If this mysterious voicemail is even connected to anyone or anything?" "The number was given to me by a man." Pamela said. "When I was working an assignment on the Marc Train."

"So, you got the number from a passenger?" Drexler asked. "On the Maryland Commuter Rail Train?" "Well, that makes me feel better." "He wasn't a passenger." Pamela said. He worked for The Black House." "The Black House?" André inquired. "I know where the White House is. I've never heard of the Black House." "That's because they didn't want you to know about them." Pamela said. "They only emerge out of the shadows when it's necessary. Right now, it's necessary." Buuuzzzzzz! The sound of an incoming text to the phone was heard. She looked at her phone and saw a text. From 202-000-0001. She tapped to open the text. It read simply; "Message received".

"See, they got the message." Pamela said. They just sent me this text to let me know." "Let me see it." André said. Pamela handed him the phone and André looked. "There is nothing there." André remarked. Pamela took the phone back from him to open the screen. "It's right here." She said. "The last message I got. Wait, it's gone." "Oh great." Drexler said. "We're getting messages that will self-destruct in 15 seconds." "What the fuck is this? Real life or a fucking Tom Cruise movie?" "It would be nice to know." Bridgette said. "That somebody is working to stop this. That we're not just sitting around doing nothing." Bridgette said. "I can work a lot of systems." Pamela said. "Modify or incapacitate computers for my needs. This stuff here is some next level stuff.

"I can do a lot of stuff as far as hacking too. That is nothing. Compared to what those people in The Black House can do." Drexler picked up the remote and turned on the television. WKBW BUFFALO BREAKING NEWS! Good evening, I'm Janie Vance. I'm Gene Millard. Anchor-woman, Janie Vance began to speak. A horrific scene just outside of Las Vegas, Nevada. A Military operation went tragically wrong. Two F-16V jets. Which were ordered into an unplanned training operation. Just minutes earlier. Erroneously fired upon a commercial U.S. jet. That jet was carrying 321 passengers. Along with 8 crew members to Las Vegas from Dulles Airport.

Among those passengers. Were three United States Congressmen and three Senators. It is unclear at this time who gave the order. Or what the F-16V planes were supposed to be firing at. Our own Melinda Richards was actually out in Vegas. To cover the fund-raising event being held for law makers. We now take you live to her location. Yes, Janie we are here. Not far from where much of the debris and remains. Of flight #1495 came down. As you can see behind me. Investigators have that area blocked off. As they search for clues. What is clear is the commercial jet. Which was carrying mothers, fathers, children and elderly. Never stood a chance.

It was struck by an AIM-120-AMRAAM. Which is an Air-Force medium range air to air missile. We're being told by a source. That spoke on condition of anonymity. As he is not authorized to speak. That the F-16Vs were not supposed to be carrying live ammunition. However, because the training exercise was put together so hastily. It may be a case of poor and improper planning. The result of that rushed decision is 329 Americans dead. Which includes the pilots, crew and six U.S. lawmakers. Obviously, there are many unanswered questions here. The NTSB, along with the FBI are on the scene. They have begun their investigations. This tragedy comes on the heels of another mystery. Also involving law makers.

Several members of Congress were traveling by train. From Washington DCs Union station to West Virginia recently. Then they all disappeared from public view. Some speculate that they are out at the Greenbrier bunker. That bunker was built for law makers. Back when there was fear of a pending cold war. That bunker has since been converted to a hotel and tourist attraction. When the current administration came to power. There was increased talk. For revamping the funding that created that facility. Of course, those of us in the public are obviously concerned. As to why some in Congress are returning their interest to this facility. A facility very expensive to upkeep.

The President, as you know. Is visiting Baltimore. He has been told of these events. He was visibly shaken when given the news. He had flown to Baltimore on Marine one. It is now reported that after the event. He will travel back to DC by limousine. As you know, that limousine is bullet and bomb proof. The White House stresses. That they have no reason to fear. That the President's life is in danger. They say he simply wishes to take the scenic route. Back to the confines of The White House. It should be noted that the six law makers on this jet. That was blown out of the sky were primary proponents. Of restarting the funding for that Greenbrier. Today, those law makers along with 321 passengers and 8 crew members are now dead.

A lot here to try and figure out, Jane. We will stay on top of this story. Until we get all the answers that we can. Pamela took the remote and turned the television volume down. "That's kind of thing." Pamela said. "Those people in The Black House do that kind of thing." Pamela said. "How do you know they could do something like this?" André asked. "Because I was on the train." She said. "With those Congress people out of DC. The man who took them. Is the one that gave me this card." "Well, who the hell is he?" Drexler demanded. "I don't know who he is." Pamela said. "Except to say. He is not the kind of dude you want to cross." Pamela replied. "When those Congress people saw him. They were scared.

"Like children who knew their father." Pamela continued. "Was about to give them the worse whipping of their lives. They were terrified. Too terrified to even ask for help. It's like they knew asking for help would be pointless." "Damn, did they have to kill all those people?" Bridgette asked. Just to get those Congressmen?" "It's probably the only way they could have killed them." André replied. Without making it look like the Congress is being targeted." "That would only make them beef up Security. They'd probably retreat to some sort of bunker. Where it would be harder to get to them. This way, it looks like somebody's incompetence. Caused a tragic accident. The remaining targets will remain accessible."

"Well, that still doesn't stop the flu vaccine." Drexler said. "That those idiots laced with deadly nerve agent. It doesn't stop their plan to kill 200 million or more citizens. Or the give-away of keys to the country." "Hold up." Bridgette said. "Turn the volume back up." The Breaking News Banner once again was flashing on screen. This is an incredible day of news here. We have yet another story involving our Military. This time. A Military convoy which was carrying some unknown freight. Has been involved in an accident in Baltimore.

We now turn to our sister station WJZ in Baltimore. For more details on this incident. Good evening. If you're just joining us from one of our affiliate stations. Here's what we know thus far. A Military convoy was traveling from the Dundalk Marine Terminal. Carrying what is yet unknown. The convoy loaded something. That was brought in by a Russian vessel called the Kislovodsk. I hope I'm pronouncing that correctly. It is unclear what or who that vessel was delivering to. Port workers who spoke on condition of anonymity. Told CBS 13 News that they were barred, from off-loading the cargo. Just from this particular vessel. Which they say is highly unusual. Instead, a Military convoy of 5 ton vehicles arrived. Military personnel with Hazmat protective gear entered the ship.

"They took over the forklifts and other machinery here." The reporter continued. "To load the cargo onto the trucks. This operation took several hours to complete. There was quite a bit of cargo offloaded according to our sources. Once the off load was complete. The convoy headed up Broening Hwy to Boston Street. It eventually made its way to the Fort McHenry tunnel. The tunnel on short notice, was closed to the public. It was presumed that the convoy was carrying some sort of toxic fumes. Or perhaps explosives as the reason to close the tunnel. Once the convoy was inside the tunnel. There was in fact, some sort of explosion. That explosion breached the very thick walls of the tunnel. This caused the tunnel to flood."

"Every member of that convoy subsequently drowned. We don't know who those individuals were. We don't know if they were from the Maryland National Guard. Perhaps the Aberdeen Proving Ground complex, which is just up the road in Harford County. Or speculation is abound they came from somewhere else. Now officials are cautious. Because they don't know what this convoy was carrying. They would like to give time. Time for the water to dilute any substance present. They have also stressed this fact. It may take up to a year, if not longer to repair and reopen the tunnel. That process won't even begin. Until they can recover the bodies and cargo from this incident. Interestingly enough. An employee here who chose not to be identified. Handed us copies of a manifest."

"He says that one of the military personnel. Came out of the ship with a clipboard. The clipboard had several documents attached. Now we have not verified the authenticity of these documents. We'd like to stress that fact. But a quick glance shows that whatever was on that ship. The President requested it to be sent here from Russia. Given all the controversy surrounded by the relationship. Between the President and Russia. This will generate some tough questions for the White House. Especially if that cargo turns out to be toxic. Or anything of detriment to U.S. citizens. This cargo would have gone virtually undetected."

"Due to much of our law enforcement and National Security tools. Are currently directed at protecting the President. In his visit here to Baltimore. Some have started to wonder. Based upon what may or may not be buried inside that tunnel. If the President's visit was timed? To coincide as a diversion. Usually, anytime any hazardous material is transported. Across a bridge or inside a tunnel here in Maryland. Officers from the Maryland Transportation Authority Police, have to provide an escort. We're being told by a spokesperson from that Agency. That the White House personally made a call. To waive any such escort. Again, we don't know the full story here. We can tell you that whatever happened here. Seems to roll right up to the doorsteps of the White House."

"If in fact this cargo was explosives or toxic agents. That were mishandled. Someone could be looking at numerous murder and attempted murder charges. Some officials tell us. Just how serious this incident is. We will not know until the water can be tested. To try and detect if any substance is present. Outside of the normal pollutants and substances that should be here. However, experts tell us. They do not believe military personnel would be wearing Hazmat clothing. If they were gathering flowers, or something innocuous from that ship. Nobody wants to go on the record here. To make a call without a full gathering of the facts."

"Privately, two Federal law enforcement personnel tell us. They have gathered enough evidence. For charges of Treason and murder to soon reign down. They say that if the facts continue. To move in the trajectory they have thus far. Tens of millions of Americans if not more. Would have died from this reckless and/or deliberate act. Some are even calling it a terrorist act. An act which may have possibly originated. From within our own Government. "Oh, they got this motherfucker now!" Drexler yelled. Bridgette, André, Pamela and Drexler were very excited. They hugged each other.

Chapter 11
Dog and Pony

At the ceremony near Baltimore's Inner Harbor. The explosion inside the tunnel rattled across the city. The shockwaves were felt by those in attendance. Everyone looked alarmed. "What the hell was that?" Commissioner Riggs asked. "According to my phone." Major Carver replied. "There was just an explosion inside the Fort McHenry tunnel." "An explosion?" Superintendent Scales repeated. "What the fuck are those folks at the Maryland Transportation Authority doing? Did somebody go into the tunnel without paying their toll? Then they blew them up?" People around them began to laugh.

"This story on WBAL is saying the tunnel has collapsed." Major Carver said. "There are several deaths." "Oh shit, this is some serious stuff." Chief Delaney said. "They're going to have to cancel this dog and pony show. I have to go. To make sure our public transportation facilities are not the next target. This might be some type of terrorist act." "That's fine Chief Delaney." Director Tolbert replied. "I just got a text. There have been some very interesting developments. We no longer need your services. Which is good for you. Because it doesn't look like your man Captain Nichols, was going to show up."

The Governor stepped up to the podium and began to speak. "Ladies and gentlemen!" He said. "We've just had an incident inside the Fort McHenry tunnel. Details are sketchy right now. So I really can't answer many questions. I will just say that all Law Enforcement personnel here. Are as of now excused. You should all contact your respective departments. Find out what it is they want you to do. The President has arrived. However he will not be exiting his limousine. Not while it is still unclear what happened. Or who is behind this. We need you all to disburse at this time."

"We don't know if there are additional attacks planned." The Governor continued. "Or if this was just a tragic accident. I have spoken with The President. He wanted me to convey his concern. Also his disappointment of not speaking to you. As soon as the roads can be checked and cleared. The President will be making his way back to Washington. We apologize for any inconvenience. This may cause to your commute. The safety of all our citizens and visitors. To this great State of Maryland is our top priority. That includes the President. Thank you all. Please be safe." The Governor then walked away from the podium.

Over at the Presidential Limousine. They were waiting for confirmation. That the roads had been cleared. Secret Service agents stood around the limousine. Keeping watch as the President waited inside. Several State Police and Baltimore City Police stood in close proximity. FBI Agents also provided a barrier to the President. Many had guns drawn on high alert. They scanned the area for any potential threats. Suddenly a man approached the limousine. Secret Service and FBI Agents immediately moved out of his way. The other law enforcement officers were stunned. Then followed the lead of the Secret Service. They allowed the man to walk up to the Limousine. The driver unlocked the door with his remote. An Agent opened the Limousine door where the President sat. The man entered and sat inside.

"Who the fuck are you?" The President asked. "Who let you into my limousine?" "Mr. President. I am Cecil." Mr. C. replied. "The President of the Black House. The house from which all of your imaginary power. Is derived and maintained. You are the first President since Reagan. We've had to make our presence known to. Trust me. When someone in my position comes to visit a sitting President. Nothing good is going to follow." "I'm the only President that matters around here." The President said. "One word for you, Mr. President." Mr. C. said. "Kislovodsk." The President looked stunned as he realized his visitor was someone serious.

"By this time next week Mr. President." Mr. C. continued. "You will have been arrested and charged with Treason. When the full extent of your misdeeds are revealed. You'll be convicted and sentenced to death. I just stopped by to deliver the news to you. Enjoy the rest of your Presidency, Mr. President. Or what's left of it." Mr. C. then exited the limousine. He walked to his waiting Town Car. "Who the fuck was that in the President's limo?" Major Carver asked. "That was nobody you want to know." Director Tolbert replied. "He's nobody none of us wants to know." "Make a hole!" A Secret Service Agent yelled. "The President is clear for departure!" Everyone cleared from standing in the street. The limousine drove away.

The next morning in Niagara Falls. André and Pamela were taking a shower together. "Don't touch me." Pamela said. "After you've been sleeping with that woman all that time." "Baby, I was just working." André responded. "Trying to get our money." "Yeah, I was listening in on some of that work." Pamela said. "Sounded like you were enjoying your job." "You know the Baltimore school of Performing Arts?" André asked. On Cathedral St." "What does that have to do with anything?" Pamela said. "I drove by there, listening to Tupac many times." André said. "Pac went to that school. I probably picked up some acting skills."

"What kind of bullshit are you...." Pamela replied. "You're lucky I love you." "You're lucky I love you and that you're rich now." They kissed passionately. Letting the water washed over their bodies. "Let's get something to eat and get on the road." André said. "We need to meet our yacht in Toronto with the rest of our money." After they got dressed, they went back into the living room. They called out to Drexler and Bridgette. "Come on, you two love birds. There will be plenty of time to do what you're doing. Once we get on the Yacht." Bridgette and Drexler soon appeared. Kissing and holding hands.

Driving on the Queen Elizabeth Way from Niagara Falls to Toronto. Both couples could hardly contain their excitement. "Little brother." Drexler said. "If I would have known it would take this long for us to be apart. I don't know if I would have made this pact with you. Then I had to let my wife. Work in that damn dirty ass strip club. So she could act like your informant." "Remember, it was her idea." André said. "By the way, that was a brilliant idea Bridgette. To come up with coded language. "If I told you to tell Drexler fuck him. He knew there was a raid coming. If I said to tell him to kiss my ass. Then he knew there was somebody talking to Police."

"It was also brilliant of you André." Bridgette said. "To get Pam that Information Technology and Cyber Security training. That way, she could plant a recording device in Deer Dog's ride. Listening to Ms. Parsons and him talk. "That was close too." Pamela added. "I had to stay close to them when they were driving to pick up what they said. I know Deer Dog noticed I was following him. Just not before I had recorded what I needed to get to Drexler. It also helped to be able to hack into Politicians and the Feds computers." When they began talking about all this unmarked money. I knew our ship had come in. "Well we also have to thank Drexler." André said. He had so many politicians in his pocket. He was able to get them to keep my Chief from investigating me.

"No problem little brother." Drexler said. "When politicians have wives addicted to heroin." They will look out for their wife's supplier so I won't talk. I made sure the Governor and legislators. Looked out for my brother." "Okay, we're coming up on Bay Street in downtown Toronto." André said. "Oh, that's where the Raptors play ball." Drexler said. "We're going to have to come here and see a game." "Man, we can come see a game or do whatever we want." Bridgette said. "For the rest of our lives." "I'll park here." André said. "We can walk over to Pier 6. Our Yacht should be there waiting."

They arrived at the Pier. Finding James standing next to the Yacht. "Hey James, my man." Drexler said. "So glad you could make it." "We truly appreciate your assistance." André said. "In getting our cargo up here. Where did you get this Yacht from?" "Oh, it belongs to a guy." James answered. "From Columbia, Maryland. He leaves it at the pier. He comes up to use it every other month. He won't know it's gone for another three weeks." "Hey we're sorry about wiring you up." Pamela said. "With explosives and a tracking device yesterday."

"We just wanted to be sure you'd make it here." "Some cop had a gun on me." James replied. "She suggested I wear something. How could I say no?" "Oh, don't look so sad James." Pamela said. "I think you're going to find. Your sacrifice was quite worth it. Let's go inside the yacht. To disarm that jacket so you can take it off. Drexler and André will make sure everything is in order. If so I believe we have a reward for you." Drexler and André went below deck to check on the money. Pamela disarmed the explosives attached to the jacket. "Good thing you made it here." Pamela said. "Before this battery died. Also good you didn't detour. To make me call this jacket." She removed a phone sewn into the interior of the jacket. "No, I wouldn't have done that." James said. "I know Drexler well enough.

André and Drexler returned from below. "Everything is down there." Drexler said. "We are good to go. This is for you James." André handed him a vehicle key. "What is it?" James asked. "Another bomb?" "No, we've unlocked one of the containers down below." André replied. "There's $20 million dollars there. To go home or wherever you want to go." André said. "That's for being loyal." Drexler said. "Letting me know what you did about Michael." "That key is to a Chevy Suburban across the street." André said. There are seven suitcases in the truck. Fill them up. With as much cash as you can get from downstairs. I'm sure you can figure out how to get home. Or wherever with what you have."

"Yes Sir. I'll be fine." James said. "I'll be more than fine." "André and I will help you load the suitcases." Drexler said." "We got you a room. At the hotel around the corner for a few nights. In that time. You should be able to figure out. How you'll get this money out of here." They helped him pack the suitcases full of cash. They then loaded them into his SUV. James drove off. "I saw this coffee house around the corner." Pamela said. "We can go over there." Pamela said. "Then get back on this boat and sail off into the sunset." Bridgette added. They locked and secured the Yacht. Then walked over to Dineen Coffee on Younge St.

They ordered coffees and Cappuccinos. Then sat and talked. Drexler handed Pamela the access code. She checked the time on her "Talley & Twine" watch. "What time is it?" André asked. "It is 8:35pm." She answered. "Almost time to go." "Are you sure you want to do the transfer here?" Drexler asked. "In Toronto? The minute you do. The Feds in Washington are going to be alerted. They will know the location of the computer terminal within two minutes. They will make a phone call. To the Royal Canadian Mounted Police. They will have Officers at that terminal within 15 minutes of the transfer." "That's why we're doing it from the library." Pamela said. "Fifteen minutes before it closes."

"We don't want them knowing where we actually are." She continued. "So let's transfer the funds before we get there." She and Bridgette walked over to the library. They were told the library would close in less than 15 minutes. "This won't take long." Pamela said. "I just need to look up something on one of your computers." "You need to be out of here in ten minutes." The custodian said. The librarian handed Pamela an internet access code. Pamela rushed quickly to a terminal. She then transferred the money. $125 million into each of their accounts. With another $80 million plus in cash. To be divided on the Yacht. "How much time do I have left?' Pamela asked. "Girl, you have a whole 60 seconds remaining."

"Okay let's walk." Pamela said. "The Canadian Feds should be getting a request right now. They'll be here in 15 minutes. It'll be 30 minutes before they can get in. Because Miss thang will be going home at 9:00pm sharp. They will have to get her to turn around and come back. Only to find out she doesn't have access to CCTV tapes. By the time they get someone down here. To show them the tapes, we'll be out of Canadian waters. Of course eventually they will see my face. They will email our pics down to DC and they will identify us. The Royal Canadian Police will cross reference our names. With border patrol entry. They'll start to search for us here in Canada.

"Our names being at a hotel down in Niagara Falls. Will send them on a goose chase. When they don't find us in Niagara Falls. They'll be praying I come back to the border. To pick up that throw away gun I left there. Good luck with that, border patrol." She laughed. They returned around the corner to the coffee house. "Are we ready to go gentlemen?" Bridgette asked. "Yes, we're ready to go." Drexler said. "Today is the first day of the rest of our lives." "Yes ladies and gentleman." André said.

"Let's all enjoy it to the fullest." Bridgette added. "Hey, I'm with the woman I love." André said. "I'm with my brother and my lovely sister-in-law. We're going to meet our other brothers in a few days. I never have to work again. How can I not enjoy that to the fullest?" They walked to and boarded the yacht. They headed east towards the Atlantic Ocean. "ALL ABOARD!" André yelled. "Welcome to the good life!"

The End!

The Black House Publishing Presents:

Angel and Christopher are long-time friends. They've built their friendship from the ground up. They love and trust one another genuinely. Love, not sex was always the foundation of their relationship. However when an argument over something silly threatens to destroy that friendship, one of them makes a play to save them. That sets in motion a passion like molten lava that flows so naturally. Exploration, Deceit, Confusion, Infidelity and Explosive Love Making. Angel and Christopher have every reason not to cross this line. Yet they have every reason why they should. They soon discover that no matter how they tried to design their friendship.....Love Makes Things Happen. There was absolutely nothing they could do but what they did.

Available at:

JonathanPMance.com,
Amazon.com,

Shop.jonathanpmance.com,
Amazon.co.uk

The Black House Publishing Inc. Presents:

A sensual collection of poetry dedicated to the most beautiful flowers on earth. Romance & Spice will Romance you, it will lace your thoughts with Spice. It will make love to your mind, tingle your body and fill your soul. Most of all it will get deep into your essence as only a black man can.

Available at:

JonathanPMance.com

Shop.jonathanpmance.com

Amazon.com, Amazon.co.uk

The Black House Publishing Inc. Proudly Presents: God Has Given

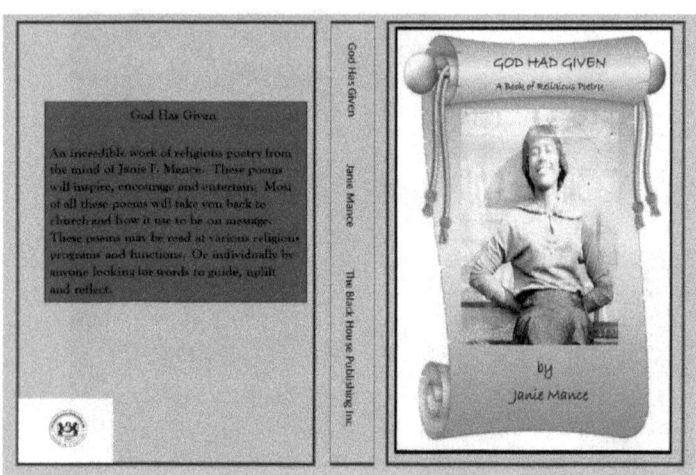

An incredible work of religious poetry from the mind of Janie F. Mance. These poems will inspire, encourage and entertain. Most of all these poems will take you back to church and how it use to be on message. These poems may be read at various church programs and functions or as an individual looking for words to uplift, guide and reflect.

Available at:

JonathanPMance.com

Shop.jonathanpmance.com

www.Amazon.com

www.Amazon.co.uk

Black Chameleons

Also Available in Ebook

Digital Audio Book Forthcoming

With Original Music Score by:

Greg "888Keyz" Mance

2018 © Copyright

Available at

Jonathanpmance.com

Shop.jonathanpmance.com

www.Amazon.com

www.Amazon.co.uk

Coming Soon From:

The Black House Publishing Inc.

Are We African-Americans Or

Euro-Centric Niggaz?

When it comes to standing up. We find a convenient excuse to lay down. We back away from struggle-The Honorable Minister Louis Farrakhan.

Without struggle there is no progress-Frederick Douglas

The Black House Publishing Inc.

Baltimore, Maryland USA

Contact

P.O. Box 941

Harrisburg, NC. 28075

443-904-0649

Email: BlackHousePublish@gmail.com

On the web

Jonathanpmance.com

www.Amazon.com

Shop.jonathanpmance.com

www.Amazon.co.uk

Thank You

To God for everything. Thank you for my late mother Janie Mance through whom you groomed me. Cendra, (Ms. Boss), Jonah, Kain Carter, Carolyn V. Mance, (Always love), The Staff at The Black House and also my dear friends. Tanya Venable (Who knew back at the NSA where we met that we'd be lifelong friends?) To Raushanah N. Butler, April Vailati, Stella Joy, Robin L. Harvin, (Simply Amazing), Myrtle Glover, (Love you) April Glover,(My smile) Tovondia Jones, (Miss you) Jerome Howard, Niecy (Hey Boo Boo), Launa MsBoop, Angela Sarah, (Hey Bookie), Kimberly Robinson Dicks, (Hi beautiful), Joseph Bell, (The Sheriff), Cascio Odell, Casey Jenkins, (Thank you) Charmin Dawns, Pearl Brawley, Veronica Gee, Valarie Mance, Justin Mance, Lincoln Mance Sr, Linda Carter, Elizabeth Green, Dee Dee, Marion, Shirley, Pamela Mance, Jackie Mance, Rob Mance, Greg 888Keyz Mance, Monie Mance, Lincoln Mance Jr, Kimberly Mance, Robyn Mance, Joshua Mance, Darryl Perfor-Mance, Keyna Mance, Larry Mance, Jonathan Mance, (my twin in Va.), To everyone in the DMV, East Baton Rouge (Home), West Baltimore (Home) and the Queen City Charlotte NC (Home). My friends from Cameroon, Nigeria and Uganda Africa. Nji Anyere, Salou, Traore, and Miriam, To Jarrad, Pauline, Moureka the NYC crew. Geneva, Redd, Mia, Chelsea, Christian, Josh, Nina, Ronnie, Glenn, Missy, Aya and everybody else in The ATL. To Michael Baisden, you are a big inspiration my brother and I thank you for what you do on the radio. To Marylen Venus (Hot Talk Radio), To April Watts 95.9 in Bmore and Triscina Grey 96.3 in DC. Sometimes I need a Fix Mix with K.K. and sometimes I want a tasty tune from the Café'. It's all about the DMV. Jeff Brown and the Original Quiet Storm from Bryant and Georgia. You are the man bro. Olympia D. from the Queen City. You have the sexiest laugh of all time. To Jonna Steward, Sassy Cassie of **Cassie's Bar & Grill on 38th** (Members only) To Colin Kapernick, thank you. Quainti Brown, André Richard, Carnell Weatherspoon, Torrence Stepteau, Thomas Watson, Jatosha Sanders, Janice Selders, Ramona Palmer, Debbie Alves, Valaries M Jackson-Saunders, Elizabeth Crawford, Tyra T. Burrell, Cynthia Black, Adrianne Williams, **The Mocha Book Club**, To Black Men, for all you do to maintain and survive in the face of enormous obstacles. To Black Women, for all you do to maintain and survive in the face of enormous obstacles. None of us are perfect and nobody perfect is coming to save us. We have to return to creation which means creating something meaningful together. Kwanzaa 24/7 365.

THANK YOU (Continued)

The Honorable Minister Louis Farrakhan, Dr. Boyce Watkins, Dr. Claude Anderson, Dr. Umar Johnson and the late great Dick Gregory. Your words are not falling on deaf ears. I know the fight is discouraging. Especially when it's the ones you're trying to help, fighting you. Don't give up on us please. To anyone I may have forgot it was not intentional. I thank any and everyone who has made a positive impact on me. To all my followers on **Facebook, @jonathanpmance on Twitter and Instagram**. I love and appreciate every one of you. To every visitor at **Jonathanpmance.com** I thank and appreciate you. Sabrina bought her clothes at **Chimesboutique.com** Check it out ladies and you will too. Tanika M. I think I love you.

For My Dark skin Sisters

Please check out our store

Shop.jonathanpmance.com/Collections

For this and other items.

For my Light skin Sisters

Please check out our store

Shop.jonathanpmance.com/collections

For this and other items

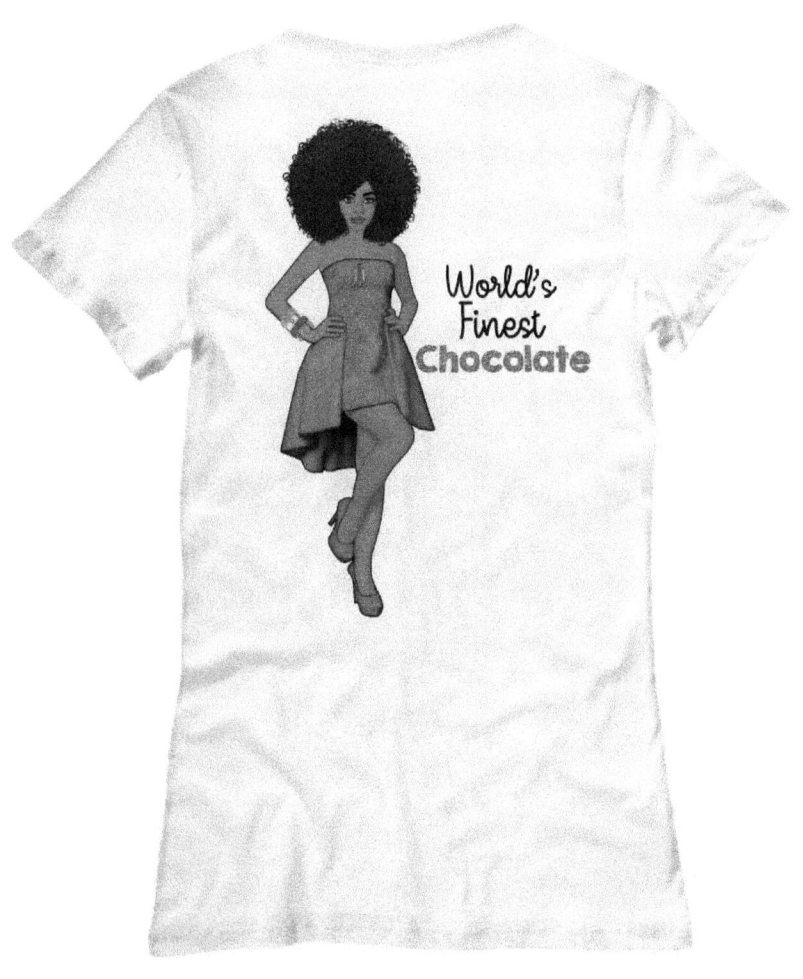

For my Brown skin Sisters

Please check out our store

Shop.jonathanpmance.com/collections

For this and other items

www.ingramcontent.com/pod-product-compliance
Lightning Source LLC
Chambersburg PA
CBHW071653090426
42738CB00009B/1514